THE AMERICAN
REVOLUTION

OPPOSING VIEWPOINTS®

Other Books in the American History Series:

THE AMERICAN REVOLUTION

OPPOSING VIEWPOINTS®

David L. Bender, *Publisher*
Bruno Leone, *Executive Editor*

Teresa O'Neill, *Series Editor*
John C. Chalberg, Ph.D., professor of history,
 Normandale Community College, *Consulting
 Editor*

William Dudley, *Book Editor*

AMERICAN HISTORY SERIES

Cover photos by Library of Congress. The following copyrighted material has been included in this book: From *The Correspondence of General Thomas Gage with the Secretaries of State, 1763-1775*, vol. 1. Clarence Edwin Carter, editor. New Haven, CT: Yale University Press, 1931. Reprinted with permission. From Charles-Louis de Montesquieu, *The Spirit of Laws*, a compendium of the first English edition, edited and translated by David Wallace Carrithers. Berkeley: University of California Press, © 1977, The Regents of the University of California. Reprinted with permission. From *The Radicalism of the American Revolution* by Gordon S. Wood. Copyright © 1992 by Gordon S. Wood. Reprinted by permission of Alfred A. Knopf, Inc. From *A People's History of the United States* by Howard Zinn. New York: Harper & Row, 1980. Copyright © 1980 by Howard Zinn. Reprinted with permission.

Library of Congress Cataloging-in-Publication Data

The American Revolution : opposing viewpoints / William
  Dudley, book editor.
      p.   cm. — (American history series)
  Includes bibliographical references (p.   ) and index.
  ISBN 1-56510-011-5 (lib. bdg. : acid-free paper) — ISBN
1-56510-010-7 (pbk. : acid-free paper)
  1. United States—History—Revolution, 1775-1783—Sources.
I. Dudley, William, 1964-   . II. Series: American history
series (San Diego, Calif.)
E208.A4395   1992   92-21795
973.3—dc20   CIP

© 1992 by Greenhaven Press, Inc., PO Box 289009,
San Diego, CA 92198-9009

Contents

Foreword

Aboard the *Arbella* as it lurched across the cold, gray Atlantic, John Winthrop was as calm as the waters surrounding him were wild. With the confidence of a born leader, Winthrop gathered his Puritan passengers around him. It was time to offer a sermon. England lay behind them, and years of strife and persecution for their religious beliefs were over, he said. But the Puritan abandonment of England, he reminded his followers, did not mean that England was beyond redemption. Winthrop wanted his followers to remember England even as they were leaving it behind. Their goal should be to create a new England, one far removed from the authority of the Anglican church and King Charles I. In Winthrop's words, their settlement in the New World ought to be a model society, a city upon a hill. He hoped his band would be able to create a just society in America for corrupt England to imitate.

Unable to find either peace or freedom within their home country, these Puritans were determined to provide England with a living example of a community that valued both. Across the hostile Atlantic Ocean would shine the bright light of a just, harmonious, and God-serving society. England may have been beset by sin and corruption, but Winthrop and the colonists believed they could still save England—and themselves. Together, they would coax out of the rocky New England soil not only food for their tables but many thriving communities dedicated to achieving harmony and justice.

On June 8, 1630, John Winthrop and his company of refugees had their first glimpse of what they came to call New England. High on the surrounding hills stood a welcoming band of fir trees whose fragrance drifted to the *Arbella* on a morning breeze. To Winthrop, the "smell off the shore [was] like the smell of a garden."

This new world would, in fact, often be compared to the Garden of Eden. In it, John Winthrop would have his opportunity to start life over again. So would his family and his shipmates. So would all those who would come after them. Victims of conflict in old England hoped to find peace in New England.

Winthrop, for one, had experienced much conflict in his life. As a Puritan, he was opposed to Catholicism and Anglicanism, both of which, he believed, were burdened by distracting rituals and distant hierarchies. A parliamentarian by conviction, he despised Charles I, who had spurned Parliament and created a private army to do his bidding. He believed in individual responsibility and fought against the loss of religious and political freedom. A gentleman landowner, he feared the rising economic power of a merchant class that seemed to value only money. Once Winthrop stepped aboard the *Arbella*, he hoped conflict would not be a part of his American future.

But his Puritan religion told Winthrop that human beings are fallen creatures and that perfection, whether communal or individual, is unachievable on this earth. Therefore, he was presented with a dilemma: On the one hand, his religion demanded that he attempt to live a perfect life in an imperfect world. On the other hand, it told him that he was destined to fail.

Soon after Winthrop disembarked from the *Arbella*, he came face-to-face with this maddening dilemma. He found himself presiding not over a utopia—an ideal community—but over a colony caught up in disputes as troubling as any that he had confronted in his English past.

John Winthrop, it seems, was not the only Puritan with a dream of perfection, with a vision of a heaven on earth. Others in the community saw the dream differently. They wanted greater political and religious freedom than their leader was prepared to grant. Often, Winthrop was able to handle this conflict diplomatically. He expanded, for example, participation in elections and allowed the voters of Massachusetts Bay greater power.

But religious conflict was another matter because it was a conflict of competing visions of the Puritan utopia. In Roger Williams and Anne Hutchinson, two of his fellow colonists, John Winthrop faced rivals unprepared to accept his definition of the perfect community. To Williams, perfection demanded that he separate himself from the Puritan institutions in his community and create an even "purer" church. Winthrop, however, disagreed and exiled Williams to Rhode Island. Hutchinson presumed that she could interpret God's will without a minister. Again, Winthrop did not agree. Hutchinson was tried on charges of heresy, convicted, and banished from Massachusetts.

John Winthrop's Massachusetts colony was the first, but far from the last, American attempt to build a unified, peaceful community that, in the end, only provoked a discord. This glimpse at its history reveals what Winthrop confronted: the unavoidable presence of conflict in American life.

American Assumptions

From America's origins in the early seventeenth century, Americans have often held several interrelated assumptions about their country. First, people believe that to be American is to be free. Second, because Americans did not have to free themselves from feudal lords or an entrenched aristocracy, conflict is often considered foreign to American life. Finally, America has been seen as a perpetual haven from the troubles and disputes that are found in the Old World.

John Winthrop, for one, lived his life as though all of these assumptions were true. But the opposing viewpoints presented in the American History Series should reveal that for many Americans, these assumptions were and are myths. Indeed, for numerous Americans, liberty has not always been guaranteed, and conflict has been a necessary, sometimes welcome aspect of their life. To these Americans, the United States is less a sanctuary than it is one more battleground for old and new ideas.

Our American landscape has been torn apart again and again by a great variety of clashes—theological, ideological, political, economic, geographical, racial, gender-based, and class-based. But to discover such a landscape is not necessarily to come upon a hopelessly divided country. If the editors desire to prove anything during the course of this series, it is not that America has been destroyed by conflict but rather that America has been enlivened, enriched, and even strengthened by Americans who have disagreed with one another.

Observers of American life, however, often see a country in which its citizens behave as though all of the basic questions of life have been settled. Over the years, they see a generation after generation of Americans who seem to blithely agree with one another. In the nineteenth century, French traveler Alexis de Tocqueville called the typical American a "venturesome conservative." According to Tocqueville, this American was willing to risk money in the marketplace but otherwise presented the drab front of someone who thought, dressed, and acted just like everyone else. To Tocqueville, Americans were individualistic risk takers when it came to playing the game of capitalism but were victims of public opinion (which he defined as the "tyranny of the majority") when it came to otherwise expressing themselves.

In the twentieth century, sociologist David Riesman has registered his agreement with Tocqueville. He has defined the modern American as "other-directed." Perhaps willing to leap into the economic arena, this American is unwilling to take risks in the marketplace of ideas. The result is either silence or assent, either because this person is unsure of his or her own beliefs or because the mass media dictate beliefs—or a bit of both. The other-directed American is fearful of standing apart from the crowd.

The editors of this series would like to suggest that Tocqueville and Riesman were too narrow in their assessment of Americans. They have found innumerable Americans who have been willing to take the trouble to disagree.

Thomas Jefferson was one of the least confrontational of Americans, but he boldly and irrevocably enriched American life with his individualistic views. Like John Winthrop before him, he had a notion of an American Eden. Like Winthrop, he offered a vision of a harmonious society. And like Winthrop, he not only became enmeshed in conflict but eventually presided over a people beset by it. But unlike Winthrop, Jefferson believed this Eden was not located in a specific community but in each individual American. His Declaration of Independence from Great Britain could also be read as a declaration of independence for each individual in American society.

Jefferson's Ideal

Jefferson's ideal world was composed of "yeoman farmers," each of whom was roughly equal to the other in society's eyes, each of whom was free from the restrictions of both government and his fellow citizens. Throughout his life, Jefferson offered a continuing challenge to Americans: advance individualism and equality or see the death of the American experiment. Jefferson believed that the strength of this experiment depended upon a society of autonomous individuals and a society without great gaps between rich and poor. His challenge to his fellow Americans to create—and sustain—such a society has itself produced both economic and political conflict.

A society whose guiding document is the Declaration of Independence is a society assured of the freedom to dream—and to disagree. We know that Jefferson himself hated conflict, whether personal or political. His tendency was to avoid confrontations of any sort, to squirrel himself away and write rather than to stand up and speak his mind. It is only through his written words that we can grasp Jefferson's utopian dream of a society of independent farmers, all pursuing their private dreams and all leading lives of sufficient prosperity.

This man of wealth and intellect lived an essentially happy life in accord with his view that Americans ought to have the right to pursue "happiness." But Jefferson's public life was much more troublesome. From the first rumblings of the American Revolution in the 1760s to the North-South skirmishes of the 1820s that ultimately produced the Civil War, Jefferson was at or near the center of American political history. The issues were almost too many—and too crucial—for one lifetime. Jefferson had to choose between supporting or rejecting the path of revolution. During and after the ensuing war, he was at the forefront of the battle for religious liberty. After endorsing the Constitution, he opposed the economic plans of Alexander Hamilton. At the end of the century, he fought the infamous Alien and Sedition Acts, which lim-

11

ited civil liberties. As president, he opposed the Federalist court, conspiracies to divide the union, and calls for a new war against England.

Throughout his life, Thomas Jefferson, slaveholder, pondered the conflict between American freedom and American slavery. And from retirement at his Monticello retreat, he frowned at the rising spirit of commercialism that he feared was dividing Americans and destroying his dream of American harmony.

No matter the issue, however, Thomas Jefferson invariably supported the rights of the individual. Worried as he was about the excesses of commercialism, he accepted them because his main concern was to live in a society where liberty and individualism could flourish. To Jefferson, Americans had to be free to worship as they desired. They also deserved to be free from an over-reaching government. To Jefferson, Americans should also be free to possess slaves.

Harmony, an Elusive Goal

Before reading the articles in this anthology, the editors ask readers to ponder the lives of John Winthrop and Thomas Jefferson. Each held a utopian vision, one based upon the demands of community and the other on the autonomy of the individual. Each dreamed of a country of perpetual new beginnings. Each found himself thrust into a position of leadership and found that conflict could not be avoided. And each lived long enough to face and express many opposing views. Harmony, whether communal or individual, was a forever elusive goal.

The opposing visions of Winthrop and Jefferson have been at the heart of many differences among Americans from many backgrounds through the whole of American history. Moreover, their visions have provoked important responses that have helped shape American society, the American character, and many an American battle.

Is the theme of community versus the individual the single defining theme in American history? No, but it is a recurring theme that provides us with a useful point of departure for showing that Americans have been more rambunctious and contentious than Tocqueville or Riesman found them to be, that blandness has not been the defining characteristic for all Americans.

In this age of mass media, the danger exists that the real issues that divide Americans will be, at best, distorted or, at worst, ignored. But by thinking honestly about the past, the real issues and real differences have often been of critical, even of life-and-death, importance to Americans. And they continue to be so today.

The editors of the American History Series have done extensive research to find representative opinions on the issues included in these volumes. They found numerous outstanding opposing viewpoints from people of all times, classes, and genders in American history. From those, they selected commentaries that best fit the nature and flavor of the period under consideration. Every attempt was made to include the most important and relevant viewpoints in each chapter. Obviously, not every notable viewpoint could be included. Therefore, a bibliography has been provided at the end of each book to aid readers in seeking out for themselves additional information.

The editors are confident that as this series reveals past conflicts, it will help revitalize the reader's views of the American present. In that spirit, the American History Series is dedicated to the proposition that American history is more complicated, more fascinating, and more troubling than John Winthrop, Thomas Jefferson, Alexis de Tocqueville, or David Riesman ever dared to imagine.

John C. Chalberg
Consulting Editor

Introduction

"Among supporters of independence, very often they agreed on little more than demanding independence. The idea of home rule may have temporarily united them. But the larger question of 'who should rule at home'—and how that rule should be exercised—was inevitably divisive."

John Adams was a worrier by nature. And America's Declaration of Independence from Great Britain had not brought an end to his worries. The events of July 4, 1776, ought to have made him a happy man, but they did not. Though a leader of the colonial opposition, Adams had not been anxious to commit himself to the final break with the mother country. John Adams was a successful lawyer and a respected politician in his town of Braintree, Massachusetts, and in the entire state. As a result, he enjoyed many of the benefits of membership in the British empire. But John Adams was also an amateur philosopher and a student of history. And history told him that empires eventually deteriorate. Their vibrant youth inevitably gives way to settled middle age, which in turn fades into a corrupt dotage.

To John Adams, signs of British economic, political, and moral corruption were everywhere. "Luxury and effeminacy" had reached appalling levels in London and threatened to engulf the American colonies in the immediate future. More ominous still was the mounting evidence that the king and Parliament were no longer interested in preserving traditional British liberties in the colonies. The notorious writs of assistance (general search warrants) and the subversion of the jury system through the use of military courts told Adams that British authorities were unwilling to protect the "rights of Englishmen." Empire and its potential riches were apparently more important than liberty.

To defend that liberty, John Adams finally set aside his considerable reservations and cast a reluctant vote for independence. He set out for his Massachusetts home with at least some hope for the American future. Among Adams's greeters as he approached Braintree, however, was a man who could barely contain his excitement. Independence would be wonderful, the man informed a startled Adams. Adams, about to nod in agreement, suddenly recalled that he had defended this man years earlier on a charge of theft. The man was imagining no more courts, no more jails, no more laws. Adams was stunned. Did independence mean free reign for common thieves? If so, then independence and the inevitable war to secure it were surely catastrophic mistakes.

John Adams was one of many American revolutionaries who wanted political independence from Great Britain without an accompanying full-scale social revolution. Fears of such a revolution made some Americans rethink their course of action. But Adams soon decided that it was too late to turn back, no matter what the risk.

Adams's brief encounter with his onetime client encapsulates one of the key issues surrounding the American Revolution. Earlier in this century, American historian Carl Becker contended that the story of the American Revolution was not simply a matter of "home rule, but of who should rule at home." Any set of opposing viewpoints must confront this key question: Was the American Revolution merely a political revolution against King George III, or was it also a social revolution against the authority of the colonial elite? If the latter, John Adams had good reason to be depressed after his impromptu meeting on the way to his Braintree home.

Many Divisions Between Americans

As John Adams's worries ought to make clear, debate before and during the American Revolution was not only between Whig supporters of independence and their Tory opponents. In temperament, background, and social standing, John Adams was much closer to any number of leading Tories than he was to his former client. There was also a small army of rather ordinary loyalists who did not fit the stereotype of the Tory gentleman. Thomas Hutchinson, man of wealth and governor of Massachusetts, was a loyalist, but so were free blacks, Indians, German-American farmers, and Dutch traders, among countless others. All preferred to remain within the British empire because they did not anticipate fair or friendly treatment at the hands of an independent American government.

Among supporters of independence, very often they agreed on little more than demanding independence. The idea of home rule

15

may have temporarily united them. But the larger question of "who should rule at home"—and how that rule should be exercised—was inevitably divisive.

Those who wrestled with the shape of government in a postrevolutionary America did presume that some version of republican government would prevail. But even here, differences quickly became apparent. John Adams, for one, was preoccupied with the potential weaknesses of republican government. He may have taken pride in his knowledge of history, but he was not encouraged by what history seemed to be telling him. Most experiments in republican government had been brief and unhappy. Some, like Greece, had succumbed to internal divisions and more powerful neighbors. Others, like Rome, had been vanquished by their own submission to the temptations of empire. The question that bothered Adams was at once simple and daunting: How could a newly independent America avoid going the way of Greece or Rome?

Though Adams thought that Great Britain had become the imperial Rome of the eighteenth century, his model of republicanism had been borrowed directly from British history. Over the preceding centuries, a body of British law had developed that emphasized individual rights over those of either an overreaching monarch or of an aggressive bureaucracy. At the same time, British history offered evidence that republican government required the stabilizing hand of a monarch and the calming influence of an aristocracy grounded in tradition and wealth. Still, by the time of the American Revolution, British common law had long established that an individual was truly free only to the extent that his person and his property were his own. Furthermore, it was assumed that anyone in full possession of his freedom would willingly fight to keep it.

Americans, Adams believed, wanted nothing more than the "rights of Englishmen." Included among these were the right to a jury trial, the right to be free of unreasonable searches, the right to be secure in one's property, and the right to be free of unwarranted taxes. Adams and those who thought as he did wanted to retain rights that they presumed had always been theirs—until Parliament began imposing restrictive measures. In this sense, these Americans were very conservative revolutionaries. They simply wanted to maintain freedoms rather than to fight for new ones.

The Virtuous Community

By the summer of 1776, however, a second strand of republican thought was weaving its way into the minds of some Americans. It placed the good of the entire community ahead of one's private interests or desires. For these republican theorists, the most note-worthy of whom was Thomas Paine, the virtuous citizen was one who thought first of the needs of the community. And the virtuous community was one composed of small farmers and urban artisans of similar background and modest wealth.

Both aspects of republicanism held that liberty was a positive good. Both also regarded liberty as a product of a very specific set of historical circumstances. Both presumed that liberty and limited government went together. And both feared that liberty could easily be lost. But republicans like Paine argued that too much emphasis on private rights, private lives, and private wealth would destroy true republicanism. To them, the purpose of the revolution was not simply to be free of interference from a distant Parliament. Nor did they think that independence from England was an excuse for amassing great personal wealth. Instead, the goal was to establish a just society of relative equality.

Adams, on the other hand, believed that individual liberties were most important and that a hierarchical society was superior. Republicanism and aristocracy coexisted in Adams's ideal world.

It was Adams's own deference to hierarchy and order that had made him a reluctant revolutionary in the first place. During the prior decade, he had carried on a running argument with those whom historian Pauline Maier has called the "old revolutionaries." They were not old in terms of age, but they were quick to challenge the British. Patrick Henry and Samuel Adams are examples of this brand of revolutionary. With the fiery rhetoric of Henry's "give me liberty or give me death" speech and the conspiratorial organization of Adams's Sons of Liberty, these revolutionaries unhesitatingly objected to British taxes and restrictions.

The "old revolutionaries" quickly translated their objections into a demand for independence. For Patrick Henry of Virginia and Samuel Adams of Massachusetts, British liberties were important. But neither Henry nor Samuel Adams placed a premium on hierarchy and order. And, unlike Samuel Adams's cousin John, neither worried greatly about the consequences a revolution might have on the social structure of the colonies.

But John Adams was far from alone in his worries. George Washington, Thomas Jefferson, and Benjamin Franklin also feared social revolution. None of these men took an early lead in the anti-British campaign. All waited at least until the passage of the Coercive Acts of 1774 to demand independence.

Passed by Parliament in response to the Boston Tea Party, the Coercive Acts (also called the Intolerable Acts) closed the port of Boston (until the dumped tea was paid for), forbade Massachusetts town meetings, removed to England all criminal trials for those accused of committing murder in the course of enforcing British laws, and installed new requirements for housing British soldiers in private American homes. Parliament then passed the Quebec Act, which annexed to the former French province the territory east of the Mississippi River and north of the Ohio River and gave more freedom to Catholics living in what had been a French possession until 1763. Suddenly, the specter of being surrounded by hated (and anti-republican) Catholics acquired new reality for the largely Protestant British colonies to the south.

Up to this point, one could argue that British laws passed after the Seven Years' War (1756-1763) were intended primarily to raise revenue or manage the empire. But these five pieces of legislation were so clearly meant to punish the colonists that many of them were suddenly forced to make serious choices. Among those who felt compelled to choose was Thomas Jefferson. No longer concerned with mere legal rights, Jefferson now argued for the natural rights of American immigrants. By leaving England and other European countries, these new "Americans" had already established their freedom from British power, he asserted. At issue no longer was the right of Parliament to legislate for the colonies. Instead, Jefferson now realized, the important issue was the natural right of American independence, obtained by having left Europe.

Thomas Paine, however, took the argument one critical step further. Paine denied the authority of the British monarch. He asserted the separateness of American interests from those of England. Here, the issue was practical: America ought to be free from England because America ought to be released from any compulsion to fight in England's colonial wars such as the recently concluded Seven Years' War against France. This war had created a huge public debt, which forced Parliament to impose taxes. Paine wrote in his pamphlet *Common Sense* that it was in America's interest to steer an independent course because England's wars were not America's wars.

Once independence had been formally declared, colonists continued to disagree among themselves. Disputes among republicans or between old and reluctant revolutionaries did not cease. And, of course, Whigs and Tories still argued. In fact, John Adams estimated that at the start of the war, one-third of the colonists favored independence, one-third were opposed, and one-third were essentially indifferent. At best, even those who were in favor of the war formed an uneasy wartime coalition against the mighty British.

Who Should Rule at Home?

After 1776, the most historically interesting debates continued to be those among American revolutionaries. Well before an

American victory was in sight, these revolutionaries were squabbling not only over who should rule at home but how that rule should be constituted and exercised. John Adams and others feared the very thing that excited Paine: Because the backbone of the day-to-day resistance would have to be provided by the ordinary people, it was likely that they would eventually demand—perhaps even seize—new freedoms from their colonial superiors. Few among these common people were students of republican theory, but Paine presumed them to be instinctive republicans. And he hoped that their version of republicanism would challenge the elite of colonial America. Paine thought that Adams and others had too long benefited from a hierarchical society in which each citizen was expected to know—and quietly remain in—his or her place. War, especially a revolutionary war, might just upset all that.

What Adams and others of his background feared could already be observed well before 1776. His cousin Samuel had relied on the common people, in fact mobs of them, to force the British to withdraw their oppressive laws. John Adams worried that once aroused, those same mobs would not be easily quieted.

In truth, mob action had dotted the historical landscape of colonial America. But it seldom threatened the prevailing social order. In the first place, such behavior was relatively infrequent. Second, because it was often directed at the royal governors, it was thought to be consistent with republicanism. Finally, it was seldom the opening event but instead was often a last resort.

But with the colonial response to the Stamp Act of 1765, urban mobs became a regular feature of colonial life. Moreover, western farmers began to express their discontent as well. And their enemies were not faraway British officeholders but the colonial legislatures, which were often dominated by large eastern landowners. From the Regulator movement in South Carolina to the Paxton Boys of Pennsylvania, geographic and class tensions appeared as conflicts grew between Great Britain and the colonies.

On many fronts, it seemed increasingly apparent to John Adams that colonial society as he knew it was threatening to disintegrate. Within Massachusetts, the Sons of Liberty contributed to that process. Composed of dissident intellectuals, skilled artisans, and small local merchants, this loose organization rapidly took on a life and political powers of its own. As the *Sons* of Liberty, the inheritors of liberty, they wanted to keep what Parliament now sought to take away. But many of them also proved to be republicans who placed the good of the community over individual liberties. And as egalitarian republicans, they rejected John Adams's world of hierarchy and deference, desiring instead a world of social, economic, and political equality.

Once the war began, many of these "sons" joined forces with those interested in pushing the revolution in a more radical direction. In city after city along the eastern seaboard, problems of unemployment, high rents, and tight money produced a revolutionary spirit very different from the original one. To such individuals, the question of who should rule at home provoked answers quite unwelcome to John Adams. He could support a revolution for political freedom but not one that threatened to upset the social and economic order.

In Pennsylvania, for example, a state constitution with radically democratic provisions was ratified. Little power was given to a governor, but great powers were reserved for a single-house legislature. Those provisions alone challenged prevailing notions of hierarchy. In addition, the new constitution required the printing of all bills "for the consideration of the people" before they were to be finally voted upon by the legislature. Clearly, in Pennsylvania, the old colonial elite was no longer in charge.

Whether the issues were constitutional or economic, notions of republican virtue inevitably crept into wartime debates. There were, in short, debates over just what the ideal society was and how it might be achieved. For some revolutionaries, John Adams among them, the Declaration of Independence and the ensuing war offered a chance to restore the "rights of Englishmen" even at the risk of destroying the old social order. For other revolutionaries, war and bloodshed were an opportunity to create a new social order. Stripped of old-fashioned notions of deference, this new order was to be founded on old ideas of public virtue and new ideas of equality, ideas that had grown directly out of the revolutionary experience.

Colonial Americans went into a revolutionary war with conflicting notions of republicanism. And the fact of war only served to intensify their differences. The result was an ongoing debate among Americans that contained far more significance for the American future than any simple division between Whigs and Tories. This debate could be heard in communities as varied as John Adams's Braintree and Thomas Paine's Philadelphia shortly after the first Fourth of July. Soon enough, it would send echoes through the difficult war years, the uncertain 1780s, and into the streets, taverns, and halls of Constitution-drafting Philadelphia in the summer of 1787. In fact, those echoes have continued to reverberate through the rest of America's turbulent history.

John C. Chalberg
Consulting Editor

CHAPTER 1

Intellectual Sources of the American Revolution

Chapter Preface

What was the source of the ideas that propelled and shaped the American Revolution? Writings from the Old World are an important part of the answer, most historians believe. From classical works by ancient Greek and Roman philosophers to contemporary radical English newspapers, many works on politics and society were read and studied by future revolutionary leaders. Historian Bernard Bailyn writes in *Faces of the Revolution*:

> The more we know about these colonial provincials, the clearer it is that among them were remarkably well-informed students of contemporary social and political thought. There never was a dark age that destroyed the cultural contacts between Europe and America. The sources of transmission had been numerous in the seventeenth century; they increased in the eighteenth. There were not only the impersonal agencies of newspapers, books, and pamphlets, but also continuous personal contact through travel and correspondence.

The most influential writings in the American Revolution were themselves largely the products of two historical events—the seventeenth-century English revolution and the spread of empirical and rationalist thinking known as the Enlightenment. The English revolution was a struggle between the king and Parliament for supreme sovereignty. King Charles I, who refused to consult Parliament on the grounds that his authority to rule came from God alone and not from the people, lost a civil war and ultimately his head in 1649. England remained without a monarch until 1660, when Charles II was restored to the throne under conditions granted by Parliament. Parliamentary sovereignty was permanently affirmed in the 1688 Glorious Revolution in which Charles II's successor, James II, was deposed and William and Mary from the Netherlands were invited to claim the throne. The result of all this struggle was a constitutionally limited monarchy that greatly increased the political power of Parliament and a 1689 Bill of Rights that gave inviolable civil and political rights to the people. The English people possessed greater freedoms than could be found in the rest of Europe. Preserving the "rights of Englishmen" was a prevailing theme of both English and American political writing leading up to the Revolution.

The Enlightenment describes the rationalist and scientific trend of eighteenth-century thought. It was a time in which people believed reason and scientific empiricism could be used to study the political as well as the natural world. Political law was rooted in natural law, it was argued, and was a law that provided for human rights and freedoms. Political systems could be rationally devised to best fulfill these natural laws and promote human freedom and progress.

John Locke and Charles-Louis de Montesquieu were two of the leading writers both influenced by and products of the English revolution and the Enlightenment. They both sought to examine the moral foundations of government and the best ways to preserve human liberty. Both writers advocated a government whose powers were divided, although their reasons for such division varied. Historian Elisha P. Douglass argues that the differences between Locke's and Montesquieu's theories on government reflected later differences between radicals and conservatives during the American Revolution:

> Locke, as well as Montesquieu, had advocated separation of powers, but the two philosophers had different views of the device which in some ways resembled those of the Revolutionary democrats and conservatives respectively. For Locke, separation of powers was primarily a means of promoting efficiency in government. The ultimate guarantee of liberty was popular sovereignty. Montesquieu . . . saw it as the sole guarantee of liberty.

Locke's and Montesquieu's writings on the foundations of government, in addition to works by John Milton, Francis Hutcheson, Edward Coke, William Blackstone, Niccolo Machiavelli, and Thomas Hobbes, were read and cited by Americans both before and after the American Revolution, and the influence of their ideas can be seen in both the Declaration of Independence and the U.S. Constitution.

VIEWPOINT 1

"The great and chief end . . . *of men's . . . putting themselves under government,* is the preservation of their property.*"*

The Basis of a Just Government Is Protection of Property

John Locke (1632-1704)

John Locke was an English philosopher whose ideas on government were influential during the American Revolution. He wrote important works on psychology, religious tolerance, and government. He epitomized the Enlightenment in his belief in reason and science, his calls for the freedom of conscience and right to property, and his belief in the essential goodness of humankind.

Locke's most famous writing on politics was the *Second Treatise of Government*, first published in 1690 as a justification of the 1688 Glorious Revolution in England, although most of it had been written years earlier. This viewpoint is excerpted from an edition of Locke's treatise published in 1980 by Hackett Publishing Company. Locke argues that the foundation of all government was a "social contract," the purpose of which is to protect a person's natural rights of life, liberty, and property. Locke asserts that the people have the right to change or even rebel against their government if it fails to carry out its duties of protecting their rights. Among the potential abuses he decried was government taxation without a person's consent. His ideas were influential in the colonists' debates over whether to break with Britain and can be seen in both the Declaration of Independence and the U.S. Constitution.

To understand political power right, and derive it from its original, we must consider, what state all men are naturally in, and that is, a *state of perfect freedom* to order their actions, and dispose of their possessions and persons, as they think fit, within the bounds of the law of nature, without asking leave, or depending upon the will of any other man.

A *state* also *of equality*, wherein all the power and jurisdiction is reciprocal, no one having more than another; there being nothing more evident, than that creatures of the same species and rank, promiscuously born to all the same advantages of nature, and the use of the same faculties, should also be equal one amongst another without subordination or subjection, unless the lord and master of them all should, by any manifest declaration of his will, set one above another, and confer on him, by an evident and clear appointment, an undoubted right to dominion and sovereignty. . . .

But though this be a *state of liberty*, yet *it is not a state of licence*: though man in that state have an uncontroulable liberty to dispose of his person or possessions, yet he has not liberty to destroy himself, or so much as any creature in his possession, but where some nobler use than its bare preservation calls for it. The *state of nature* has a law of nature to govern it, which obliges every one: and reason, which is that law, teaches all mankind, who will but consult it, that being all *equal and independent*, no one ought to harm another in his life, health, liberty, or possessions: for men being all the workmanship of one omnipotent, and infinitely wise maker; all the servants of one sovereign master, sent into the world by his order, and about his business; they are his property, whose workmanship they are, made to last during his, not one another's pleasure: and being furnished with like faculties, sharing all in one community of nature, there cannot be supposed any such *subordination* among us, that may authorize us to destroy one another, as if we were made for one another's uses, as the inferior ranks of creatures are for our's. Every one, as he is *bound to preserve himself*, and not to quit his station wilfully, so by the like reason, when his own preservation comes not in competition, ought he, as much as he can, *to preserve the rest of mankind*, and may not, unless it be to do justice on an offender, take away, or impair the life, or what tends to the preservation of the life, the liberty, health, limb, or goods of another. . . .

Of the Ends of Political Society and Government

If man in the state of nature be so free, as has been said; if he be absolute lord of his own person and possessions, equal to the greatest, and subject to no body, why will he part with his free-

Cato's Letters

John Trenchard and Thomas Gordon were Englishmen whose joint writings The Independent Whig *and* Cato's Letters, *first published in the early 1720s, were widely read in America. Influenced by Locke, they helped popularize his ideas in the colonies. In the fifty-ninth of* Cato's Letters, *which first appeared January 6, 1721, they argued that government's powers to deprive liberties are limited by natural law.*

All Governments, under whatsoever Form they are administered, ought to be administered for the Good of the Society; when they are otherwise administered, they cease to be government, and become Usurpation. This being the End of all Government, even the most despotick have this Limitation to their Authority: In this Respect, the only Difference between the most absolute Princes and limited Magistrates, is, that in free Governments there are Checks and Restraints appointed and expressed in the Constitution itself: In despotick Governments, the People submit themselves to the Prudence and Discretion of the Prince alone: But there is still this tacit Condition annexed to his Power, that he must act by the unwritten Laws of Discretion and Prudence, and employ it for the sole Interest of the People, who give it to him, or suffer him to enjoy it, which they ever do for their own Sakes. . . .

I have said thus much, to shew that no Government can be absolute in the Sense, or rather Nonsense, of our modern Dogmatizers, and indeed in the Sense too commonly practised. No barbarous Conquest; no extorted Consent of miserable People, submitting to the Chain to escape the Sword; no repeated and hereditary Acts of Cruelty, though called Succession, no Continuation of Violence, though named Prescription; can alter, much less abrogate, these fundamental Principles of Government itself, or make the Means of Preservation the Means of Destruction, and render the Condition of Mankind infinitely more miserable than that of the Beasts of the Field, by the sole Privilege of that Reason which distinguishes them from the Brute Creation.

dom? why will he give up this empire, and subject himself to the dominion and controul of any other power? To which it is obvious to answer, that though in the state of nature he hath such a right, yet the enjoyment of it is very uncertain, and constantly exposed to the invasion of others: for all being kings as much as he, every man his equal, and the greater part no strict observers of equity and justice, the enjoyment of the property he has in this state is very unsafe, very unsecure. This makes him willing to quit a condition, which, however free, is full of fears and continual dangers: and it is not without reason, that he seeks out, and is willing to join in society with others, who are already united, or have a mind to unite, for the mutual *preservation* of their lives, liberties and estates, which I call by the general name, *property*.

The great and *chief end*, therefore, of men's uniting into common-wealths, and putting themselves under government, *is the preservation of their property*. To which in the state of nature there are many things wanting.

First, There wants an *established*, settled, known *law*, received and allowed by common consent to be the standard of right and wrong, and the common measure to decide all controversies between them: for though the law of nature be plain and intelligible to all rational creatures; yet men being biased by their interest, as well as ignorant for want of study of it, are not apt to allow of it as a law binding to them in the application of it to their particular cases.

Secondly, In the state of nature there wants *a known and indifferent judge*, with authority to determine all differences according to the established law: for every one in that state being both judge and executioner of the law of nature, men being partial to themselves, passion and revenge is very apt to carry them too far, and with too much heat, in their own cases; as well as negligence, and unconcernedness, to make them too remiss in other men's.

Thirdly, In the state of nature there often wants *power* to back and support the sentence when right, and to *give it due execution*. They who by any injustice offended, will seldom fail, where they are able, by force to make good their injustice; such resistance many times makes the punishment dangerous, and frequently destructive, to those who attempt it.

Thus mankind, notwithstanding all the privileges of the state of nature, being but in an ill condition, while they remain in it, are quickly driven into society. Hence it comes to pass, that we seldom find any number of men live any time together in this state. The inconveniences that they are therein exposed to, by the irregular and uncertain exercise of the power every man has of punishing the transgressions of others, make them take sanctuary under the established laws of government, and therein seek *the preservation of their property*. It is this makes them so willingly give up every one his single power of punishing, to be exercised by such alone, as shall be appointed to it amongst them; and by such rules as the community, or those authorized by them to that purpose, shall agree on. And in this we have the original *right and rise of both the legislative and executive power*, as well as of the governments and societies themselves. . . .

The great end of men's entering into society, being the enjoyment of their properties in peace and safety, and the great instrument and means of that being the laws established in that society;

the *first and fundamental positive law* of all common-wealths *is the establishing of the legislative* power; as the *first and fundamental natural law*, which is to govern even the legislative itself, *is the preservation of the society*, and (as far as will consist with the public good) of every person in it. This *legislative* is not only *the supreme power* of the common-wealth, but sacred and unalterable in the hands where the community have once placed it; nor can any edict of any body else, in what form soever conceived, or by what power soever backed, have the force and obligation of a *law*, which has not its *sanction from* that *legislative* which the public has chosen and appointed: for without this the law could not have that, which is absolutely necessary to its being a *law, the consent of the society*, over whom no body can have a power to make laws, but by their own consent, and by authority received from them; and therefore all the *obedience*, which by the most solemn ties any one can be obliged *to* pay, ultimately terminates in this *supreme power*, and is directed by those laws which it enacts: nor can any oaths to any foreign power whatsoever, or any domestic subordinate power, discharge any member of the society from his *obedience to the legislative*, acting pursuant to their trust; nor oblige him to any obedience contrary to the laws so enacted, or farther than they do allow; it being ridiculous to imagine one can be tied ultimately to *obey* any *power* in the society, which is not the *supreme*.

Though the *legislative*, whether placed in one or more, whether it be always in being, or only by intervals, though it be the *supreme* power in every common-wealth; yet,

First, It is *not*, nor can possibly be absolutely *arbitrary* over the lives and fortunes of the people: for it being but the joint power of every member of the society given up to that person, or assembly, which is legislator; it can be no more than those persons had in a state of nature before they entered into society, and gave up to the community: for no body can transfer to another more power than he has in himself; and no body has an absolute arbitrary power over himself, or over any other, to destroy his own life, or take away the life or property of another. A man, as has been proved, cannot subject himself to the arbitrary power of another; and having in the state of nature no arbitrary power over the life, liberty, or possession of another, but only so much as the law of nature gave him for the preservation of himself, and the rest of mankind; this is all he doth, or can give up to the common-wealth, and by it to the *legislative power*, so that the legislative can have no more than this. Their power, in the utmost bounds of it, is *limited to the public good* of the society. It is a power, that hath no other end but preservation, and therefore can never have a right to destroy, enslave, or designedly to impoverish the subjects. The obligations of the law of nature cease not in society, but only in many cases are drawn closer, and have by human laws known penalties annexed to them, to inforce their observation. Thus the law of nature stands as an eternal rule to all men, *legislators* as well as others. The *rules* that they make for other men's actions, must, as well as their own and other men's actions, be conformable to the law of nature, *i.e.* to the will of God, of which that is a declaration, and the *fundamental law of nature being the preservation of mankind,* no human sanction can be good, or valid against it.

In his writings, John Locke developed the idea that revolution against an unjust government was not only a right but an obligation.

Secondly, The *legislative,* or supreme authority, cannot assume to its self a power to rule by extemporary arbitrary decrees, but *is bound to dispense justice,* and decide the rights of the subject *by promulgated standing laws, and known authorized judges:* for the law of nature being unwritten, and so no where to be found but in the minds of men, they who through passion or interest shall miscite, or misapply it, cannot so easily be convinced of their mistake where there is no established judge: and so it serves not, as it ought, to determine the rights, and fence the properties of those that live under it, especially where every one is judge, interpreter, and executioner of it too, and that in his own case: and he that has right on his side, having ordinarily but his own single strength, hath not force enough to defend himself from injuries, or to punish delinquents. To avoid these inconveniences, which disorder men's properties in the state of nature, men unite into societies, that they may have the united strength of the whole society to secure and defend their properties, and may have *standing rules* to bound it, by which every one may know what is his. To this end it is that men give up all their natural power to the society which they enter into, and the community put the legislative power into such hands as they think fit, with this trust, that they shall be governed by *declared laws*, or else their peace, quiet, and property will still be at the same uncertainty, as it was in the state of nature. . . .

Thirdly, The *supreme power cannot take* from any man any part of his *property* without his own consent: for the preservation of property being the end of government, and that for which men enter into society, it necessarily supposes and requires, that the people should *have property*, without which they must be supposed to lose that, by entering into society, which was the end for which they entered into it; too gross an absurdity for any man to own. *Men* therefore *in society having property*, they have such a right to the goods, which by the law of the community are their's, that no body hath a right to take their substance or any part of it from them, without their own consent: without this they have no *property* at all; for I have truly no *property* in that, which another can by right take from me, when he pleases, against my consent. Hence it is a mistake to think, that the *supreme or legislative power* of any common-wealth, can do what it will, and dispose of the estates of the subject *arbitrarily*, or take any part of them at pleasure. . . .

Fourthly, The *legislative cannot transfer the power of making laws* to any other hands: for it being but a delegated power from the people, they who have it cannot pass it over to others. The people alone can appoint the form of the common-wealth, which is by constituting the legislative, and appointing in whose hands that shall be. And when the people have said, We will submit to rules, and be governed by *laws* made by such men, and in such forms, no body else can say other men shall make *laws* for them; nor can the people be bound by any *laws*, but such as are enacted by those whom they have chosen, and authorized to make *laws* for them. The power of the *legislative*, being derived from the people by a positive voluntary grant and institution, can be no other than what that positive grant conveyed, which being only to make *laws*, and not to make *legislators*, the *legislative* can have no power to transfer their authority of making laws, and place it in other hands.

These are the *bounds* which the trust, that is put in them by the society, and the law of God and nature, have *set to the legislative* power of every common-wealth, in all forms of government.

First, They are to govern by *promulgated established laws*, not to be varied in particular cases, but to have one rule for rich and poor, for the favourite at court, and the country man at plough.

Secondly, These *laws* also ought to be designed *for* no other end ultimately, but *the good of the people.*

Thirdly, They must *not raise taxes* on the *property of the people, without the consent of the people,* given by themselves, or their deputies. And this properly concerns only such governments where the *legislative* is always in being, or at least where the people have not reserved any part of the legislative to deputies, to be from time to time chosen by themselves.

Fourthly, The *legislative* neither must *nor can transfer the power of making laws* to any body else, or place it any where, but where the people have.

VIEWPOINT 2

"Democracy hath therefore two excesses to avoid, the spirit of inequality which leads to aristocracy or monarchy; and the spirit of extreme equality, which leads to despotic power."

The Basis of a Just Government Is Virtue

Charles-Louis de Montesquieu (1689-1755)

Charles-Louis de Montesquieu was a French jurist and political philosopher. His most famous and influential work was *The Spirit of the Laws*, first published in 1748, and excerpted here. The work, an examination of republican, monarchical, and despotic forms of government, helped lay the foundations of modern political science. Translated into English by Thomas Nugent in 1750, it was read by many leaders of the American Revolution, including Thomas Jefferson and John Adams.

Montesquieu favorably compares the government of England to the monarchy of his native France, in which the king reigned supreme. He promulgates the idea of checks and balances among differing branches of government to check tyranny. He emphasizes virtue as the fundamental attribute of republics and argues that public virtue is something that must be continually cultivated for democracies to work. Democracies can be threatened by too much license and equality, he asserts.

There are three species of government; *republican, monarchical,* and *despotic*. In order to discover their nature, 'tis sufficient to recollect the common notion, which supposes three definitions or rather three facts, that the *republican government is that in which the body or only a part of the people is possessed of the supreme power: monarchy that in which a single person governs but by fixt and established laws: a despotic government, that in which a single person directs every thing by his own will and caprice. . . .*

This is what I call the nature of each government; we must examine now which are those laws that follow this nature directly, and consequently are the first fundamental laws. . . .

Laws Relative to Democracy

When the body of the people in a republic are possessed of the supreme power, this is called a *democracy*.

In a democracy the people are in some respects the sovereign, and in others the subject.

There can be no sovereign but by suffrages, which are their own will; and the sovereign's will is the sovereign himself. The laws therefore which establish the right of suffrage, are fundamental to this government. In fact, 'tis as important to regulate in a republic, in what manner, by whom, to whom, and concerning what, suffrages are to be given, as it is in a monarchy to know who is the prince and after what manner he ought to govern. . . .

'Tis an essential point to fix the number of citizens that are to form the public assemblies; otherwise it might be uncertain whether the whole body or only a part of the people have voted. At Sparta the number was fixt to ten thousand. But at Rome, that had sometimes all its inhabitants without its walls, and sometimes all Italy and a great part of the world within them; at Rome, I say, this number was never fixt, which was one of the principal causes of its ruin.

The people in whom the supreme power resides, ought to do of themselves whatever conveniently they can; and what they cannot well do, they must commit to the management of ministers.

The ministers are not properly their's, unless they have the nomination of them: 'tis therefore a fundamental maxim in this government, that the people should chuse their ministers, that is, their magistrates.

They have occasion as well as monarchs, and even more than they, to be directed by a council or senate. But to have a proper confidence in them, they should have the chusing of the members; whether the election be made by themselves, as at Athens; or by some magistrate deputed for the purpose, as was customary at Rome on certain occasions.

The people are extremely well qualified for chusing those whom they are to intrust with part of their authority. They can tell when a person has been often in battle, and has had particular success; they are therefore very capable of electing a general. They can tell when a judge is assiduous in his office, when he gives general satisfaction, and has never been charged with bribery. These are all facts of which they can have better information in a public forum, than a monarch in his palace. But are they able to manage an affair, to find out and make a proper use of places, occasions, moments? No, this is beyond their capacity. . . .

Six Types of Government

Niccolo Machiavelli, an Italian political philosopher whose writings date from the early 1500s, wrote extensively on politics and morality. He is considered by some historians to be the first modern political philosopher. His views on the fragility of democracies, expressed here in an excerpt from his work The Discourses, *were shared by many leaders of the American Revolution.*

Those who have written about republics declare that there are in them three kinds of governments, which they call principality, aristocracy, and democracy; and that those who organize a city most often turn to one of these, depending upon whichever seems more appropriate to them. Others—and wiser men, according to the judgment of many—are of the opinion that there are six types of government: three of these are very bad; three others are good in themselves but are so easily corruptible that they, too, can become pernicious. Those which are good are the three mentioned above; those which are bad are three others which depend upon the first three, and each of them is, in a way, similar to its good counterpart, so that they easily jump from one form to another. For the principality easily becomes tyrannical; aristocrats can very easily produce an oligarchy; democracy is converted into anarchy with no difficulty. So that if a founder of a republic organizes one of these three governments in a city, he organizes it there for a brief period of time only, since no precaution can prevent it from slipping into its contrary on account of the similarity, in such a case, of the virtue and the vice. . . .

Let me say, therefore, that all the forms of government listed are defective: the three good ones because of the brevity of their lives, the three bad ones because of their inherent harmfulness. Thus, those who were prudent in establishing laws recognized this fact and, avoiding each of these forms in themselves, chose one that combined them all, judging such a government to be steadier and more stable, for when there is in the same city-state a principality, an aristocracy, and a democracy, one form keeps watch over the other.

The public business must however be carried on, with a certain motion neither too quick nor too slow. But the action of the common people is always either too remiss or too violent. Sometimes with a hundred thousand arms they overturn all before them; and sometimes with a hundred thousand feet they creep like insects. . . .

There is no great share of probity necessary to support a monarchical or despotic government. The force of laws in one, and the prince's arm in the other, are sufficient to direct and maintain the whole. But in a popular state, one spring more is necessary, namely *virtue*.

What I have here advanced, is confirmed by the unanimous testimony of historians, and is extremely agreeable to the nature of things. For it is clear that in a monarchy, where he who commands the execution of the laws generally thinks himself above them, there is less need of virtue than in a popular government, where the person intrusted with the execution of the laws, is sensible of his being subject to their direction, and that he must submit to their authority.

Clear it is also that a monarch, who through bad council or indolence ceases to enforce the execution of the laws, may easily repair the evil; he has only to change his council; or to shake off this indolence. But when in a popular government, there is a suspension of the laws, as this can proceed only from the corruption of the republic, the state is certainly undone.

A very droll spectacle it was in the last century to behold the impotent efforts the English made for the establishment of democracy. As those who had a share in the direction of public affairs were void of all virtue, as their ambition was inflam'd by the success of the most daring of their members, as the spirit of a faction was suppressed only by that of a succeeding faction, the government was continually changing; the people amazed at so many revolutions fought every where for a democracy without being able to find it. At length after a series of tumultuary motions and violent shocks, they were obliged to have recourse to the very government they had so odiously proscribed. . . .

When virtue is banished, ambition invades the hearts of those who are capable of receiving it, and avarice possesses the whole community. Desires then change their objects; what they were fond of before, becomes now indifferent; they were free with laws, and they want to be free without them; every citizen is like a slave who has escaped from his master's house; what was maxim is called rigor; to rule they give the name of constraint; and of fear to attention. Frugality then, and not the thirst of gain, passes for avarice. . . .

The principle of democracy is corrupted, not only when the spirit of equality is extinct, but likewise when they fall into a spirit of extreme equality, and when every citizen wants to be upon a level with those he has chosen to command him. Then the people, incapable of bearing the very power they have intrusted, want to do every thing of themselves, to debate for the senate, to execute for the magistrate, and to strip the judges.

When this is the case, virtue can no longer subsist in the republic. The people want to exercise the functions of the magistrates; who cease to be revered. The deliberations of the senate are slighted; all respect is then laid aside for the senators, and consequently for old age. If respect ceases for old age, it will cease also for parents; deference to husbands will be likewise thrown off, and submission to masters. This licentiousness will soon captivate the mind; and the restraint of command be as fatiguing as that of obedience. Wives, children, slaves, will shake off all subjection. No longer will there be any such thing as manners, order, or virtue. . . .

Democracy hath therefore two excesses to avoid, the spirit of inequality which leads to aristocracy or monarchy; and the spirit of extreme equality, which leads to despotic power, as the latter is compleated by conquest. . . .

As distant as heaven is from earth, so is the true spirit of equality from that of extreme equality. The former does not consist in managing so that every body should command, or that no one should be commanded; but in obeying and commanding our equals. It endeavours not to be without a master, but that its masters should be none but its equals.

In the state of nature indeed, all men are born equal; but they cannot continue in this equality. Society makes them lose it, and they recover it only by means of the laws.

Such is the difference between a well and an ill policied democracy, that in the former men are equal only as citizens, but in the latter they are equal also as magistrates, senators, judges, fathers, husbands, masters.

The natural place of virtue is near to liberty; but it is not nearer to extreme liberty than to servitude. . . .

The Word *Liberty*

There is no word whatsoever that has admitted of more various significations, and has made more different impressions on human minds, than that of *Liberty*. Some have taken it for a facility of deposing a person on whom they had conferred a tyrannical authority; others for the power of chusing a person whom they are obliged to obey; others for the right of bearing arms, and of being thereby enabled to use violence; others in fine for the privilege of being governed by a native of their own country or by their own laws. A certain nation, for a long time thought liberty consisted in the privilege of wearing a long beard. Some have annexed this name to one form of government, in exclusion of others: Those who had a republican taste, applied it to this government; those who liked a monarchical state, gave it to monarchies. Thus they all have applied the name of *Liberty* to the government most conformable to their own customs and inclinations: and as in a republic people have not so constant and so present a view of the instruments of the evils they complain of, and likewise as the laws seem there to speak more, and the executors of the laws less, it is generally attributed to republics, and excluded from monarchies. In fine as in democracies the people seem to do very near whatever they please, liberty has been placed in this sort of government, and the power of the people has been confounded with their liberty.

It is true that in democracies the people seem to do what they please; but political liberty does not consist in an unrestrained freedom. In governments, that is, in societies directed by laws, liberty can consist only in the power of doing what we ought to will, and in not being constrained to do what we ought not to will.

We must have continually present to our minds the difference between independence and liberty. Liberty is a right of doing whatever the laws permit; and if a citizen could do what they forbid, he would no longer be possest of liberty, because all his fellow citizens would have the same power. . . .

Democratic and aristocratic states are not necessarily free. Political liberty is to be met with only in moderate governments: yet even in these it is not always met with. It is there only when there is no abuse of power: but constant experience shews us, that every man invested with power is apt to abuse it; he pushes on till he comes to the utmost limit. Is it not strange, tho' true, to say, that virtue itself has need of limits?

To prevent the abuse of power, 'tis necessary that by the very disposition of things power should be a check to power. A government may be so constituted, as no man shall be compelled to do things to which the law does not oblige him, nor forced to abstain from things which the law permits. . . .

The Constitution of England

In every government there are three sorts of power: the legislative; the executive in respect to things dependent on the law of nations; and the executive, in regard to things that depend on the civil laws.

By virtue of the first, the prince or magistrate enacts temporary or perpetual laws, and amends or abrogates those that have been already enacted. By the second, he makes peace or war, sends or receives embassies, establishes the public security, and provides against invasions. By the third, he punishes crimes, or determines the disputes that arise between individuals. The latter we shall call the judiciary power, and the other simply the executive power of the state.

The political liberty of the subject is a tranquillity of mind, arising from the opinion each person has of his safety. In order to have this liberty, it is requisite the government be so constituted as one man need not be afraid of another.

When the legislative and executive powers are united in the same person, or in the same body of magistracy, there can be then no liberty; because apprehensions may arise, lest the same monarch or senate should enact tyrannical laws, to execute them in a tyrannical manner.

Again, there is no liberty, if the power of judging be not separated from the legislative and executive powers. Were it joined with the legislative, the life and liberty of the subject would be exposed to arbitrary control; for the judge would be then the legislator. Were it joined to the executive power, the judge might behave with all the violence of an oppressor.

Miserable indeed would be the case, were the same man, or the same body whether of the nobles or of the people, to exercise those three powers, that of enacting laws, that of executing the public resolutions, and that of judging the crimes or differences of individuals.

CHAPTER 2

Early Disputes Between England and the Colonies

Chapter Preface

On the surface, prospects for the British Empire in America seemed excellent in 1763. The Seven Years' War ended in February with the Treaty of Paris, in which France ceded all of her North American territory to Britain. The American colonies seemed to be thriving, loyal provinces of the empire. Historian Jack P. Greene writes:

> Among the old colonies stretched along the Atlantic seaboard from Nova Scotia to Florida the inhabitants had never been happier to be part of so vast and so thriving an institution, and British nationalism had never been greater. To have suggested that these colonies during the next quarter century would openly revolt against Britain, weld themselves together in a loose confederation, make good a bid for independence, and embark upon a grand experiment in federalism would have seemed, except possibly to the most acute observer at the time, preposterous.

What were the disputes between the colonies and Great Britain that eventually led to open rebellion? On one level, the differences can be traced to specific laws and actions of the British government after 1763 as it attempted to revamp its colonial system. On a deeper level, these new laws and the American reactions to them revealed fundamental differences that had developed between the colonies and Britain over their status in the empire and their political rights of self-government.

Over the previous 150 years, the policy of Great Britain toward the American colonies was characterized by what British Parliament member Edmund Burke called "salutary neglect." Britain did not directly tax the colonies. It enacted some restrictive trade regulations and duties such as the 1733 Navigation Act, but these were avoided by colonial smuggling (helped by lax enforcement by the British). Long-standing tensions did exist between the governors, usually appointed by the Crown, and the colonial legislatures, elected by the colonists. However, by the 1760s most of the colonial assemblies had established their power to pass laws, raise taxes, and authorize military operations without British interference. Historian Richard Hofstadter writes:

> By the 1760s, the colonials held to the position that they enjoyed certain rights of self-government by reason of their being Englishmen; these rights, they believed, could not be rescinded. In contrast, the British held to the view that any practice of self-government exercised by the colonials was a privilege extended

to them by the royal grace and favor, privileges that could be withdrawn without colonial consultation.

These disagreements came rushing to the surface following the French and Indian War. Great Britain found itself saddled with great debts and with new western territory to manage. It determined to tighten its administration over the colonies and to ensure that the colonies pay part of the British war debts and the costs of maintaining British soldiers in the colonies. Between 1763 and 1765 it passed a series of acts for these purposes. Among the new laws were prohibitions against settling the western territories and the colonial coining of money, measures designed to tighten the enforcement of trade and tariff regulations, and the Stamp Act, a direct tax on legal papers, pamphlets, and newspapers that colonists had to pay for the papers to have legal standing.

Colonial reaction to the new measures, especially the Stamp Act, was far more angry than the British had expected. The colonial legislatures and a specially called Stamp Act Congress submitted petitions of protest to Parliament. Urban crowds used public intimidation and sometimes violence against the colonial agents sent to collect the tax. Pamphlets and newspaper editorials decried the tax. The colonies organized an economic boycott of British goods. For many colonists, both those who later advocated independence and those who later became loyalists, the issue was maintaining the traditional rights of English citizens, especially the rights of "no taxation without representation." The British Parliament believed that it had full sovereign authority over all the British Empire, including the colonies. American protesters held that without representation Parliament had no power to tax them.

The colonial protests, especially the economic boycott, proved effective. Parliament repealed the Stamp Act in 1766, causing much celebration in the colonies. However, Parliament refused to relinquish in principle its ultimate authority to tax. This sequence of events was repeated following the 1767 Townshend Acts, in which Parliament passed heavy import duties on a variety of British goods. Again the colonists protested, pamphlets and newspapers decried the measure and defended the rights of the colonists, and an economic boycott was organized. Again Parliament repealed most of the measures in 1770 while refusing to compromise on the principle of its authority. Parliament let stand a small tax on tea, a tax which three years later caused a chain of events that ultimately led to the colonies' decision for independence.

Viewpoint 1

"The right of the Legislature of Great Britain to impose taxes on her American colonies . . . [is] indisputably clear."

The British Parliament Has the Right to Tax the Colonies

Soame Jenyns (1704-1787)

Soame Jenyns was a poet and a member of the British Parliament from 1741 to 1780. He served for many years on the Board of Trade, an influential committee of British merchants, royal officials, and others who advised Parliament on colonial matters. In 1765 he wrote a pamphlet defending Parliament's right to tax the colonies called *The Objections to the Taxation of Our American Colonies by the Legislature of Great Britain, Briefly Considr'd* published in London. The pamphlet was reprinted in colonial newspapers and otherwise distributed throughout the colonies, further inflaming debate on the Stamp Act and other acts of Parliament on the colonies.

The right of the Legislature of Great Britain to impose taxes on her American colonies, and the expediency of exerting that right in the present conjuncture, are propositions so indisputably clear that I should never have thought it necessary to have undertaken their defence, had not many arguments been lately flung out both in papers and conversation, which with insolence equal to their absurdity deny them both. As these are usually mixt up with several patriotic and favorite words such as liberty, property, Englishmen, etc., which are apt to make strong impressions on that more numerous part of mankind who have ears but no understanding, it will not, I think, be improper to give them some answers. To this, therefore, I shall singly confine myself, and do it in as few words as possible, being sensible that the fewest will give least trouble to myself, and probably most information to my reader.

Taxation and Consent

The great capital argument which I find on this subject, and which, like an elephant at the head of a Nabob's army, being once overthrown must put the whole into confusion, is this; that no Englishman is, or can be taxed, but by his own consent: by which must be meant one of these three propositions; either that no Englishman can be taxed without his own consent as an individual; or that no Englishman can be taxed without the consent of the persons he chuses to represent him; or that no Englishman can be taxed without the consent of the majority of all those who are elected by himself and others of his fellow subjects to represent them. Now let us impartially consider whether any one of these propositions are in fact true: if not, then this wonderful structure which has been erected upon them falls at once to the ground, and like another Babel, perishes by a confusion of words, which the builders themselves are unable to understand.

First then, that no Englishman is or can be taxed but by his own consent as an individual: this is so far from being true, that it is the very reverse of truth; for no man that I know of is taxed by his own consent, and an Englishman, I believe, is as little likely to be so taxed as any man in the world.

Secondly, that no Englishman is or can be taxed but by the consent of those persons whom he has chosen to represent him. For the truth of this I shall appeal only to the candid representatives of those unfortunate counties which produce cyder, and shall willingly acquiesce under their determination.

Lastly, that no Englishman is or can be taxed without the consent of the majority of those who are elected by himself and others of his fellow subjects to represent them. This is certainly as false as the other two; for every Englishman is taxed, and not one in twenty represented: copyholders, leaseholders, and all men possessed of personal property only, chuse no representatives; Manchester, Birmingham, and many more of our richest and most flourishing trading towns send no members to Parliament, consequently cannot consent by their representatives, because they chuse none to represent them; yet are they not Englishmen?

A Mob's Disgraceful Acts

Francis Bernard served as colonial governor of New Jersey and Massachusetts. In a letter to the Earl of Halifax in England, dated August 31, 1765, Bernard describes some of the mob activity Bostonians engaged in while protesting the Stamp Act.

The lieutenant governor had been apprised that there was an evil spirit gone forth against him, but being conscious that he had not in the least deserved to be made a party in regard to the Stamp Act or the Custom House, he rested in full security that the mob would not attack him, and he was at supper with his family when he received advice that the mob were coming to him. He immediately sent away his children and determined to stay in the house himself, but happily his eldest daughter returned and declared she would not stir from the house unless he went with her; by which means she got him away, which was undoubtedly the occasion of saving his life. For as soon as the mob had got into the house, with a most irresistible fury they immediately looked about for him to murder him, and even made diligent inquiry wither he was gone. They went to work with a rage scarce to be exemplified by the most savage people. Everything movable was destroyed in the most minute manner except such things of value as were worth carrying off, among which was near £1,000 sterling in specie, besides a great quantity of family plate, etc.

or are they not taxed?

I am well aware that I shall hear Locke, Sidney, Selden, and many other great names quoted to prove that every Englishman, whether he has a right to vote for a representative or not, is still represented in the British Parliament, in which opinion they all agree. On what principle of common-sense this opinion is founded I comprehend not, but on the authority of such respectable names I shall acknowledge its truth; but then I will ask one question, and on that I will rest the whole merits of the cause. Why does not this imaginary representation extend to America as well as over the whole Island of Great Britain? If it can travel three hundred miles, why not three thousand? If it can jump over rivers and mountains, why cannot it sail over the ocean? If the towns of Manchester and Birmingham, sending no representatives to Parliament, are notwithstanding there represented, why are not the cities of Albany and Boston equally represented in that Assembly? Are they not alike British subjects? are they not Englishmen? or are they only Englishmen when they sollicit for protection, but not Englishmen when taxes are required to enable this country to protect them?

But it is urged that the colonies are by their charters placed under distinct Governments each of which has a legislative power within itself, by which alone it ought to be taxed; that if this privilege is once given up, that liberty which every Englishman has a right to, is torn from them, they are all slaves, and all is lost.

English Liberty

The liberty of an Englishman is a phrase of so various a signification, having within these few years been used as a synonymous term for blasphemy, bawdy, treason, libels, strong beer, and cyder, that I shall not here presume to define its meaning; but I shall venture to assert what it cannot mean; that is, an exemption from taxes imposed by the authority of the Parliament of Great Britain; nor is there any charter that ever pretended to grant such a privilege to any colony in America; and had they granted it, it could have had no force; their charters being derived from the Crown, and no charter from the Crown can possibly supersede the right of the whole legislature. Their charters are undoubtedly no more than those of all corporations, which impower them to make byelaws, and raise duties for the purposes of their own police, for ever subject to the superior authority of Parliament; and in some of their charters the manner of exercising these powers is specifyed in these express words, "according to the course of other corporations in Great Britain". And therefore they can have no more pretence to plead an exemption from this parliamentary authority, than any other corporation in England.

It has been moreover alleged, that though Parliament may have power to impose taxes on the colonies, they have no right to use it, because it would be an unjust tax; and no supreme or legislative power can have a right to enact any law in its nature unjust. To this, I shall only make this short reply, that if Parliament can impose no taxes but what are equitable, and if the persons taxed are to be the judges of that equity, they will in effect have no power to lay any tax at all. No tax can be imposed exactly equal on all, and if it is not equal it cannot be just, and if it is not just, no power whatever can impose it; by which short syllogism all taxation is at an end; but why it should not be used by Englishmen on this side the Atlantic as well as by those on the other, I do not comprehend.

Thus much for the right. Let us now a little inquire into the expediency of this measure, to which two objections have been made; that the time is improper, and the manner wrong.

The Proper Time

As to the first, can any time be more proper to require some assistance from our colonies, to preserve to themselves their present safety, than when this country is almost undone by procuring it? Can any time be more proper to impose some tax upon their trade, than when they are enabled to rival us in our manufactures, by the encouragement and protection which we have given them? Can any time be more proper to oblige them to settle handsome incomes on their Governors, than when we find them unable to procure a subsistence on any other terms than those of breaking all their instructions, and betraying the rights of their sovereign? Can there be a more proper time to compel them to fix certain salaries on their judges, than when we see them so dependent on the humours of their Assemblies, that they can obtain a livelihood no longer than *quam diu se male gesserint* [through continual misconduct]? Can there be a more proper time to force them to maintain an army at their expence, than when that army is necessary for their own protection, and we are utterly unable to support it? Lastly; can there be a more proper time for this mother country to leave off feeding out of her own vitals these children whom she has nursed up, than when they are arrived at such strength and maturity as to be well able to provide for themselves and ought rather with filial duty to give some assistance to her distresses?

As to the manner; that is, the imposing taxes on the colonies by the authority of Parliament, it is said to be harsh and arbitrary; and that it would have been more consistent with justice, at least with maternal tenderness, for administration here to have settled quotas on each of the colonies, and have then transmitted them with injunctions that the sums allotted should be immediately raised by their respective legislatures, on the penalty of their being imposed by Parliament in case of their non-compliance. But was this to be done, what would be the consequence? Have their Assemblies shewn so much obedience to the orders of the Crown, that we could reasonably expect that they would immediately tax themselves on the arbitrary command of a minister? Would it be possible here to settle those quotas with justice, or would any one of the colonies submit to them, were they ever so just? Should we not be compared to those Roman tyrants, who used to send orders to their subjects to murder themselves within so many hours, most obligingly leaving the method to their own choice, but on their disobedience threatening a more severe fate from the hands of an executioner? And should we not receive votes, speeches, resolutions, petitions, and remonstrances in abundance, instead of taxes? In short, we either have a right to tax the colonies, or we have not. If Parliament is possessed of this right, why should it be exercised with more delicacy in America than it has ever been even in Great Britain itself? If on the other hand, they have no such right, sure it is below the dignity as well as the justice of the Legislature to intimidate the colonies with vain threats, which they have really no right to put in execution.

One method indeed has been hinted at, and but one, that might render the exercise of this power in a British Parliament just and legal, which is the introduction of representatives from the several colonies into that body; but as this has never seriously been proposed, I shall not here consider the impracticability of this method, nor the effects of it if it could be practised; but only say that I have lately seen so many specimens of the great powers of speech of which these American gentlemen are possessed, that I should be much afraid that the sudden importation of so much eloquence at once, would greatly endanger the safety and government of this country; or in terms more fashionable, though less understood, this our most excellent Constitution. If we can avail ourselves of these taxes on no other condition, I shall never look upon it as a measure of frugality; being perfectly satisfyed that in the end it will be much cheaper for us to pay their army than their orators.

I cannot omit taking notice of one prudential reason which I

America Must Pay for Its Protection

George Grenville was prime minister of Great Britain from 1763 to 1765, a time when the Stamp Act and other laws unpopular with the colonies were passed. In this excerpt taken from a January 14, 1766, debate, Grenville asserts that Parliament has the right and the duty to impose taxes on America to help defray Great Britain's military expenditures. His arguments were preserved in William Cobbett's 1803 Parliamentary History of England.

That this kingdom has the sovereign, the supreme legislative power over America, is granted. It cannot be denied; and taxation is a part of that sovereign power. It is one branch of the legislation. It is, it has been exercised, over those who are not, who were never represented. It is exercised over the India Company, the merchants of London, and the proprietors of the stocks, and over great manufacturing towns. It was exercised over the county palatine of Chester, and the bishoprick of Durham, before they sent any representatives to parliament. . . .

Protection and obedience are reciprocal. Great Britain protects America, America is bound to yield obedience. If not, tell me when the Americans were emancipated? When they want the protection of this kingdom, they are always very ready to ask it. That protection has always been afforded them in the most full and ample manner. The nation has run itself into an immense debt to give them this protection; and now they are called upon to contribute a small share towards the public expence.

have heard frequently urged against this taxation of the colonies, which is this: That if they are by this means impoverished, they will be unable to purchase our manufactures, and consequently we shall lose that trade from which the principal benefit which we receive from them must arise. But surely, it requires but little sagacity to see the weakness of this argument; for should the colonies raise taxes for the purposes of their own government and protection, would the money so raised be immediately annihilated? What some pay, would not others receive? Would not those who so receive it, stand in need of as many of our manufactures, as those who pay? Was the army there maintained at the expence of the Americans, would the soldiers want fewer coats, hats, shirts, or shoes than at present? Had the judges salaries ascertained to them, would they not have occasion for as costly perriwigs, or robes of as expensive scarlet, as marks of their legal abilities, as they now wear in their present state of dependency? Or had their Governors better incomes settled on them for observing their instructions, than they can now with difficulty obtain for disobeying them, would they expend less money in their several Governments, or bring home at their return less riches to lay out in the manufactories of their native country? . . .

From what has been here said, I think that not only the right of the legislature of Great Britain to impose taxes on her colonies, not only the expediency, but the absolute necessity of exercising that right in the present conjuncture, has been so clearly though concisely proved, that it is to be hoped that in this great and important question all parties and factions, or in the more polite and fashionable term, all connections will most cordially unite; that every member of the British Parliament, whether in or out of humour with Administration, whether he has been turned out because he has opposed, or whether he opposes because he has been turned out, will endeavour to the utmost of his power to support this measure. A measure which must not only be approved by every man who has any property or common sense, but which ought to be required by every English subject of an English Administration.

VIEWPOINT 2

"A right to impose an internal tax on the colonies without their consent for the single purpose of revenue is denied."

The British Parliament Has No Right to Tax the Colonies

Daniel Dulany (1722-1797)

Daniel Dulany was a wealthy lawyer and Maryland public official. Born in Maryland, he received his higher education in England. In October 1765, seven months after the British Parliament passed the controversial Stamp Act, he published the pamphlet *Considerations on the Propriety of Imposing Taxes in the British Colonies,* which was reprinted in vol. 2 of *The Annals of America,* published in 1968 by Encyclopædia Britannica. The pamphlet attempted to expand on the argument that the British Parliament, having no elected colonial representatives, had no right to tax the colonies. The arguments were in part a refutation of assertions made by some British officials that the colonies were "virtually represented" in Parliament much the same as were people in Great Britain who lacked the right to vote. The pamphlet went through five editions in the colonies and was widely praised. It was also reprinted in England, and its influence has been credited as one reason the Stamp Act was repealed in 1766.

Dulany attempts to steer a moderate course in British-colonial relations, rejecting both Parliament's power to tax the colonies and total independence of the colonies from England. His views remained relatively constant until his death; he refused to support American independence and remained neutral during the revolutionary war.

I shall undertake to disprove the supposed similarity of situation, whence the same kind of representation is deduced of the inhabitants of the colonies, and of the British nonelectors; and, if I succeed, the notion of a virtual representation of the colonies must fail, which, in truth, is a mere cobweb spread to catch the unwary and entangle the weak. I would be understood. I am upon a question of propriety, not of power; and though some may be inclined to think it is to little purpose to discuss the one when the other is irresistible, yet are they different considerations; and, at the same time that I invalidate the claim upon which it is founded, I may very consistently recommend a submission to the law, whilst it endures. . . .

Nonelectors

Lessees for years, copyholders, proprietors of the public funds, inhabitants of Birmingham, Leeds, Halifax, and Manchester, merchants of the City of London, or members of the corporation of the East India Company, are, as such, under no personal incapacity to be electors; for they may acquire the right of election, and there are actually not only a considerable number of electors in each of the classes of lessees for years, etc., but in many of them, if not all, even members of Parliament. The interests, therefore, of the nonelectors, the electors, and the representatives are individually the same; to say nothing of the connection among neighbors, friends, and relations. The security of the nonelectors against oppression is that their oppression will fall also upon the electors and the representatives. The one cannot be injured and the other indemnified.

Further, if the nonelectors should not be taxed by the British Parliament, they would not be taxed at all; and it would be iniquitous, as well as a solecism in the political system, that they should partake of all the benefits resulting from the imposition and application of taxes, and derive an immunity from the circumstance of not being qualified to vote. Under this constitution, then, a double or virtual representation may be reasonably supposed.

The electors, who are inseparably connected in their interests with the nonelectors, may be justly deemed to be the representatives of the nonelectors, at the same time they exercise their personal privilege in their right of election, and the members chosen, therefore, the representatives of both. This is the only rational explanation of the expression "virtual representation." None has been advanced by the assertors of it, and their meaning can only be inferred from the instances by which they endeavor to elucidate it; and no other meaning can be stated to which the instances apply. . . .

The inhabitants of the colonies are, as such, incapable of being electors, the privilege of election being exercisable only in person, and, therefore, if every inhabitant of America had the requisite freehold, not one could vote but upon the supposition of his ceasing to be an inhabitant of America and becoming a resident in Great Britain, a supposition which would be impertinent because it shifts the question—Should the colonies not be taxed by parliamentary impositions; their respective legislatures have a regular, adequate, and constitutional authority to tax them; and therefore there would not necessarily be an iniquitous and absurd exemption from their not being represented by the House of Commons?

There is not that intimate and inseparable relation between the electors of Great Britain and the inhabitants of the colonies, which must inevitably involve both in the same taxation. On the contrary, not a single actual elector in England might be immediately affected by a taxation in America, imposed by a statute which would have a general operation and effect upon the properties of the inhabitants of the colonies.

Internal Taxes

But though it has been admitted that the Stamp Act is the first statute that has imposed an internal tax upon the colonies *for the single purpose of revenue*, yet the advocates for that law contend that there are many instances of the Parliament's exercising a supreme legislative authority over the colonies and actually imposing *internal taxes* upon their properties—that the duties upon any exports or imports are internal taxes; that an impost on a foreign commodity is as much an internal tax as a duty upon any production of the plantations; that no distinction can be supported between one kind of tax and another, an authority to impose the one extending to the other.

If these things are really as represented by the advocates for the Stamp Act, why did the chancellor of the Exchequer make it a question for the consideration of the House of Commons, whether the Parliament could impose an *internal tax* in the colonies or not for the *single purpose of revenue*?

It appears to me that there is a clear and necessary distinction between an act imposing a tax for the single purpose of revenue and those acts which have been made for the regulation of trade and have produced some revenue in consequence of their effect and operation as regulations of trade.

The colonies claim the privileges of British subjects. It has been proved to be inconsistent with those privileges to tax them without their own consent, and it has been demonstrated that a tax imposed by Parliament is a tax *without their consent*.

The subordination of the colonies and the authority of Parlia-

51

The Stamp Act Congress

In October 1765, the Stamp Act Congress, consisting of twenty-eight delegates from nine colonies, met and wrote fourteen declarations, eight of which appear here. The declarations asserted colonial rights and attacked the Stamp Act. The Stamp Act Congress was the first intercolonial congress to meet in America.

I. That His Majesty's subjects in these colonies, owe the same allegiance to the Crown of Great-Britain, that is owing from his subjects born within the realm, and all due subordination to that august body the Parliament of Great-Britain.

II. That His Majesty's liege subjects in these colonies, are entitled to all the inherent rights and liberties of his natural born subjects within the kingdom of Great-Britain.

III. That it is inseparably essential to the freedom of a people, and the undoubted right of Englishmen, that no taxes be imposed on them, but with their own consent, given personally, or by their representatives.

IV. That the people of these colonies are not, and from their local circumstances cannot be, represented in the House of Commons in Great-Britain.

V. That the only representatives of the people of these colonies, are persons chosen therein by themselves, and that no taxes ever have been, or can be constitutionally imposed on them, but by their respective legislatures.

VI. That all supplies to the Crown, being free gifts of the people, it is unreasonable and inconsistent with the principles and spirit of the British Constitution, for the people of Great-Britain to grant to His Majesty the property of the colonists.

VII. That trial by jury is the inherent and invaluable right of every British subject in these colonies.

VIII. That the late Act of Parliament, entitled, *An Act for granting and applying certain Stamp Duties, and other Duties, in the British colonies and plantations in America, etc.*, by imposing taxes on the inhabitants of these colonies, and the said Act, and several other Acts, by extending the jurisdiction of the courts of Admiralty beyond its ancient limits, have a manifest tendency to subvert the rights and liberties of the colonists.

ment to preserve it have been fully acknowledged. Not only the welfare but perhaps the existence of the mother country, as an independent kingdom, may depend upon her trade and navigation, and these so far upon her intercourse with the colonies that if this should be neglected, there would soon be an end to that commerce, whence her greatest wealth is derived and upon which her maritime power is principally founded. From these considerations, the right of the British Parliament to regulate the trade of the colonies may be justly deduced; a denial of it would contradict the admission of the subordination and of the authority to preserve it, resulting from the nature of the relation between the mother country and her colonies. It is a common and frequently the most proper method to regulate trade by duties on imports and exports. The authority of the mother country to regulate the trade of the colonies being unquestionable, what regulations are the most proper are to be of course submitted to the determination of the Parliament; and if an incidental revenue should be produced by such regulations, these are not therefore unwarrantable.

A right to impose an internal tax on the colonies without their consent for the single purpose of revenue is denied; a right to regulate their trade without their consent is admitted. The imposition of a duty may, in some instances, be the proper regulation. If the claims of the mother country and the colonies should seem on such an occasion to interfere and the point of right to be doubtful (which I take to be otherwise), it is easy to guess that the determination will be on the side of power and that the inferior will be constrained to submit. . . .

Not only as a friend to the colonies but as an inhabitant having my all at stake upon their welfare, I desire an exemption from taxes imposed *without my consent*, and I have reflected longer than a moment upon the consequences. I value it as one of the dearest privileges I enjoy. I acknowledge dependence on Great Britain, but I can perceive a degree of it without slavery, and I disown all other. I do not expect that the interests of the colonies will be considered by some men but in subserviency to other regards. The effects of luxury, and venality, and oppression, posterity may perhaps experience, and *sufficient for the day will be the evil thereof.*

VIEWPOINT 3

"From what hath been shown, it will appear beyond a doubt, that the British subjects in America, have equal rights with those in Britain."

Parliament Is Abusing the Rights of Americans

Stephen Hopkins (1707-1785)

Stephen Hopkins was colonial governor of Rhode Island at the time of the Stamp Act controversy. Unlike the governors of many other colonies who were appointed by the king or queen of England, Hopkins was elected governor of Rhode Island by members of the colonial assembly. In November 1764 Hopkins called a special session of the legislature to warn about the proposed Stamp Act. The legislature responded by sending a petition to King George III listing economic grievances and denying the right of Parliament to enact the Stamp Act. The legislature also endorsed a pamphlet Hopkins had written entitled *The Rights of Colonies Examined*, published in Providence in 1764. The pamphlet was widely acclaimed and reprinted several times in the colonies and in Great Britain.

In his pamphlet, excerpted here, Hopkins argues that Americans fully shared with the citizens of Great Britain the rights and liberties granted under the British constitution. This constitution, although not a written document, was a common law constitution, the cumulative result of British law and the fundamental rights and freedoms that had evolved in England over the previous centuries. Hopkins asserts that recent British actions such as the Stamp Act were jeopardizing these rights.

Hopkins at this juncture did not advocate total independence from Great Britain. Later, however, he did serve as a member of the Continental Congress and he was a signer of the Declaration of Independence.

Liberty is the greatest blessing that men enjoy, and slavery the heaviest curse that human nature is capable of.—This being so, makes it a matter of the utmost importance to men, which of the two shall be their portion. Absolute liberty is, perhaps, incompatible with any kind of government.—The safety resulting from society, and the advantage of just and equal laws, hath caused men to forego some part of their natural liberty, and submit to government. This appears to be the most rational account of its beginning; although, it must be confessed, mankind have by no means been agreed about it. Some have found its origin in the divine appointment; others have thought it took its rise from power; enthusiasts have dreamed that dominion was founded in grace. Leaving these points to be settled by the descendants of Filmer, Cromwell and Venner, we will consider the British constitution, as it at present stands, on revolution principles; and from thence endeavor to find the measure of the magistrate's power and the people's obedience.

This glorious constitution, the best that ever existed among men, will be confessed by all, to be founded by compact, and established by consent of the people. By this most beneficent compact, British subjects are governed only agreeable to laws to which themselves have some way consented; and are not to be compelled to part with their property, but as it is called for by the authority of such laws. The former, is truly liberty; the latter is really to be possessed of property, and to have something that may be called one's own.

The Rights of Colonists

On the contrary, those who are governed at the will of another, or of others, and whose property may be taken from them by taxes, or otherwise, without their own consent, and against their will, are in the miserable condition of slaves. "For liberty solely consists in an independency upon the will of another; and by the name of slave, we understand a man who can neither dispose of his person or goods, but enjoys all at the will of his master," says Sidney, on government. These things premised, whether the British American colonies, on the continent, are justly entitled to like privileges and freedom as their fellow subjects in Great Britain are, shall be the chief point examined. In discussing this question, we shall make the colonies in New England, with whose rights we are best acquainted, the rule of our reasoning; not in the least doubting but all the others are justly entitled to like rights with them.

New England was first planted by adventurers, who left England, their native country, by permission of King Charles the First; and, at their own expense, transported themselves to America, with great risk and difficulty settled among savages, and in a very surprising manner formed new colonies in the wilderness. Before their departure, the terms of their freedom, and the relation they should stand in to the mother country, in their emigrant state, were fully settled; they were to remain subject to the King, and dependent on the kingdom of Great Britain. In return, they were to receive protection, and enjoy all the rights and privileges of free-born Englishmen.

Taxes Destroy Liberty

In 1764 the Connecticut Assembly asked a committee headed by Thomas Fitch, the colonial governor, to draft a resolution in opposition to the Stamp Act. Fitch's report was published in the form of a pamphlet entitled Reasons Why the British Colonies in America Should Not Be Charged with Internal Taxes. *The pamphlet was widely distributed in both Great Britain and the colonies.*

If these internal taxations take place, and the principles upon which they must be founded are adopted and carried into execution, the colonies will have no more than a show of legislation left, nor the King's subjects in them any more than the shadow of true English liberty; for the same principles which will justify such a tax of a penny will warrant a tax of a pound, a hundred, or a thousand pounds, and so on without limitations; and if they will warrant a tax on one article, they will support one on as many particulars as shall be thought necessary to raise any sum proposed. And all such subjections, burdens, and deprivations, if they take place with respect to the King's subjects abroad, will be without their consent, without their having opportunity to be represented or to show their ability, disability, or circumstances. They will no longer enjoy that fundamental privilege of Englishmen whereby, in special, they are denominated a free people. The legislative authority of the colonies will in part actually be cut off; a part of the same will be taken out of their own assemblies, even such part as they have enjoyed so long and esteem most dear.

This is abundantly proved by the charter given to the Massachusetts colony, while they were still in England, and which they received and brought over with them, as the authentic evidence of the conditions they removed upon. The colonies of Connecticut and Rhode Island, also, afterwards obtained charters from the crown, granting them the like ample privileges. By all these charters, it is in the most express and solemn manner granted, that these adventurers, and their children after them for ever, should have and enjoy all the freedom and liberty that the subjects in England enjoy; that they might make laws for their own government, suitable to their circumstances not repugnant to, but as near as might be, agreeable to the laws of England; that they might purchase lands, acquire goods, and use trade for their advantage, and have an absolute property in whatever they justly acquired. These, with many other gracious privileges, were granted them by several kings; and they were to pay, as an acknowledgment to the crown, only one-fifth part of the ore of gold and silver, that should at any time be found in the said colonies, in lieu of, and full satisfaction for, all dues and demands of the crown and kingdom of England upon them.

There is not any thing new or extraordinary in these rights granted to the British colonies; the colonies from all countries, at all times, have enjoyed equal freedom with the mother state. Indeed, there would be found very few people in the world, willing to leave their native country, and go through the fatigue and hardship of planting in a new uncultivated one, for the sake of losing their freedom. They who settle new countries, must be poor; and, in course, ought to be free. Advantages, pecuniary or agreeable, are not on the side of emigrants; and surely they must have something in their stead.

To illustrate this, permit us to examine what hath generally been the condition of colonies with respect to their freedom; we will begin with those who went out from the ancient commonwealths of Greece, which are the first, perhaps, we have any good account of. Thucidides, that grave and judicious historian, says of one of them, "they were not sent out to be slaves, but to be the equals of those who remain behind;" and again, the Corinthians gave public notice, "that a new colony was going to Epidamus, into which, all that would enter, should have equal and like privileges with those who stayed at home." This was uniformly the condition of all the Grecian colonies; they went out and settled new countries; they took such forms of government as themselves chose, though it generally nearly resembled that of the mother state, whether democratical or oligarchical. . . .

When we come down to the latter ages of the world, and consider the colonies planted in the three last centuries, in America, from several kingdoms in Europe, we shall find them, says Puffendorf, very different from the ancient colonies, and gives us an instance in those of the Spaniards. Although it be confessed, these fall greatly short of enjoying equal freedom with the ancient Greek and Roman ones; yet it will be said truly, they enjoy equal freedom with their countrymen in Spain; but as they are all under the government of an absolute monarch, they have no reason to complain that one enjoys the liberty the other is deprived of. The

French colonies will be found nearly in the same condition, and for the same reason, because their fellow subjects in France, have also lost their liberty. And the question here is not whether all colonies, as compared one with another, enjoy equal liberty, but whether all enjoy as much freedom as the inhabitants of the mother state; and this will hardly be denied in the case of the Spanish, French, or other modern foreign colonies.

By this, it fully appears, that colonies, in general, both ancient and modern, have always enjoyed as much freedom as the mother state from which they went out; and will any one suppose the British colonies in America, are an exception to this general rule? Colonies that came out from a kingdom renowned for liberty; from a constitution founded on compact; from a people, of all the sons of men, the most tenacious of freedom; who left the delights of their native country, parted from their homes, and all their conveniences, searched out and subdued a foreign country, with the most amazing travail and fortitude, to the infinite advantage and emolument of the mother state; that removed on a firm reliance of a solemn compact, and royal promise and grant, that they, and their successors for ever, should be free; should be partakers and sharers in all the privileges and advantages of the then English, now British constitution.

Equal Liberty

If it were possible a doubt could yet remain, in the most unbelieving mind, that these British colonies are not every way justly and fully entitled to equal liberty and freedom with their fellow subjects in Europe, we might show, that the parliament of Great Britain, have always understood their rights in the same light.

By an act passed in the thirteenth year of the reign of his late majesty King George the Second, entitled an act for naturalizing foreign protestants, &c.; and by another act passed in the twentieth year of the same reign, for nearly the same purposes, by both which it is enacted and ordained, "that all foreign protestants, who had inhabited, and resided for the space of seven years, or more, in any of his majesty's colonies, in America," might, on the conditions therein mentioned, be naturalized, and thereupon should "be deemed, adjudged and taken to be his majesty's natural born subjects of the kingdom of Great Britain, to all intents, constructions and purposes, as if they, and every one of them, had been, or were born within the same." No reasonable man will here suppose the parliament intended by these acts to put foreigners, who had been in the colonies only seven years, in a better condition than those who had been born in them, or had removed from Britain thither, but only to put these foreigners on an equality with them; and to do this, they are obliged to give them all the rights of natural born subjects of Great Britain.

From what hath been shown, it will appear beyond a doubt, that the British subjects in America, have equal rights with those in Britain; that they do not hold those rights as a privilege granted them, nor enjoy them as a grace and favor bestowed; but possess them as an inherent indefeasible right; as they, and their ancestors, were free-born subjects, justly and naturally entitled to all the rights and advantages of the British constitution.

New Laws

And the British legislative and executive powers have considered the colonies as possessed of these rights, and have always heretofore, in the most tender and parental manner, treated them as their dependent, though free, condition required. The protection promised on the part of the crown, with cheerfulness and great gratitude we acknowledge, hath at all times been given to the colonies. The dependence of the colonies to Great Britain, hath been fully testified by a constant and ready obedience to all the commands of His present Majesty, and his royal predecessors; both men and money having been raised in them at all times when called for, with as much alacrity and in as large proportions as hath been done in Great Britain, the ability of each considered. It must also be confessed with thankfulness, that the first adventurers and their successors, for one hundred and thirty years, have fully enjoyed all the freedoms and immunities promised on their first removal from England. But here the scene seems to be unhappily changing. The British ministry, whether induced by a jealousy of the colonies, by false informations, or by some alteration in the system of political government, we have no information; whatever hath been the motive, this we are sure of, the parliament in their last session, passed an act, limiting, restricting and burdening the trade of these colonies, much more than had ever been done before; as also for greatly enlarging the power and jurisdiction of the courts of admiralty in the colonies; and also came to a resolution, that it might be necessary to establish stamp duties, and other internal taxes, to be collected within them. This act and this resolution, have caused great uneasiness and consternation among the British subjects on the continent of America; how much reason there is for it, we will endeavor, in the most modest and plain manner we can, to lay before our readers.

In the first place, let it be considered, that although each of the colonies hath a legislature within itself, to take care of it's interests, and provide for it's peace and internal government; yet there are many things of a more general nature, quite out of the reach of these particular legislatures, which it is necessary should be

Parliamentary Powers and Natural Law

James Otis was a Massachusetts lawyer and one of the most prominent early opponents to British policies in the colonies. In his 1764 pamphlet The Rights of the British Colonies Asserted and Proved, *Otis declared that Parliament's authority over the colonies was limited by natural law and that Parliament could not abridge natural rights. These ideas later became the cornerstone of America's* Declaration of Independence.

To say the Parliament is absolute and arbitrary is a contradiction. The Parliament cannot make 2 and 2, 5: omnipotency cannot do it. The supreme power in a state is *jus dicere* [to declare the law] only: *jus dare* [to give the law], strictly speaking, belongs alone to God. Parliaments are in all cases to declare what is for the good of the whole; but it is not the declaration of Parliament that makes it so. There must be in every instance a higher authority, viz., God. Should an act of Parliament be against any of His natural laws, which are immutably true, their declaration would be contrary to eternal truth, equity, and justice, and consequently void; and so it would be adjudged by the Parliament itself when convinced of their mistake. Upon this great principle, parliaments repeal such acts as soon as they find they have been mistaken in having declared them to be for the public good when in fact they were not so. When such mistake is evident and palpable, as in the instances in the appendix, the judges of the executive courts have declared the act "of a whole Parliament void." See here the grandeur of the British constitution! See the wisdom of our ancestors!

regulated, ordered and governed. One of this kind is, the commerce of the whole British empire, taken collectively, and that of each kingdom and colony in it, as it makes a part of that whole. Indeed, every thing that concerns the proper interest and fit government of the whole commonwealth, of keeping the peace, and subordination of all the parts towards the whole, and one among another, must be considered in this light. Amongst these general concerns, perhaps, money and paper credit, those grand instruments of all commerce, will be found also to have a place. These, with all other matters of a general nature, it is absolutely necessary should have a general power to direct them; some supreme and over ruling authority, with power to make laws, and form regulations for the good of all, and to compel their execution and observation. It being necessary some such general power should exist somewhere, every man of the least knowledge of the British constitution, will be naturally led to look for, and find it in the parliament of Great Britain; that grand and august legislative body, must, from the nature of their authority, and the necessity of the thing, be justly vested with this power. Hence, it becomes the indispensable duty of every good and loyal subject, cheerfully to obey and patiently submit to all the acts, laws, orders and regulations that may be made and passed by parliament, for directing and governing all these general matters.

Here it may be urged by many, and indeed, with great appearance of reason, that the equity, justice, and beneficence of the British constitution, will require, that the separate kingdoms and distant colonies, who are to obey and be governed by these general laws and regulations, ought to be represented, some way or other, in parliament; at least whilst these general matters are under consideration. Whether the colonies will ever be admitted to have representatives in parliament,—whether it be consistent with their distant and dependent state,—and whether if it were admitted, it would be to their advantage,—are questions we will pass by; and observe, that these colonies ought in justice, and for the very evident good of the whole commonwealth, to have notice of every new measure about to be pursued, and new act that is about to be passed, by which their rights, liberties, or interests will be affected; they ought to have such notice, that they may appear and be heard by their agents, by council, or written representation, or by some other equitable and effectual way. . . .

Unfair Taxes

The resolution of the house of commons, come into during the same session of parliament, asserting their rights to establish stamp duties, and internal taxes, to be collected in the colonies without their own consent, hath much more, and for much more reason, alarmed the British subjects in America, than any thing that had ever been done before. These resolutions, carried into execution, the colonies cannot help but consider as a manifest violation of their just and long enjoyed rights. For it must be confessed by all men, that they who are taxed at pleasure by others, cannot possibly have any property, can have nothing to be called their own; they who have no property, can have no freedom, but are indeed reduced to the most abject slavery; are in a condition far worse than countries conquered and made tributary; for these have only a fixed sum to pay, which they are left to raise among themselves, in the way that they may think most equal and easy; and having paid the stipulated sum, the debt is discharged, and what is left is their own. This is much more tolerable than to be taxed at the mere will of others, without any bounds, without any stipulation and agreement, contrary to their consent, and against their will. If we are told that those who lay these taxes upon the colonies, are men of the highest character for their wisdom, justice and integrity, and therefore cannot be supposed to deal hardly, unjustly, or unequally by any; admitting, and really believing that all this is true, it will make no alteration in the nature of the case; for one who is bound to obey the will of another, is as really a slave, though he may have a good master, as if he had a bad one; and this is stronger in politic bodies than in natural ones, as the former have perpetual succession, and remain the same; and although they may have a very good master at one time, they may have a very bad one at another. And indeed, if the people in America, are to be taxed by the representatives of the people in Britain, their malady is an increasing evil, that must always grow greater by time. Whatever burdens are laid upon the Americans, will be so much taken off the Britons; and the doing this, will soon be extremely popular; and those who put up to be members of the house of commons, must obtain the votes of the people, by promising to take more and more of the taxes off them, by putting it on the Americans. This must most assuredly be the case, and it will not be in the power even of the parliament to prevent it; the people's private interest will be concerned, and will govern them; they will have such, and only such representatives as will act agreeable to this their interest; and these taxes laid on Americans, will be always a part of the supply bill, in which the other branches of the Legislature can make no alteration; and in truth, the subjects in the colonies will be taxed at the will and pleasure of their fellow subjects in Britain.—How equitable, and how just this may be, must be left to every impartial man to determine.

But it will be said, that the monies drawn from the colonies by duties, and by taxes, will be laid up and set apart to be used for their future defence. This will not at all alleviate the hardship, but serves only more strongly to mark the servile state of the people. Free people have ever thought, and always will think, that the money necessary for their defence, lies safest in their own hands, until it be wanted immediately for that purpose. To take the money of the Americans, which they want continually to use in their trade, and lay it up for their defence, at a thousand leagues distance from them, when the enemies they have to fear, are in their own neighborhood, hath not the greatest probability of friendship or of prudence. . . .

In an imperial state, which consists of many separate governments, each of which hath peculiar privileges, and of which kind it is evident the empire of Great Britain is; no single part, though greater than another part, is by that superiority entitled to make laws for, or to tax such lesser part; but all laws, and all taxations, which bind the whole, must be made by the whole. This may be fully verified by the empire of Germany, which consists of many states; some powerful, and others weak; yet the powerful never make laws to govern or to tax the little and weak ones; neither is it done by the emperor, but only by the diet, consisting of the representatives of the whole body. Indeed, it must be absurd to suppose, that the common people of Great Britain have a sovereign and absolute authority over their fellow subjects in America, or even any sort of power whatsoever, over them; but it will be still more absurd to suppose they can give a power to their representatives, which they have not themselves. If the house of commons do not receive this authority from their constituents, it will be difficult to tell by what means they obtained it, except it be vested in them by mere superiority and power.

Should it be urged, that the money expended by the mother country, for the defence and protection of America, and especially during the late war, must justly entitle her to some retaliation from the colonies; and that the stamp duties and taxes, intended to be raised in them, are only designed for that equitable purpose; if we are permitted to examine how far this may rightfully vest the parliament with the power of taxing the colonies, we shall find this claim to have no sort of equitable foundation. In many of the colonies, especially those in New England, who were planted, as is before observed, not at the charge of the crown or kingdom of England, but at the expense of the planters themselves; and were not only planted, but also defended against the savages, and other enemies, in long and cruel wars, which continued for an hundred years, almost without intermission, solely at their own charge; and in the year 1746, when the Duke D'Anville came out from France, with the most formidable French fleet that ever was in the American seas, enraged at these colonies for the loss of Louisbourg, the year before, and with orders to make an attack on them; even in this greatest exigence, these colonies were left to the protection of Heaven and their own efforts. These colonies having thus planted and defended themselves, and removed all enemies from their borders, were in hopes to enjoy peace, and recruit their state, much exhausted by these long struggles; but they were soon called upon to raise men, and send out to the defence of other colonies, and to make conquests for the crown; they dutifully obeyed the requisition, and with ardor entered into those services, and continued in them, until all encroachments were removed, and all Canada, and even the Havana, conquered. They most cheerfully complied with every call of the crown; they rejoiced, yea, even exulted, in the prosperity and exaltation of the British empire. But these colonies, whose bounds were fixed, and whose borders were before cleared from enemies, by their own fortitude, and at their own expense, reaped no sort of advantage by these conquests; they are not enlarged, have not gained a single acre of land, have no part in the Indian or interior trade; the immense tracts of land subdued, and no less immense and profitable commerce acquired, all belong to Great Britain; and not the least share or portion to these colonies, though thousands of their men have lost their lives, and millions of their money have been expended in the purchase of them for great part of which we are yet in debt, and from which we shall not in many years be able to extricate ourselves. Hard will be the fate, yea, cruel the destiny, of these unhappy colonies, if the reward they are to receive for all this, is the loss of their freedom; better for them Canada still remained French; yea, far more eligible that it ever should remain so, than that the price of its reduction should be their slavery.

If the colonies are not taxed by parliament, are they therefore exempted from bearing their proper share in the necessary burdens of government? This by no means follows. Do they not support a regular internal government in each colony, as expensive to the people here, as the internal government of Britain is to the people there? Have not the colonies here, at all times when called upon by the crown, raised money for the public service, done it as cheerfully as the parliament have done on like occasions? Is not this the most easy, the most natural, and most constitutional way of raising money in the colonies? What occasion then to distrust the colonies? What necessity to fall on an invidious and unconstitutional method, to compel them to do what they have ever done freely? Are not the people in the colonies as loyal and dutiful subjects as any age or nation ever produced? And are they not as useful to the kingdom, in this remote quarter of the world, as their fellow subjects are who dwell in Britain? The parliament, it is confessed, have power to regulate the trade of the whole empire; and hath it not full power, by this means, to draw all the money and all the wealth of the colonies into the mother country, at pleasure? What motive, after all this, can remain, to induce the parliament to abridge the privileges, and lessen the rights of the most loyal and dutiful subjects; subjects justly entitled to ample freedom, who have long enjoyed, and not abused or forfeited their liberties; who have used them to their own advantage, in dutiful subserviency to the orders and interests of Great Britain? Why should the gentle current of tranquillity, that has so long run with peace through all the British states, and flowed with joy and with happiness in all her countries, be at last obstructed, be turned out of its true course, into unusual and winding channels, by which many of those states must be ruined; but none of them can possibly be made more rich or more happy?

VIEWPOINT 4

"The several New England charters ascertain, define, and limit the respective rights and privileges of each colony, and I cannot conceive how it has come to pass that the colonies now claim any other or greater rights than are therein expressly granted to them."

Parliament Is Not Abusing the Rights of Colonists

Martin Howard (1720?-1781)

In February 1765, a pamphlet was published sharply attacking Rhode Island governor Stephen Hopkins's tract *The Rights of Colonies Examined*. The anonymous writer purported to be a gentleman from Halifax, Nova Scotia, but was in fact Martin Howard, a resident of Newport, Rhode Island. Howard was a lawyer and landowner involved in a political faction opposed to Hopkins.

Howard's pamphlet, called *A Letter from a Gentleman at Halifax, to His Friend in Rhode Island, Containing Remarks Upon a Pamphlet Entitled The Rights of the Colonies Examined*, was published in Rhode Island and is excerpted in the following viewpoint. In it Howard sharply attacks both Hopkins's writing style and his arguments. Howard asserts that the political rights of colonists are limited by their colonial charters, and he refutes Hopkins's arguments that the colonists share equal rights with the English.

Howard did succeed in getting Hopkins and other colonial writers such as James Otis to retract some of their earlier and stronger opinions concerning colonial rights. However, he was forced to flee Rhode Island following the August 1765 Stamp Act riots. Appointed chief justice of North Carolina, he again had to flee to England in 1777, where he died destitute.

M y Dear Sir,

I thank you very kindly for the pamphlets and newspapers you was so obliging as to send me. I will, according to your request, give you a few miscellaneous strictures on that pamphlet, wrote by Mr. H—p—s, your governor, entitled *The Rights of Colonies Examined*. . . .

The Rights of Colonies Examined is a labored, ostentatious piece, discovers its author to be totally unacquainted with style or diction, and eagerly fond to pass upon the world for a man of letters. . . .

However disguised, polished, or softened the expression of this pamphlet may seem, yet everyone must see that its professed design is sufficiently prominent throughout, namely, to prove *that the colonies have rights independent of, and not controllable by the authority of Parliament*. It is upon this dangerous and indiscreet position I shall communicate to you my real sentiments.

Parliament and the Colonies

To suppose a design of enslaving the colonies by Parliament is too presumptuous; to propagate it in print is perhaps dangerous. Perplexed between a desire of speaking all he thinks and the fear of saying too much, the honorable author is obliged to entrench himself in obscurity and inconsistency in several parts of his performance: I shall bring one instance.

In page eleven he says, "It is the indispensable duty of every good and loyal subject cheerfully to obey, and patiently submit to, all the laws, orders, etc., that may be passed by Parliament."

I do not much admire either the spirit or composition of this sentence. Is it the duty *only* of good and loyal subjects to obey? Are the wicked and disloyal subjects absolved from this obligation? Else why is this passage so marvelously penned? Philoleutherus Lipsiensis would directly pronounce this a figure in rhetoric called nonsense. Believe me, my friend, I did not quote this passage to show my skill in criticism, but to point out a contradiction between it and another passage in page twenty, which runs thus: "It must be absurd to suppose that the common people of Great Britain have a sovereign and absolute authority over their fellow subjects of America, *or even any sort of power whatso-*

ever over them; but it will be still more absurd to suppose they can give a power to their representatives which they have not themselves," etc. Here it is observable that the first cited passage expresses a full submission to the authority of Parliament; the last is as explicit a denial of that authority. The sum of His Honor's argument is this: the people of Great Britain have not any sort of power over the Americans; the House of Commons have no greater authority than the people of Great Britain who are their constituents; *ergo*, the House of Commons *have not any sort of power over the Americans*. This is indeed a curious invented syllogism, the sole merit of which is due to the first magistrate of an English colony.

The Declaratory Act

Recognizing that American resistance had made the Stamp Act unenforceable, and under pressure from London merchants hurting from the American boycott of British goods, the British Parliament repealed the unpopular tax on March 18, 1766. Not wishing to concede their authority in principle to tax the colonies, Parliament also passed the Declaratory Act asserting Great Britain's power over America.

Whereas *several of the houses of representatives in his Majesty's colonies and plantations in* America, *have of late, against law, claimed to themselves, or to the general assemblies of the same, the sole and exclusive right of imposing duties and taxes upon his Majesty's subjects in the said colonies and plantations; and have, in pursuance of such claim, passed certain votes, resolutions, and orders, derogatory to the legislative authority of parliament, and inconsistent with the dependency of the said colonies and plantations upon the crown of* Great Britain: . . . be it declared . . . , That the said colonies and plantations in *America* have been, are, and of right ought to be, subordinate unto, and dependent upon the imperial crown and parliament of *Great Britain*; and that the King's majesty, by and with the advice and consent of the lords spiritual and temporal, and commons of *Great Britain*, in parliament assembled, had, hath, and of right ought to have, full power and authority to make laws and statutes of sufficient force and validity to bind the colonies and people of *America*, subjects of the crown of *Great Britain*, in all cases whatsoever.

I have endeavored to investigate the true natural relation, if I may so speak, between colonies and their mother state, abstracted from compact or positive institution, but here I can find nothing satisfactory. Till this relation is clearly defined upon a rational and natural principle, our reasoning upon the measure of the colonies' obedience will be desultory and inconclusive. Every connection in life has its reciprocal duties; we know the relation between a parent and child, husband and wife, master and servant, and from thence are able to deduce their respective obligations. But we have no notices of any such precise natural relation between a mother state and its colonies, and therefore cannot reason with so much certainty upon the power of the one or the duty of the others. The ancients have transmitted to us nothing that is applicable to the state of modern colonies because the relation between these is formed by political compact, and the condition of each, variant in their original and from each other. The honorable author has not freed this subject from any of its embarrassments: vague and diffuse talk of rights and privileges, and ringing the changes upon the words liberty and slavery only serve to convince us that words may affect without raising images or affording any repose to a mind philosophically inquisitive. For my own part, I will shun the walk of metaphysics in my inquiry, and be content to consider the colonies' rights upon the footing of their charters, which are the only plain avenues that lead to the truth of this matter.

The several New England charters ascertain, define, and limit the respective rights and privileges of each colony, and I cannot conceive how it has come to pass that the colonies now claim any other or greater rights than are therein expressly granted to them. I fancy when we speak or think of the rights of freeborn Englishmen, we confound those rights which are personal with those which are political: there is a distinction between these which ought always to be kept in view.

Personal and Political Rights

Our personal rights, comprehending those of life, liberty, and estate, are secured to us by the common law, which is every subject's birthright, whether born in Great Britain, on the ocean, or in the colonies; and it is in this sense we are said to enjoy all the rights and privileges of Englishmen. The political rights of the colonies or the powers of government communicated to them are more limited, and their nature, quality, and extent depend altogether upon the patent or charter which first created and instituted them. As individuals, the colonists participate of every blessing the English constitution can give them: as corporations created by the crown, they are confined within the primitive views of their institution. Whether, therefore, their indulgence is scanty or liberal can be no cause of complaint; for when they accepted of their charters they tacitly submitted to the terms and conditions of them.

The colonies have no rights independent of their charters; they can claim no greater than those give them; by those the Parliamentary jurisdiction over them is not taken away, neither could

The Right to Impose Taxes

Thomas Whately was one of the secretaries of George Grenville, British prime minister from 1763 to 1765. Whately's 1765 pamphlet The Regulations Lately Made Concerning the Colonies and the Taxes Imposed upon Them, Considered *was an official defense of Parliament and was widely debated in the colonies.*

The Instances that have been mentioned prove, that the Right of the Parliament of *Great Britain* to impose Taxes of every kind on the Colonies, has been always admitted; but were there no Precedents to support the Claim, it would still be incontestable, being founded on the Principles of our Constitution; for the Fact is, that the Inhabitants of the Colonies are represented in Parliament: they do not indeed chuse the Members of that Assembly; neither are Nine Tenths of the People of *Britain* Electors; for the Right of Election is annexed to certain Species of Property, to peculiar Franchises, and to Inhabitancy in some particular Places; but these Descriptions comprehend only a very small Part of the Land, the Property, and the People of this Island: all Copyhold, all Leasehold Estates, under the Crown, under the Church, or under private Persons, tho' for Terms ever so long; all landed Property in short, that is not Freehold, and all monied Property whatsoever are excluded: the Possessors of these have no Votes in the Election of Members of Parliament; Women and Persons under Age be their Property ever so large, and all of it Freehold, have none. The Merchants of *London,* a numerous and respectable Body of Men, whose Opulence exceeds all that *America* could collect; the Proprietors of that vast Accumulation of Wealth, the public Funds; the Inhabitants of *Leeds,* of *Halifax,* of *Birmingham,* and of *Manchester,* Towns that are each of them larger than the Largest in the Plantations; . . . are all in the same Circumstances; none of them chuse their Representatives; and yet are they not represented in Parliament? Is their vast Property subject to Taxes without their Consent? Are they all arbitrarily bound by Laws to which they have not agreed? The Colonies are in exactly the same Situation: All *British* Subjects are really in the same; none are actually, all are virtually represented in Parliament; for every Member of Parliament sits in the House, not as Representative of his own Constituents, but as one of that august Assembly by which all the Commons of *Great Britain* are represented.

any grant of the King abridge that jurisdiction, because it is founded upon common law, as I shall presently show, and was prior to any charter or grant to the colonies: every Englishman, therefore, is subject to this jurisdiction, and it follows him wherever he goes. It is of the essence of government that there should be a supreme head, and it would be a solecism in politics to talk of members independent of it.

With regard to the jurisdiction of Parliament, I shall endeavor to show that it is attached to every English subject wherever he be, and I am led to do this from a clause in page nine of His Honor's pamphlet, where he says "That the colonies do not hold their rights as a privilege granted them, nor enjoy them as a grace and favor bestowed, but possess them as an inherent, indefeasible right." This postulatum cannot be true with regard to political rights, for I have already shown that these are derived from your charters, and are held by force of the King's grant; therefore these inherent, indefeasible rights, as His Honor calls them, must be personal ones, according to the distinction already made. Permit me to say that inherent and indefeasible as these rights may be, the jurisdiction of Parliament over every English subject is equally as inherent and indefeasible: that both have grown out of the same stock, and that if we avail ourselves of the one we must submit to and acknowledge the other.

It might here be properly enough asked, Are these personal rights self-existent? Have they no original source? I answer, They are derived from the constitution of England, which is the common law; and from the same fountain is also derived the jurisdiction of Parliament over us.

British Common Law

But to bring this argument down to the most vulgar apprehension: The common law has established it as a rule or maxim that the plantations are bound by British acts of Parliament if particularly named; and surely no Englishman in his senses will deny the force of a common law maxim. One cannot but smile at the inconsistency of these inherent, indefeasible men: if one of them has a suit at law, in any part of New England, upon a question of land, property, or merchandise, he appeals to the common law to support his claim or defeat his adversary, and yet is so profoundly stupid as to say that an act of Parliament does not bind him when perhaps the same page in a law book which points him out a remedy for a libel or a slap in the face would inform him that it does. In a word, the force of an act of Parliament over the colonies is predicated upon the common law, the origin and basis of all those inherent rights and privileges which constitute the boast and felicity of a Briton.

Can we claim the common law as an inheritance, and at the same time be at liberty to adopt one part of it and reject the other? Indeed we cannot. The common law, pure and indivisible in its nature and essence, cleaves to us during our lives and follows us from Nova Zembla to Cape Horn; and therefore, as the jurisdiction of Parliament arises out of and is supported by it, we may as well renounce our allegiance or change our nature as to be exempt from the jurisdiction of Parliament. Hence it is plain to me that in denying this jurisdiction we at the same time take leave of the common law, and thereby, with equal temerity and folly, strip ourselves of every blessing we enjoy as Englishmen: a flagrant proof, this, that shallow drafts in politics and legislation confound and distract us, and that an extravagant zeal often defeats its own purposes.

I am aware that the foregoing reasoning will be opposed by the maxim "That no Englishman can be taxed but by his own consent or by representatives."

It is this dry maxim, taken in a literal sense and ill understood, that, like the song of "Lillibullero," has made all the mischief in the colonies; and upon this the partisans of the colonies' rights chiefly rest their cause. I don't despair, however, of convincing you that this maxim affords but little support to their argument when rightly examined and explained.

It is the opinion of the House of Commons, and may be considered as a law of Parliament, that they are the representatives of every British subject, wheresoever he be. In this view of the matter, then, the aforegoing maxim is fully vindicated in practice, and the whole benefit of it, in substance and effect, extended and applied to the *colonies*. Indeed the maxim must be considered in this latitude, for in a literal sense or construction it ever was, and ever will be, impracticable. Let me ask, Is the Isle of Man, Jersey, or Guernsey represented? What is the value or amount of each man's representation in the kingdom of Scotland, which contains near two millions of people, and yet not more than three thousand have votes in the election of members of Parliament? But to show still further that in fact and reality this right of representation is not of that consequence it is generally thought to be, let us take into the argument the moneyed interest of Britain, which, though immensely great, has no share in this representation. A worthless freeholder of forty shillings per annum can vote for a member of Parliament, whereas a merchant, though worth one hundred thousand pounds sterling, if it consist only in personal effects, has no vote at all. But yet let no one suppose that the interest of the latter is not equally the object of Parliamentary attention with the former. Let me add one example more. Copyholders in England of one thousand pounds sterling per annum, whose estates in land are nominally but not intrinsically inferior to a freehold cannot, by law, vote for members of Parliament; yet we never hear that these people *"murmur with submissive fear, and mingled rage."* They don't set up their private humor against the constitution of their country, but submit with cheerfulness to those forms of government which providence, in its goodness, has placed them under.

71

Suppose that this Utopian privilege of representation should take place. I question if it would answer any other purpose but to bring an expense upon the colonies, unless you can suppose that a few American members could bias the deliberations of the whole British legislature. In short, this right of representation is but a phantom, and if possessed in its full extent would be of no real advantage to the colonies; they would, like Ixion, embrace a cloud in the shape of Juno.

The Danger of Innovations

In addition to this head, I could further urge the danger of innovations. Every change in a constitution in some degree weakens its original frame, and hence it is that legislators and statesmen are cautious in admitting them. The goodly building of the British constitution will be best secured and perpetuated by adhering to its original principles. Parliaments are not of yesterday; they are as ancient as our Saxon ancestors. Attendance in Parliament was originally a duty arising from a tenure of lands, and grew out of the feudal system, so that the privilege of sitting in it is territorial and confined to Britain only. Why should the beauty and symmetry of this body be destroyed and its purity defiled by the unnatural mixture of representatives from every part of the British dominions? *Parthians, Medes, Elamites, and the dwellers of Mesopotamia, etc.*, would not, in such a case, speak the same language. What a heterogeneous council would this form? What a monster in government would it be? In truth, my friend, the matter lies here: the freedom and happiness of every British subject depends not upon his share in elections but upon the sense and virtue of the British Parliament, and these depend reciprocally upon the sense and virtue of the whole nation. When virtue and honor are no more, the lovely frame of our constitution will be dissolved. Britain may one day be what Athens and Rome now are; but may Heaven long protract the hour!

The jurisdiction of Parliament being established, it will follow that this jurisdiction cannot be apportioned; it is transcendent and entire, and may levy internal taxes as well as regulate trade. There is no essential difference in the rights: a stamp duty is confessedly the most reasonable and equitable that can be devised, yet very far am I from desiring to see it established among us; but I fear the shaft is sped and it is now too late to prevent the blow.

The examples cited by His Honor with regard to ancient colonies may show his reading and erudition, but are of no authority in the present question. I am not enough skilled in the Grecian history to correct the proofs drawn from thence, though they amount to very little. If the Grecian colonies, as His Honor says, "took such forms of government as themselves chose," there is no kind of similitude between them and the English colonies, and therefore to name them is nothing to the purpose. The English colonies take their forms of government from the crown; hold their privileges upon condition that they do not abuse them; and hold their lands by the tenure of common socage, which involves in it fealty and obedience to the King. Hence it is plain His Honor's argument is not strengthened by the example of the Grecian colonies; for what likeness is there between independent colonies, as those must be which "took such forms of government as themselves chose," and colonies like ours, which are in a manner feudatory, and holden of a superior? . . .

Hopkins's Arguments Answered

The act of the thirteenth of his late Majesty, entitled An Act for Naturalizing of Foreign Protestants, had better have been omitted by His Honor; for if that act is to be the measure of the colonists' rights they will be more circumscribed than he would willingly choose. In that act there is a proviso that no person who shall become a natural-born subject by virtue of that act should be of the Privy Council, or a member of either house of Parliament, or capable of enjoying in Great Britain or Ireland any place of trust, civil or military, etc. This statute confirms the distinction I have set up between personal and political rights. After naturalization, foreign Protestants are here admitted subjects to all intents and purposes, that is, to the full enjoyment of those rights which are connected with the person, liberty, or estate of Englishmen; but by the proviso they are excluded from bearing offices or honors. . . .

Believe me, my friend, it gives me great pain to see so much ingratitude in the colonies to the mother country, whose arms and money so lately rescued them from a French government. I have been told that some have gone so far as to say that they would, as things are, prefer such a government to an English one. Heaven knows I have but little malice in my heart, yet, for a moment, I ardently wish that these spurious, unworthy sons of Britain could feel the iron rod of a Spanish inquisitor or a French farmer of the revenue; it would indeed be a punishment suited to their ingratitude. Here I cannot but call to mind the adder in one of the fables of Pilpay, which was preparing to sting the generous traveler who had just rescued him from the flames.

You'll easily perceive that what I have said is upon the general design of His Honor's pamphlet; if he had divided his argument with any precision, I would have followed him with somewhat more of method. The dispute between Great Britain and the colonies consists of two parts: first, the jurisdiction of Parliament, and, secondly, the exercise of that jurisdiction. His Honor hath blended these together, and nowhere marked the division between them. The first I have principally remarked upon. As to the second, it can only turn upon the expediency or utility of those schemes which may, from time to time, be adopted by Parliament relative to the colonies. Under this head, I readily grant, they are at full liberty to remonstrate, petition, write pamphlets and newspapers without number, to prevent any improper or unreasonable imposition. Nay, I would have them do all this with that spirit of freedom which Englishmen always have, and I hope ever will, exert; but let us not use our liberty for a cloak of maliciousness. Indeed I am very sure the loyalty of the colonies has ever been irreproachable; but from the pride of some and the ignorance of others the cry against mother country has spread from colony to colony; and it is to be feared that prejudices and resentments are kindled among them which it will be difficult ever thoroughly to soothe or extinguish. It may become necessary for the supreme legislature of the nation to frame some code, and therein adjust the rights of the colonies with precision and certainty, otherwise Great Britain will always be teased with new claims about liberty and privileges.

I have no ambition in appearing in print, yet if you think what is here thrown together is fit for the public eye you are at liberty to publish it. I the more cheerfully acquiesce in this because it is with real concern I have observed that, notwithstanding the frequent abuse poured forth in pamphlets and newspapers against the mother country, not one filial pen in America hath as yet been drawn, to my knowledge, in her vindication.

VIEWPOINT 5

"There was a general combination among the soldiers ... to commit some extraordinary act of violence upon the town."

The Boston Massacre Was an Example of British Oppression

James Bowdoin (1726-1790), Joseph Warren (1741-1775), and Samuel Pemberton (1723-1779)

One of the incidents that greatly increased tension between Great Britain and the American colonies was the Boston Massacre in 1770. The incident was the culmination of a buildup of tension between citizens of Boston and British soldiers. The soldiers were stationed in Boston in 1768 at the request of British customs officials, who had been beleaguered in their attempts to enforce the British Townshend Acts. Bostonians harassed the highly unpopular troops in an effort to force their removal. On March 5, 1770, during a confrontation between a mob and some British troops, the British opened fire. Five people were killed.

At a March 13 town meeting, three prominent citizens sympathetic to the American cause were appointed to investigate the incident and to ensure that the guilty were punished. The three committee members were James Bowdoin, a wealthy merchant and future Massachusetts governor, Joseph Warren, a physician who was later killed in 1775 at the Battle of Bunker Hill, and Samuel Pemberton, a Massachusetts judge. The three took depositions from citizens and presented their findings on March 19, 1770. Their report was published in pamphlet form later in the year. The committee's stance could be seen in the pamphlet's title: *A Short Narrative Of The Horrid Massacre In Boston . . . & With Some Observations On The State Of Things Prior To That Catastrophe* (Boston, 1770). The committee argued that the guilt for the violence lay heavily with the British soldiers. The pamphlet asserts that the British intended to provoke an incident and do violence to the colonists. The tract was reprinted in Frederic Kidder's *History of the Boston Massacre* (Albany, 1870) with modernized spelling and punctuation.

It may be a proper introduction to this narrative, briefly to represent the state of things for some time previous to the said massacre; and this seems necessary in order to the forming a just idea of the causes of it.

Recent History

At the end of the late war, in which this province bore so distinguished a part, a happy union subsisted between Great Britain and the colonies. This was unfortunately interrupted by the Stamp Act; but it was in some measure restored by the repeal of it. It was again interrupted by other acts of parliament for taxing America; and by the appointment of a board of commissioners, in pursuance of an act, which by the face of it was made for the relief and encouragement of commerce, but which in its operation, it was apprehended, would have, and it has in fact had, a contrary effect. By the said act the said commissioners were "to be resident in some convenient part of his majesty's dominions in America." This must be understood to be in some part convenient for the whole. But it does not appear that, in fixing the place of their residence, the convenience of the whole was at all consulted, for Boston, being very far from the centre of the colonies, could not be the place most convenient for the whole. Judging by the act, it may seem this town was intended to be favored, by the commissioners being appointed to reside here; and that the consequence of that residence would be the relief and encouragement of commerce; but the reverse has been the constant and uniform effect of it; so that the commerce of the town, from the embarrassments in which it has been lately involved, is greatly reduced. . . .

The residence of the commissioners here has been detrimental, not only to the commerce, but to the political interests of the town and province; and not only so, but we can trace from it the causes of the late horrid massacre. Soon after their arrival here in

November, 1767, instead of confining themselves to the proper business of their office they became partisans of Governor [Francis] Bernard in his political schemes; and had the weakness and temerity to infringe upon one of the most essential rights of the house of commons of this province—that of giving their votes with freedom, and not being accountable therefor but to their constituents. One of the members of that house, Capt. Timothy Folger, having voted in some affair contrary to the mind of the said commissioners, was for so doing dismissed from the office he held under them.

Never Forgotten

In 1772 Joseph Warren used the occasion of the commemoration of the Boston Massacre to attack British rule. His speech was reprinted in Hezekiah Niles' collection Principles and Acts of the Revolution in America, *published in Baltimore in 1822.*

The fatal 5th of March, 1770, can never be forgotten. The horrors of that dreadful night are but too deeply impressed on our hearts. Language is too feeble to paint the emotion of our souls when our streets were stained with the blood of our brethren, when our ears were wounded by the groans of the dying, and our eyes were tormented with the sight of mangled bodies of the dead. . . .

The immediate actors in the tragedy of that night were surrendered to justice. It is not mine to say how far they were guilty. They have been tried by the country and *acquitted* of murder! And they are not to be again arraigned at an earthly bar; but, surely the men who have promiscuously scattered death amidst the innocent inhabitants of a populous city ought to see well to it that they be prepared to stand at the bar of an omniscient judge! And all who contrived or encouraged the stationing troops in this place have reasons of eternal importance to reflect with deep contrition on their base designs, and humbly to repent of their impious machinations.

These proceedings of theirs, the difficulty of access to them on office business, and a supercilious behavior, rendered them disgustful to people in general, who in consequence thereof treated them with neglect. This probably stimulated them to resent it; and to make their resentment felt, they and their coadjutor, Governor Bernard, made such representations to his majesty's ministers as they thought best calculated to bring the displeasure of the nation upon the town and province; and in order that those representations might have the more weight, they are said to have contrived and executed plans for exciting disturbances and tumults, which otherwise would probably never have existed; and, when excited, to have transmitted to the ministry the most exaggerated accounts of them.

These particulars of their conduct his majesty's council of this province have fully laid open in their proceeding in council, and in their address to General Gage, in July and October, 1768; and in their letter to Lord Hillsborough of the 15th of April, 1769. Unfortunately for us, they have been too successful in their said representations, which, in conjunction with Governor Bernard's, have occasioned his majesty's faithful subjects of this town and province to be treated as enemies and rebels, by an invasion of the town by sea and land; to which the approaches were made with all the circumspection usual where a vigorous opposition is expected. While the town was surrounded by a considerable number of his majesty's ships of war, two regiments landed and took possession of it; and to support these, two other regiments arrived some time after from Ireland; one of which landed at Castle Island, and the other in the town.

Troops Forced upon Us

Thus were we, in aggravation of our other embarrassments, embarrassed with troops, forced upon us contrary to our inclination—contrary to the spirit of Magna Charta—contrary to the very letter of the Bill of Rights, in which it is declared, that the raising or keeping a standing army within the kingdom in time of peace, unless it be with the consent of parliament, is against law, and without the desire of the civil magistrates, to aid whom was the pretence for sending the troops hither; who were quartered in the town in direct violation of an act of parliament for quartering troops in America; and all this in consequence of the representations of the said commissioners and the said governor, as appears by their memorials and letters lately published.

As they were the procuring cause of troops being sent hither, they must therefore be the remote and a blameable cause of all the disturbances and bloodshed that have taken place in consequence of that measure. . . .

We shall next attend to the conduct of the troops, and to some circumstances relative to them. Governor Bernard without consulting the council, having given up the State-house to the troops at their landing, they took possession of the chambers, where the representatives of the province and the courts of law held their meetings; and (except the council-chamber) of all other parts of that house; in which they continued a considerable time, to the great annoyance of those courts while they sat, and of the merchants and gentlemen of the town, who had always made the lower floor of it their exchange. They had a right so to do, as the property of it was in the town; but they were deprived of that right by mere power. The said governor soon after, by every stratagem and by every method but a forcible entry, endeavored to get possession of the Manufactory house, to make a barrack of it for the troops; and for that purpose caused it to be besieged by the troops, and the people in it to be used very cruelly; which extraordinary proceedings created universal uneasiness, arising from the apprehension that the troops under the influence of such a man would be employed to effect the most dangerous purposes; but failing of that, other houses were procured, in which, contrary to act of parliament, he caused the troops to be quartered. After their quarters were settled, the main guard was posted at one of the said houses, directly opposite to, and not twelve yards from, the State-house (where the general court, and all the law courts for the county were held), with two field pieces pointed to the State-house. This situation of the main guard and field pieces seemed to indicate an attack upon the constitution, and a defiance of law; and to be intended to affront the legislative and executive authority of the province.

The general court, at the first session after the arrival of the troops, viewed it in this light, and applied to Governor Bernard to cause such a nuisance to be removed; but to no purpose. Disgusted at such an indignity, and at the appearance of being under duress, they refused to do business in such circumstances; and in consequence thereof were adjourned to Cambridge, to the great inconvenience of the members.

Besides this, the challenging the inhabitants by sentinels posted in all parts of the town before the lodgings of officers, which (for about six months, while it lasted), occasioned many quarrels and uneasiness.

Capt. Wilson, of the 59th, exciting the negroes of the town to take away their masters' lives and property, and repair to the army for protection, which was fully proved against him—the attack of a party of soldiers on some of the magistrates of the town—the repeated rescues of soldiers from peace officers—the firing of a loaded musket in a public street, to the endangering a great number of peaceable inhabitants—the frequent wounding of persons by their bayonets and cutlasses, and the numerous instances of bad behavior in the soldiery, made us early sensible that the troops were not sent here for any benefit to the town or province, and that we had no good to expect from such conservators of the peace.

It was not expected, however, that such an outrage and massacre, as happened here on the evening of the fifth instant, would have been perpetrated. There were then killed and wounded, by a discharge of musketry, eleven of his majesty's subjects. . . .

What gave occasion to the melancholy event of that evening

seems to have been this. A difference having happened near Mr. Gray's ropewalk, between a soldier and a man belonging to it, the soldier challenged the ropemakers to a boxing match. The challenge was accepted by one of them, and the soldier worsted. He ran to the barrack in the neighborhood, and returned with several of his companions. The fray was renewed, and the soldiers were driven off. They soon returned with recruits, and were again worsted. This happened several times, till at length a considerable body of soldiers was collected, and they also were driven off, the ropemakers having been joined by their brethren of the contiguous ropewalks. By this time Mr. Gray being alarmed interposed, and with the assistance of some gentlemen prevented any further disturbance. To satisfy the soldiers and punish the man who had been the occasion of the first difference, and as an example to the rest, he turned him out of his service; and waited on Col. Dalrymple, the commanding officer of the troops, and with him concerted measures for preventing further mischief. Though this affair ended thus, it made a strong impression on the minds of the soldiers in general, who thought the honor of the regiment concerned to revenge those repeated repulses. For this purpose they seemed to have formed a combination to commit some outrage upon the inhabitants of the town indiscriminately; and this was to be done on the evening of the 5th instant or soon after; as appears by the depositions of the following persons, viz:

William Newhall declares, that on Thursday night the 1st of March instant, he met four soldiers of the 29th regiment, and that he heard them say, "there were a great many that would eat their dinners on Monday next, that should not eat any on Tuesday."

Daniel Calfe declares, that on Saturday evening the 3d of March, a camp-woman, wife to James McDeed, a grenadier of the 29th, came into his father's shop, and the people talking about the affrays at the ropewalks, and blaming the soldiers for the part they had acted in it, the woman said, "the soldiers were in the right"; adding, "that before Tuesday or Wednesday night they would wet their swords or bayonets in New England people's blood.". . .

Butchery in King Street

By the foregoing depositions it appears very clearly, there was a general combination among the soldiers of the 29th regiment at least, to commit some extraordinary act of violence upon the town; that if the inhabitants attempted to repel it by firing even one gun upon those soldiers, the 14th regiment were ordered to be in readiness to assist them; and that on the late butchery in King street they actually were ready for that purpose, had a single gun been fired on the perpetrators of it.

It appears by a variety of depositions, that on the same evening between the hours of six and half after nine (at which time the firing began), many persons, without the least provocation, were in various parts of the town insulted and abused by parties of armed soldiers patrolling the streets. . . .

Samuel Drowne declares that, about nine o'clock of the evening of the fifth of March current, standing at his own door in Cornhill, he saw about fourteen or fifteen soldiers of the 29th regiment, who came from Murray's barracks, armed with naked cutlasses, swords, &c., and came upon the inhabitants of the town, then standing or walking in Cornhill, and abused some, and violently assaulted others as they met them; most of whom were without so much as a stick in their hand to defend themselves, as he very clearly could discern, it being moonlight, and himself being one of the assaulted persons. All or most of the said soldiers he saw go into King street (some of them through Royal Exchange lane), and there followed them, and soon discovered them to be quarrelling and fighting with the people whom they saw there, which he thinks were not more than a dozen, when the soldiers came there first, armed as aforesaid. Of those dozen people, the most of them were gentlemen, standing together a little below the Town-house, upon the Exchange. At the appearance of those soldiers so armed, the most of the twelve persons went off, some of them being first assaulted.

The violent proceedings of this party, and their going into King street, "quarrelling and fighting with the people whom they saw there" (mentioned in Mr. Drowne's deposition), was immediately introductory to the grand catastrophe.

These assailants, who issued from Murray's barracks (so called), after attacking and wounding divers persons in Cornhill, as above mentioned, being armed, proceeded (most of them) up the Royal Exchange lane into King street; where, making a short stop, and after assaulting and driving away the few they met there, they brandished their arms and cried out, "Where are the boogers! where are the cowards!" At this time there were very few persons in the street beside themselves. This party in proceeding from Exchange lane into King street, must pass the sentry posted at the westerly corner of the Custom-house which butts on that lane and fronts on that street. This is needful to be mentioned, as near that spot and in that street the bloody tragedy was acted, and the street actors in it were stationed: their station being but a few feet from the front side of the said Custom-house. The outrageous behavior and the threats of the said party occasioned the ringing of the meeting-house bell near the head of King street, which bell ringing quick, as for fire, it presently brought out a number of the inhabitants, who being soon sensible of the occa-

Paul Revere's depiction of grinning redcoats purposely firing into helpless colonists fueled anti-British sentiment.

sion of it, were naturally led to King street, where the said party had made a stop but a little while before, and where their stopping had drawn together a number of boys, round the sentry at the Custom-house. Whether the boys mistook the sentry for one of the said party, and thence took occasion to differ with him, or whether he first affronted them, which is affirmed in several depositions; however that may be, there was much foul language between them, and some of them, in consequence of his pushing at them with his bayonet, threw snowballs at him, which occasioned him to knock hastily at the door of the Custom-house. From hence two persons thereupon proceeded immediately to the mainguard, which was posted (opposite to the State-house) at a small distance, near the head of the said street. The officer on guard was Capt. Preston, who with seven or eight soldiers, with fire-arms and charged bayonets, issued from the guard house, and in great haste posted himself and his soldiers in the front of the Custom-house, near the corner aforesaid. In passing to this station the soldiers pushed several persons with their bayonets, driving through the people in so rough a manner that it appeared they intended to create a disturbance. This occasioned some snowballs to be thrown at them, which seems to have been the only provocation that was given. Mr. Knox (between whom and Capt. Preston there was some conversation on the spot) declares, that while he was talking with Capt. Preston, the soldiers of his detachment had attacked the people with their bayonets; and that there was not the least provocation given to Capt. Preston or his party; the backs of the people being toward them when the people were attacked. He also declares that Capt. Preston seemed to be in great haste and much agitated, and that, according to his opinion, there were not then present in King street above seventy or eighty persons at the extent.

The said party was formed into a half circle; and within a short time after they had been posted at the Custom-house, began to fire upon the people.

Capt. Preston is said to have ordered them to fire, and to have repeated that order. One gun was fired first; then others in succession, and with deliberation, till ten or a dozen guns were fired; or till that number of discharges were made from the guns that were fired. By which means eleven persons were killed and wounded, as above represented. . . .

One happy effect has arisen from this melancholy affair, and it is the general voice of the town and province it may be a lasting one—all the troops are removed from the town. They are quartered for the present in the barracks at Castle Island; from whence it is hoped they will have a speedy order to remove entirely out of the province, together with those persons who were the occasion of their coming hither.

"Had... those who have influence over the populace in Boston taken as much trouble to appease and restrain as they have on too many occasions to inflame and excite the people to tumults and mischief, I am as confident that no blood would have been shed."

The Boston Massacre Was Provoked by the Colonists

Thomas Gage (1721-1787)

Thomas Gage was commander in chief of all British forces in North America from 1763 to 1775. In 1768 he was stationed in Boston, Massachusetts, to help quell any disturbances that might arise from the stationing of troops in that city. The antagonism between the townspeople and the British troops erupted on March 5, 1770, when troops fired into a rioting mob, killing five people. A general uprising was averted only when troops were withdrawn from the town to islands in the harbor. The event became known in the colonies as the Boston Massacre and was frequently cited in anti-British speeches and writings.

The following viewpoint is taken from a letter written on April 10, 1770, by Gage to the Earl of Hillsborough, one of King George III's leading ministers. Gage provides his version of what occurred on March 5 and the reasons for the violence. He argues that the soldiers were largely acting in self-defense against a dangerous and abusive mob. He asserts that the mobs in Boston were being orchestrated by colonial leaders wishing to drive the troops out of Boston.

The eight soldiers and their captain, Thomas Preston, were arrested and charged with manslaughter. Gage expresses doubts that they could receive a fair trial. However, defended in court by two patriot leaders, John Adams and Josiah Quincy, Preston and six soldiers were acquitted; the other soldiers were found guilty, branded on the hand, and released.

With the withdrawal of British soldiers, Boston entered a period of relative calm. Gage was named governor of Massachusetts in 1774, but gained criticism for his actions leading to the battles of Lexington and Concord in 1775. He was recalled to England in October 1775. His letters were later collected and edited by Clarence E. Carter and published in two volumes in 1931 and 1933 under the title *The Correspondence of General Thomas Gage with the Secretaries of State 1763-1775.*

Your Lordship will have received by the way of Boston much earlier intelligence than it has been in my power to transmit, of an unhappy quarrel between the people of that town and the soldiers, in which several of the former were killed and wounded. But I take the first opportunity to send Your Lordship the best account I have been able to procure of this unfortunate accident, as well as to represent the critical situation of the troops, and the hatred of the people towards them.

Prejudice Against the Troops

The occasion which brought the regiments to Boston rendered them obnoxious to the people, and they may have increased the odium themselves, as the disorders of that place have mostly sprung from disputes with Great Britain. The officers and soldiers are Britons, and the people found no advocates amongst them. It was natural for them, without examining into the merits of a political dispute, to take the part of their country; which probably they have often done with more zeal than discretion, considering the circumstances of the place they were in; for in matters of dispute with the mother country, or relative thereto, government is at end in Boston, and in the hands of the people, who have only to assemble to execute any designs. No person dares to oppose them, or call them to account; the whole authority of government, the governor excepted, and magistracy supporting them. The people, prejudiced against the troops, laid every snare to entrap and distress them, and frequent complaints have been made that the soldiers were daily insulted, and the people encouraged to insult them even by magistrates; that no satisfaction could be obtained, but the soldier, if found in fault, punished with the rigor of the law. Such proceedings could not fail to irritate, but the troops were restrained by their discipline; and though accidental quarrels happened, matters were prevented going to extremities.

In my letter to Your Lordship . . . I mentioned a misunderstanding between the inhabitants and soldiers in this town, soon after which advice was transmitted from Boston that the people there had quarreled with the troops, and lay in wait for them in the streets to knock them down; insomuch that it was unsafe for officers or soldiers to appear in the streets after dark. A particular quarrel happened at a rope walk with a few soldiers of the 29th Regiment; the provocation was given by the ropemakers, though it may be imagined in the course of it that there were faults on both sides. This quarrel, it is supposed, excited the people to concert a general rising on the night of March 5. They began by falling upon a few soldiers in a lane, contiguous to a barrack of the 29th Regiment, which brought some officers of the said regiment out of their quarters; who found some of their men greatly hurt, but carried all the soldiers to their barrack. The mob followed, menacing and brandishing their clubs over the officers' heads, to the barrack door, the officers endeavoring to pacify them, and desiring them to retire. Part of the mob broke into a meetinghouse and rang the fire bell, which appears to have been the alarm concerted; for numerous bodies immediately assembled in the streets, armed, some with muskets, but most with clubs, bludgeons, and suchlike weapons.

Mob Provocations

Many people came out of their houses supposing a fire in the town, and several officers on the same supposition were repairing to their posts; but meeting with mobs were reviled, attacked, and those who could not escape, knocked down, and treated with great inhumanity. Different mobs paraded through the streets, passing the several barracks, and provoking the soldiers to come out. One body went to the main guard, where every provocation was given, without effect, for the guard remained quiet. From thence the mob proceeded to a sentinel posted upon the customhouse, at a small distance from the guard, and attacked him. He defended himself as well as he could, calling out for help; and people ran to the guard to give information of his danger. Captain Preston of the 29th Regiment, being Captain of the Day, his duty upon the alarm carried him to the main guard, and hearing the sentinel was in danger of being murdered, he detached a sergeant and twelve men to relieve him, and soon after followed himself, to prevent any rash act on the part of the troops. This party as well as the sentinel was immediately attacked, some throwing bricks, stones, pieces of ice and snowballs at them, whilst others advanced up to their bayonets, and endeavored to close with them, to use their bludgeons and clubs; calling out to them to fire if they dared, and provoking them to it by the most opprobrious language.

The Captain's Account

Capt. Thomas Preston, the British officer in charge of the soldiers involved in the Boston Massacre, provides his own version of events. His account was reprinted in the Publications *of the Colonial Society of Massachusetts, 1900.*

The mob still increased, and were more outragious, striking their clubs on bludgeons one against another, and calling out, "Come on, you rascals, you bloody backs, you lobster scoundrels; fire if you dare, G—d damn you, fire and be damn'd; we know you dare not;" and much more such language was used. At this time I was between the soldiers and the mob, parleying with and endeavouring all in my power to persuade them to retire peaceably; but to no purpose. They advanced to the points of the bayonets, struck some of them, and even the muzzles of the pieces, and seemed to be endeavouring to close with the soldiers. On which some well-behaved persons asked me if the guns were charged: I replied, yes. They then asked me if I intended to order the men to fire; I answered no, by no means; observing to them, that I was advanced before the muzzles of the men's pieces, and must fall a sacrifice if they fired; that the soldiers were upon the half cock and charged bayonets, and my giving the word fire, under those circumstances, would prove me no officer. While I was thus speaking, one of the soldiers, having received a severe blow with a stick, stept a little on one side, and instantly fired, on which turning to and asking him why he fired without orders, I was struck with a club on my arm, which for sometime deprived me of the use of it; which blow, had it been placed on my head, most probably would have destroyed me. On this a general attack was made on the men by a great number of heavy clubs, and snow-balls being thrown at them, by which all our lives were in imminent danger; some persons at the same time from behind calling out, "Damn your bloods, why don't you fire?" Instantly three of four of the soldiers fired, one after another, and directly after three more in the same confusion and hurry.

Captain Preston stood between the soldiers and the mob, parleying with the latter, and using every conciliating method to persuade them to retire peaceably. Some amongst them asked him if he intended to order the men to fire, he replied by no means, and observed he stood between the troops and them. All he could say had no effect, and one of the soldiers, receiving a violent blow, instantly fired. Captain Preston turned round to see who fired, and received a blow upon his arm, which was aimed at his head; and the mob, at first seeing no execution done, and imagining the soldiers had only fired powder to frighten, grew more bold and attacked with greater violence, continually striking at the soldiers and pelting them, and calling out to them to fire. The soldiers at length perceiving their lives in danger, and hearing the word fire all round them, three or four of them fired one after another, and again three more in the same hurry and confusion. Four or five persons were unfortunately killed, and more wounded. Captain Preston and the party were soon afterward delivered into the hands of the magistrates, who committed them to prison.

The misunderstanding between the people and the troops in this place was contrived by one party, not only to wound their adversaries who had voted to supply the troops according to act of Parliament through the sides of the soldiers, by making them and their measures odious to the people, but also to have a pretence to desire the removal of the troops; which I am assured was mentioned, if not moved at the time, in the Council. This plan of getting the troops removed by quarreling with them was soon transmitted to Boston; where they immediately put it in execution, by endeavors to bring on a general quarrel between them and the townspeople. We fortunately found not only magistrates but many people of consequence in this place, who discovered the designs of the adverse party, and exerted themselves in keeping the people quiet and, preventing mischief; without whose assistance I am confident something very disagreeable must have happened here, notwithstanding the uncommon pains taken with the soldiers. And had the magistrates and those who have influence over the populace in Boston taken as much trouble to appease and restrain as they have on too many occasions to inflame and excite the people to tumults and mischief, I am as confident that no blood would have been shed in that place. But it appears, unfortunately, that their schemes were not to be brought about through peace and tranquility, but by promoting disorders.

Some have sworn that Captain Preston gave orders to fire; others who were near, that the soldiers fired without orders from the provocation they received. None can deny the attack made upon the troops, but differ in the degree of violence in the attack.

I hope and believe that I have given Your Lordship in general a true relation of this unhappy affair; and sorry I am to say, there is too much reason to apprehend neither Captain Preston nor the soldiers, can have a fair and impartial trial for their lives. The utmost malice and malevolence has been shown already, in endeavors to bring on the trials whilst the people are heated by resentment, and the thirst of revenge. And attempts have been made to overawe the judges. . . .

Conceiving the troops to be of no use at the island, I proposed to the lieutenant governor to remove them out of the province, and one of them immediately. The last measure I shall be obliged to take shortly, or run the risk of some contagious disorders getting amongst the men from their being so much crowded in small rooms. Not finding the proposal agreeable, I have consented to let both regiments remain till the arrival of the February mail from England; though I can't perceive any service is hoped for from them, unless it is to serve in the last extremity as an asylum, to which the officers of the Crown might fly for the security of their persons. But if there are any reasons to apprehend dangers of the kind, I am ignorant of them. It has indeed been proved that they were of no other use in the town of Boston, for the people were as lawless and licentious after the troops arrived as they were before. The troops could not act by military authority, and no person in civil authority would ask their aid. They were there contrary to the wishes of the Council, Assembly, magistrates and people, and seemed only offered to abuse and ruin, and the soldiers were either to suffer ill usage, and even assaults upon their persons till their lives were in danger, or by resisting and defending themselves, to run almost a certainty of suffering by the law.

VIEWPOINT 7

"[We] think it our duty . . . to Express our firm resolution . . . to oppose . . . [the tea tax] as dangerous to the liberty & commerce of this country."

Americans Should Resist the Tea Tax

Residents of Plymouth, Massachusetts (1773)

For a few years following the British repeal of the Townshend Acts in 1770 and the removal of British troops from Boston following the 1770 Boston Massacre, relative political calm existed between Britain and her colonies. The British cancelled all taxes except a three-penny tax on East India Company tea, but the colonists got around this by illegally smuggling Dutch tea instead.

The calm was shattered when the British Parliament passed the Tea Act on May 10, 1773, in an effort to rescue the financially strapped East India Company. By adjusting import duties and trade regulations the British were able to undersell the colonial tea smugglers. A half million pounds of tea were shipped to the colonies.

Many Americans, egged on by colonial leaders including Samuel Adams of Massachusetts, viewed this act of Parliament as an attempt to bribe the colonists into buying the tea and paying the tax—thus opening the door to further taxation and oppression. Ships carrying the tea were refused permission to dock in New York, Philadelphia, and Charleston. In Boston the ships were docked but in a famous episode the tea was dumped into the harbor by Boston townspeople on December 16, 1773.

The following viewpoint is taken from a set of resolutions passed by the town of Plymouth, Massachusetts, on December 7, 1773, and later collected in *Records of The Town of Plymouth*, vol. 3 1743-1783 (Plymouth: Memorial Press, 1903). Plymouth was one of many communities that debated and passed resolutions on the tea controversy. The resolutions attacked the tax and called for colonial resistance.

The Inhabitants of this town ever attentive to the rights & Interest of their country, having been repeatedly alarmed with the measures of late years, adopted & pursued by the British Administration under various forms Evidently repugnant to Every principall of our Constitution, & after flattering ourselves from time to time with hopes that from a Change of men or some other happy Circumstance

Such new measures might be adopted as would put an End to the unhappy contest between Britain and the colonies & leave us in the full enjoyment of those rights, which no power on Earth can reasonably dispute; much less pretend to deprive us of, have yet the misfortune to find the British ministry so far from relaxing, that they are still pursueing with assiduity the Same destructive measures, a recent Instance of which we see in Their attempt by virtue of an Act of the last Session of Parliament, to Enable the east India company in London to Export their tea to America in Such Quantity as the Lords of the Treasury shall think proper subject to the same unconstitutional Tax or tribute, which we have upon other occasions & Under differant appearances with firmness & resolution opposd as dangerous to that liberty which our fathers claimed & Enjoyed which we have a right to Enjoy & which our posterity may Expect we transmit to them Inviolate, do think it our duty on this as on Severall other Similar occasions to Express our firm resolution not only to oppose this step as dangerous to the liberty & commerce of this country, but allso to Aid & Support all our brethren in their opposition to this & Every Violation of our rights; and Therefore resolve.

1 That the dangerous nature & tendency of Importing teas here by any person or persons Especially the India company as proposd subject to a tax upon us without our consent, & the Steps Incumbent on Every one Concerned for the true Interest of America to take on the occasion, as well as the sentiments & conduct they should observe with regard to all aiders & abettors of that measure are Extremely well Expressed by the late Judicious resolves of the Worthy Citizens of Philadelphia.

2dly That the persons to whom the sd India company have consigned the tea they propose to send to Boston, have by their wickedness & obstinacy in Endeavoring to accept of & Execute their Commission contrary to the almost universall sense & desire of the whole province, & in still continueing to refuse to gratify the reasonable request of their countrymen forfeited that protection Every Good Citizen is Intitled to & Expos'd themselves & their abettors to the Indignation & resentment of all Good men.

3dly That it is an affront to the common sense & understanding of mankind & to the Majesty of the people, who are under God the Source from whence is derived all powers & magistracy in Every community to assert that any meeting of the people to consult measures for their common Security & hapiness on very Extreordinary & alarming occasions, is Either Unlawfull or Irregular

Since no legislature could be supposed to Establish rules of conduct in such cases as no man could even Suppose would take place in a free & Good Government.

Gratitude for Boston

4thly That the late meetings of a verry large & respectfull body of the Inhabitants of Boston & the ajacent towns, & their conduct & determination at sd meetings relative to the Importation & reshiping of any teas that have or may be sent here Subject to a Duty on Importation was both necessary & laudable & highly deserving the Gratitude of all who are Interested in or with the prosperity of America; & that whoever have attempted (by any means whatever) to Interrupt their proceedings & prevent the full operation of their determinations have in that Instance shown themselves Inimical to the freedom & Interest of the Country.

5thly That we are in duty & Gratitude bound not only to acknowledge our obligations to the body who composd that meeting for their noble, Generous & spirited Conduct in the common cause, but allso to aid & Support them in carrying their votes & resolves into Execution & that we will not only aid & support them in Executing the said Votes & resolves, but at the hazard of our lives & fortunes will Exert our whole force to defend them against the violence & wickedness of our Common Enemies.

6thly That the town clerk immediately record these votes & resolutions & deliver a fair copy of them to the Committe of Correspondence of this town to be by them Transmitted to the Committe of correspondence for the town of Boston.

VIEWPOINT 8

"We suppose it our indispensible duty ... to manifest our ... detestation of every measure which has a tendency to introduce anarchy, confusion, and disorder into the state."

Americans Should Not Provoke Britain

Massachusetts Gazette (1773)

On December 7, 1773, the residents of Plymouth, Massachusetts, passed a set of strong resolutions against the Tea Act, an attempt by the British to ship and sell, with tax, tea to the colonies. One week later some residents of the town, fearing reprisal from the British, attempted to have the resolutions reconsidered. When they failed, they published the following protest on December 23, 1773, in the *Massachusetts Gazette*.

The article attacks the resolutions passed earlier in the month as being dangerous to liberty and calls for a more conciliatory attitude aimed at solving the crisis. It argues that meetings calling for resistance were dominated by radicals and were not representative of all Americans.

That it is not only our right but our duty frankly and freely to express our sentiments on every matter which essentially concerns the safety and welfare of our country, is a trust which we apprehend cannot be denied.

Therefore, We who are inhabitants of the town of Plymouth neither captivated by sounds and declamations, nor deceived by the cunning stratagems of men who under the specious masque of patriotism have attempted to delude an innocent and loyal people; But firmly and steadily fix'd and determin'd to defend our rights and privileges, and to endeavour to hand to our posterity the blessings of peace and good government which were procured by our fathers and transmitted to Us,—Having taken into serious consideration the dangerous and fatal consequences which may arise from the late resolves pass'd at a meeting of this town on the seventh day of this instant December; Fearing that they may bring upon us the vengeance of affronted Majesty and his insulted authority, We cannot answer it to our God and our consciences unless we protest against the proceedings of said meetings, and publish to the world that we were not instrumental in procuring those mischiefs which may naturally be expected from such conduct.—And we do by these presents solemnly protest against the whole of said resolves as being repugnant to our ideas of Liberty, law and reason. With the first of said resolves we will not concern ourselves further than to observe that we cannot see the necessity of this town's adopting similar measures with the citizens of Philadelphia.

The 2d. contains a censure upon a number of gentlemen (who are appointed consignees by the East-India company) which we cannot think either decent or just. Nor can we suppose that they have forfeited that protection to which good citizens are entitled, or exposed themselves to the indignation of good men.

To the 3d. and 4th. We say that we think it an affront to the common sense of mankind and to the dignity of the laws, to assert that such a meeting as was held in the town of *Boston* on the first of this instant December, was either lawful or regular: And further that the said meeting and the conduct and determination therein do not appear to us to be either necessary or laudable, or in any degree meriting the gratitude of those who wish Well to America: But in our opinion those who by constitutional and lawful means have endeavoured to hinder their proceedings and to prevent the bad effects thereof, have in this instance shewn themselves to be firm friends to the freedom and *true* interests of this Country.

To the fifth we must observe, That we do not think ourselves bound either in duty or gratitude to acknowledge any obligations to the body who composed that meeting, nor to aid and support them in carrying their votes and resolves into execution, nor do we intend to hazard our lives and fortunes in their defence: But on the contrary We suppose it our indispensible duty (as the faithful and loyal subjects of his most gracious Majesty King GEORGE the third) to manifest our abhorrence and detestation of every measure which has a tendency to introduce anarchy, confusion, and disorder into the state, whether the same be proposed by Bodies of Men or by an individual.

Chapter 3

Debates over Independence

Chapter Preface

Great Britain reacted angrily to the Boston Tea Party and its destruction of private property. Its responses raised the division between the colonies and the mother country to a new level, ultimately culminating in the previously unthinkable step of a colonial war for independence. Parliament's responses to the Boston Tea Party included a series of laws known in the colonies as the Intolerable Acts. The Boston Port Act closed the entire port of Boston until the East India Company was compensated for the tea thrown in the harbor. The Administration of Justice Act transferred legal suits against Crown officials from Massachusetts to England, depriving the colony of important judicial powers. The Massachusetts Government Act further revamped the colonial government by transferring more legislative and executive powers from the elected assembly to officials appointed by England. A new Quartering Act authorized the quartering of troops in private dwellings, not only in Massachusetts but in all the colonies.

Great Britain had hoped to isolate Massachusetts from the rest of the colonies and to have its actions serve as a warning to other colonies not to carry resistance too far. Instead the colonists interpreted the actions as evidence of a plan to totally subvert their rights as English citizens. The Intolerable Acts in large part inspired greater colonial unity. One result was the creation of the First Continental Congress, an advisory council with no official governmental powers that met in Philadelphia in the fall of 1774 to develop a common response to the Intolerable Acts. The Congress, after debating and rejecting a revised plan of union between the colonies and Britain proposed by delegate Joseph Galloway, called on Britain to repeal the Intolerable Acts and all other objectionable laws and taxes. It also drew up a Declaration of Rights, organized yet another boycott of British goods, advised each colony to form a militia, and recommended that Massachusetts form an independent government. While conceding Parliament's authority to regulate trade, the Congress officially declared that Parliament had no right to tax or legislate for the colonies, which lacked representation in Parliament.

Parliament refused to recognize the Continental Congress and rejected its proposals. In February 1775 it officially authorized King George III to use force to enforce British laws. British general Thomas Gage, appointed governor of Massachusetts, received orders in April to use force "to restore the vigour of Government" in Massachusetts. The colony's assembly, in defiance of Gage, had kept itself in session as a provincial congress and formed almost a shadow government. Gage directed a British regiment to seize a cache of arms being stored by the colonial militia in Concord. The militia and the British troops clashed in Concord and in Lexington, Massachusetts, on April 19, resulting in 99 British killed and 174 wounded, while the Americans had 52 dead and 41 wounded. It was the first battle of the Revolution. Historian Alden T. Vaughn writes:

> Resistance by the colonists brought more and more redcoated British regulars into American towns. The bolder colonists armed themselves; the officers of the imperial troops tried to prevent rebel armaments from becoming a threat to imperial authority. Had the first clash not come at Lexington in mid-April 1775 it would surely have occurred elsewhere—in Virginia, in New York, in South Carolina—not long after.

The Second Continental Congress met shortly after the battles at Lexington and Concord. Under the leadership and influence of John Dickinson, who had replaced Joseph Galloway as the leading advocate against open rebellion, it drafted an "Olive Branch Petition" to King George III asking for peaceful settlement of differences. It also drafted a "Declaration of the Causes and Necessities of Taking Up Arms." The latter resolution, coauthored by Dickinson and Virginia delegate Thomas Jefferson, justified colonial military resistance while also declaring that the colonies did not desire independence. However, on August 23, 1775, King George III formally rejected Dickinson's Olive Branch Petition and declared the colonies in a state of rebellion.

Despite King George's actions, many members of the Continental Congress and the general public still professed loyalty to the Crown while objecting to the authoritarian rule of Parliament. Perhaps the most important event that changed this view was the publication of the pamphlet *Common Sense* by Thomas Paine in January 1776. The pamphlet, which sold more than 120,000 copies over the next three months, in clear language forcefully advocated complete independence of the American colonies from both Britain's Parliament and its king. In part because of *Common Sense* and its influence, the fighting between the colonies and Britain changed from a defense of the colonists' rights as English citizens to a move for independence as Americans. The change in public sentiment inspired by *Common Sense* eventually resulted in the Continental Congress voting for independence on July 2 and adopting the Jefferson-authored Declaration of Independence on July 4, 1776.

VIEWPOINT 1

"I have prepared . . . a plan for uniting America more intimately, in constitutional policy, with Great Britain. . . . I am certain when dispassionately considered, it will be found to be the most perfect union in power and liberty with the Parent State."

The Colonies Should Seek a Revised Union with Great Britain

Joseph Galloway (1731-1803)

The first Continental Congress assembled in Carpenter's Hall in Philadelphia, Pennsylvania, on September 5, 1774. One of the leading delegates was Joseph Galloway, a wealthy lawyer and member of the Pennsylvania Assembly. He was speaker of that colonial legislature from 1766 to 1775.

Galloway was a chief exponent of a moderate position toward Great Britain, and he was opposed to the more radical and inflammatory pronouncements of people such as Samuel Adams of Massachusetts. At the Continental Congress he argued that the delegates were facing two bleak choices: restoring British-colonial relations to the way they were prior to 1763, which he argued was not possible, and total independence from Britain, which he did not support. He instead proposed a Plan of Union between Great Britain and the colonies. His plan called for a grand council representing all the American colonies to share power with Parliament. Legislation affecting all colonies and relations with Britain could be formulated by both bodies and become law only if passed on both sides of the Atlantic.

Galloway's plan was warmly received by many of the delegates. Edward Rutledge of South Carolina declared the plan to be "almost perfect." Opponents to the plan included Patrick Henry of Virginia, who argued that the proposed grand council might usurp the power of the colonial assemblies, and John Adams of Massachusetts, who wrote in his diary: "Among all the difficulties in the way of effective and united action in 1774 . . . no more alarming one happened than the plan of a proposed union between Great Britain and the Colonies presented . . . by Mr. Joseph Galloway." Adams and others thought the plan might strengthen the British Empire and blunt the drive for greater colonial independence. The Congress, voting by colonies, defeated the Galloway proposal by a vote of six to five, and subsequently expunged all records of the proposal and the debate from its official records. Whether it would have been approved by Great Britain is unknown.

Galloway eventually moved to England in 1778, where he became a chief spokesman and writer for the American loyalists. His holdings in the United States were confiscated, and his request to return to America in 1793 was denied. He died in England in 1803.

The following viewpoint is in two parts. The first is a speech by Joseph Galloway in support of his proposal and was taken from *Journals of the Continental Congress* (edited by W. C. Ford, Washington, DC, 1904). Like all speeches of the Congress, it is reconstructed from notes. The speech is followed by the text of the plan itself, which is excerpted here from *American Archives*, vol. 1 (edited by Peter Force, Washington, DC, 1837-1946).

I

There are two propositions before the Congress for restoring the wished-for harmony: one, that Parliament should be requested to place the Colonies in the state they were in in the year 1763; the other, that a non-exportation and non-importation agreement should be adopted. I will consider these propositions, and venture to reject them both; the first, as indecisive, tending to mislead both countries, and to lay a foundation for further discontent and quarrel; the other, as illegal, and ruinous to America.

The first proposition is indecisive, because it points out no ground of complaint—asks for a restoration of no right, settles no principle, and proposes no plan for accommodating the dispute.

There is no statute which has been passed to tax or bind the Colonies since the year 1763, which was not founded on precedents and statutes of a similar nature before that period; and therefore the proposition, while it expressly denies the right of Parliament, confesses it by the strongest implication. In short, it is nugatory, and without meaning; and however it may serve, when rejected by Parliament, as it certainly will be, to form a charge of injustice upon, and to deceive and inflame the minds of the people hereafter, it cannot possibly answer any other purpose.

The second proposition is undutiful and illegal: it is an insult on the supreme authority of the State; it cannot fail to draw on the Colonies the united resentment of the Mother Country. If we will not trade with Great Britain, she will not suffer us to trade at all. Our ports will be blocked up by British men of war, and troops will be sent to reduce us to reason and obedience. A total and sudden stagnation of commerce is what no country can bear: it must bring ruin on the Colonies: the produce of labour must perish on their hands, and not only the progress of industry be stopped, but industry and labour will cease, and the country itself be thrown into anarchy and tumult. I must therefore reject both the propositions; the first as indecisive, and the other as inadmissible upon any principle of prudence or policy.

Facts to Consider

If we sincerely mean to accommodate the difference between the two countries, and to establish their union on more firm and constitutional principles, we must take into consideration a number of facts which led the Parliament to pass the acts complained of, since the year 1763, and the real state of the Colonies. A clear and perfect knowledge of these matters only can lead us to the ground of substantial redress and permanent harmony. I will therefore call your recollection to the dangerous situation of the Colonies from the intrigues of France, and the incursions of the Canadians and their Indian allies, at the commencement of the last war. None of us can be ignorant of the just sense they then entertained of that danger, and of their incapacity to defend themselves against it, nor of the supplications made to the Parent State for its assistance, nor of the cheerfulness with which Great Britain sent over her fleets and armies for their protection, of the millions she expended in that protection, and of the happy consequences which attended it.

In this state of the Colonies, it was not unreasonable to expect that Parliament would have levied a tax on them proportionate to their wealth, and the sums raised in Great Britain. Her ancient right, so often exercised, and never controverted, enabled her, and the occasion invited her, to do it. And yet, not knowing their wealth, a generous tenderness arising from the fear of doing them injustice, induced Parliament to forbear to levy aids upon them. It left the Colonies to do justice to themselves and to the nation. And moreover, in order to allure them to a discharge of their duty, it offered to reimburse those Colonies which should generously grant the aids that were necessary to their own safety. But what was the conduct of the Colonies on this occasion, in which their own existence was immediately concerned? However painful it may be for me to repeat, or you to hear, I must remind you of it. You all know there were Colonies which at some times granted liberal aids, and at others nothing; other Colonies gave nothing during the war; none gave equitably in proportion to their wealth, and all that did give were actuated by partial and self interested motives, and gave only in proportion to the approach or remoteness of the danger. These delinquencies were occasioned by the want of the exercise of some supreme power to ascertain, with equity, their proportions of aids, and to over-rule the particular passions, prejudices, and interests, of the several Colonies.

Joseph Galloway sought a compromise solution between total independence and capitulation to Great Britain.

To remedy these mischiefs, Parliament was naturally led to exercise the power which had been, by its predecessors, so often exercised over the Colonies, and to pass the Stamp Act. Against this act, the Colonies petitioned Parliament, and denied its authority.

Instead of proposing some remedy, by which that authority should be rendered more equitable and more constitutional over the Colonies, the petitions rested in a declaration that the Colonies could not be represented in that body. This justly alarmed the British Senate. It was thought and called by the ablest men and Britain, a clear and explicit declaration of the American Independence, and compelled the Parliament to pass the Declaratory Act, in order to save its ancient and incontrovertible right of supremacy over all the parts of the empire. By this injudicious step the cause of our complaints became fixed, and instead of obtaining a constitutional reformation of the authority of Parliament over the Colonies, it brought on an explicit declaration of a right in Parliament to exercise absolute and unparticipated power over them. Nothing now can be wanting to convince us, that the Assemblies have pursued measures which have produced no relief, and answered no purpose but a bad one. I therefore hope that the collected wisdom of Congress will perceive and avoid former mistakes; that they will candidly and thoroughly examine the real merits of our dispute with the Mother Country, and take such ground as shall firmly unite us under one system of polity, and make us one people.

Looking at Both Sides

In order to establish those principles, upon which alone American relief ought, in reason and policy, to be founded, I will take a brief view of the arguments on both sides of the great question between the two countries—a question in its magnitude and importance exceeded by none that has been ever agitated in the councils of any nation. The advocates for the supremacy of Parliament over the Colonies contend, that there must be one supreme legislative head in every civil society, whose authority must extend to the regulation and final decision of every matter susceptible of human direction; and that every member of the society, whether political, official, or individual, must be subordinate to its supreme will, signified in its laws: that this supremacy and subordination are essential in the constitution of all States, whatever may be their forms; that no society ever did or could exist, without it; and that these truths are solidly established in the practice of all governments, and confirmed by the concurrent authority of all writers on the subject of civil society.

These advocates also assert, what we cannot deny—That the discovery of the Colonies was made under a commission granted by the supreme authority of the British State, that they have been settled under that authority, and therefore are truly the property of that State. Parliamentary jurisdiction has been constantly exercised over them from their first settlement; its executive authority has ever run through all their inferior political systems: the Colonists have ever sworn allegiance to the British State, and have been considered, both by the State and by themselves, as subjects of the British Government. Protection and allegiance are reciprocal duties; the one cannot exist without the other. The Colonies cannot claim the protection of Britain upon any principle of reason or law, while they deny its supreme authority. Upon this ground the authority of Parliament stands too firm to be shaken by any arguments whatever; and therefore to deny that authority, and at the same time to declare their incapacity to be represented, amounts to a full and explicit declaration of independence.

In regard to the political state of the Colonies, you must know that they are so many inferior societies, disunited and unconnected in polity. That while they deny the authority of Parliament, they are, in respect to each other, in a perfect state of nature, destitute of any supreme direction or decision whatever, and incompetent to the grant of national aids, or any other general measure whatever, even to the settlement of differences among themselves. This they have repeatedly acknowledged, and particularly by their delegates in Congress in the Beginning of the last war; and the aids granted by them since that period, for their own protection, are a proof of the truth of that acknowledgment.

You also knew that the seeds of discord are plentifully sowed in the constitution of the Colonies; that they are already grown to maturity, and have more than once broke out into open hostilities. They are at this moment only suppressed by the authority of the Parent State; and should that authority be weakened or annulled, many subjects of unsettled disputes, and which in that case, can only be settled by an appeal to the sword must involve us in all the horrors of civil war. You will now consider whether you wish to be destitute of the protection of Great Britain, or to see a renewal of the claims of France upon America; or to remain in our present disunited state, the weak exposed to the force of the strong. I am sure no honest man can entertain wishes so ruinous to his country.

Having thus briefly stated the arguments in favour of parliamentary authority, and considered the state of the Colonies, I am free to confess that the exercise of that authority is not perfectly constitutional in respect to the Colonies. We know that the whole landed interest of Britain is represented in that body, while neither the land nor the people of America hold the least participation in the legislative authority of the State. Representation, or a participation in the supreme councils of the State, is the great principle upon which the freedom of the British Government is established and secured. I also acknowledge, that that territory whose people have no enjoyment of this privilege, are subject to an authority unrestrained and absolute; and if the liberty of the subject were not essentially concerned in it, I should reject a distinction so odious between members of the same state, so long as it shall be continued. I wish to see it exploded, and the right to participate in the supreme councils of the State extended, in some form, not only to America, but to all the British dominions; otherwise I fear that profound and excellent fabrick of civil polity will, ere long, crumble to pieces.

The case of the Colonies is not a new one. It was formerly the very situation of Wales, Durham and Chester.

As to the tax, it is neither unjust or oppressive, it being rather a relief than a burthen; but it is want of constitutional principle in the authority that passed it, which is the ground for complaint. This, and this only, is the source of American grievances. Here, and here only, is the defect; and if this defect were removed, a foundation would be laid for the relief of every American complaint; the obnoxious statutes would of course be repealed, and others would be made, with the assent of the Colonies, to answer the same and better purposes; the mischiefs arising from the disunion of the Colonies would be removed; their freedom would be established, and their subordination fixed on solid constitutional principles.

A Way to Avoid War

Desirous as I am to promote the freedom of the Colonies, and to prevent the mischiefs which will attend a military contest with Great Britain, I must intreat you to desert the measures which have been so injudiciously and ineffectually pursued by antecedent Assemblies. Let us thoroughly investigate the subject matter in dispute, and endeavour to find from that investigation the means of perfect and permanent redress. In whatever we do, let us be particular and explicit, and not wander in general allegations. These will lead us to no point, nor can produce any relief; they are besides dishonourable and insidious. I would therefore acknowledge the neccessity of the supreme authority of Parliament over the Colonies, because it is a proposition which we cannot deny without manifest contradiction, while we confess that we are subjects of the British Government; and if we do not approve of a representation in Parliament, let us ask for a participation in the freedom and power of the English constitution in some other mode of incorporation: for I am convinced, by long attention to the subject, that let us deliberate, and try what other expedients we may, we shall find none that can give to the Colonies substantial freedom, but some such incorporation. I therefore beseech you, by the respect you are bound to pay to the instructions of your constituents, by the regard you have for the honour and safety of your country, and as you wish to avoid a war with Great Britain, which must terminate, at all events in the ruin of America, not to rely on a denial of the authority of Parliament, a refusal to be represented, and on a non-importation agreement; because whatever protestations, in that case, may be made to the contrary, it will prove to the world that we intend to throw off our allegiance to the State, and to involve the two countries in all the horrors of a civil war.

With a view to promote the measure I have so earnestly recommended, I have prepared the draught of a plan for uniting America more intimately, in constitutional policy, with Great Britain. It contains the great outlines or principles only, and will require many additions in case those should be approved. I am certain when dispassionately considered, it will be found to be the most perfect union in power and liberty with the Parent State, next to a representation in Parliament, and I trust it will be approved of by both countries. In forming it, I have been particularly attentive to the rights of both; and I am confident that no American, who wishes to continue a subject of the British State, which is what we all uniformly profess, can offer any reasonable objection against it.

II

Resolved, that this Congress will apply to His Majesty for a redress of grievances under which his faithful subjects in America labor; and assure him that the colonies hold in abhorrence the idea of being considered independent communities on the British government, and most ardently desire the establishment of a political union, not only among themselves but with the mother state, upon those principles of safety and freedom which are essential in the constitution of all free governments, and particularly that of the British legislature. And as the colonies from their local circumstances cannot be represented in the Parliament of Great Britain, they will humbly propose to His Majesty and his two houses of Parliament the following plan, under which the strength of the whole empire may be drawn together on any emergency, the interest of both countries advanced, and the rights and liberties of America secured: *A Plan for a Proposed Union between Great Britain and the Colonies of New Hampshire, the Massachusetts Bay, Rhode Island, Connecticut, New York, New Jersey, Pennsylvania, Maryland, the Three Lower Counties on the Delaware, Virginia, North Carolina, South Carolina, and Georgia.*

That a British and American legislature, for regulating the administration of the general affairs of America, be proposed and established in America, including all the said colonies; within and under which government each colony shall retain its present constitution and powers of regulating and governing its own internal police, in all cases whatever.

That the said government be administered by a president general, to be appointed by the King, and a Grand Council, to be chosen by the representatives of the people of the several colonies, in their respective assemblies, once in every three years.

That the several assemblies shall choose members for the Grand Council. . . .

That there shall be a new election of members for the Grand Council every three years; and on the death, removal, or resignation of any member, his place shall be supplied by a new choice at the next sitting of assembly of the colony he represented.

That the Grand Council shall meet once in every year if they shall think it necessary, and oftener if occasions shall require, at such time and place as they shall adjourn to at the last preceding meeting, or as they shall be called to meet at by the president general on any emergency.

All Rights and Liberties

That the Grand Council shall have power to choose their speaker, and shall hold and exercise all the like rights, liberties, and privileges as are held and exercised by and in the House of Commons of Great Britain.

That the president general shall hold his office during the pleasure of the King and his assent shall be requisite to all acts of the Grand Council, and it shall be his office and duty to cause them to be carried into execution.

That the president general, by and with the advice and consent of the Grand Council, hold and exercise all the legislative rights, powers, and authorities necessary for regulating and administering all the general police and affairs of the colonies in which Great Britain and the colonies, or any of them, the colonies in general, or more than one colony, are in any manner concerned, as well civil and criminal as commercial.

That the said president general and the Grand Council be an inferior and distinct branch of the British legislature, united and incorporated with it for the aforesaid general purposes; and that any of the said general regulations may originate and be formed and digested, either in the Parliament of Great Britain or in the said Grand Council, and being prepared, transmitted to the other for their approbation or dissent; and that the assent of both shall be requisite to the validity of all such general acts and statutes.

That in time of war, all bills for granting aid to the Crown, prepared by the Grand Council and approved by the president general, shall be valid and passed into a law, without the assent of the British Parliament.

VIEWPOINT 2

"To these grievous acts and measures Americans cannot submit, but . . . we have for the present only resolved to pursue . . . peaceable measures."

Great Britain Must Change Its Policies Toward the Colonies

The First Continental Congress (1774)

After weeks of debate, which included the introduction and rejection of the Galloway Plan of Union, the Continental Congress adopted the following resolutions on October 14, 1774. The original draft of this declaration was the work of Major John Sullivan, delegate from New Hampshire. The version here is excerpted from *Journals of the American Congress*, volume 1 (Washington, DC, 1823).

In this statement the Congress declared that the American colonists possessed personal rights, including life, liberty, and property, based upon "the immutable laws of nature, the principles of the English constitution, and the several charters or compacts." The declaration calls for the repeal of British laws passed since 1763 which, according to the Congress, had violated these rights. Rather than declare independence, the Congress sought to list their grievances to Great Britain in the hope of obtaining relief from its oppressive laws. Historians Winthrop D. Jordan and Leon F. Litwack write, "In effect, its members asked the clock be turned back eleven years to the situation that had prevailed until 1763."

John Adams wrote in his autobiography of two points that were heavily debated in the Congress. One was whether to base the colonial claims of rights on the "law of nature" in addition to the British constitution and the colonial charters. "Mr. Galloway and Mr. [James] Duane were for excluding the laws of nature. I was very strenuous for retaining and insisting on it." The other issue of debate was how much authority the colonies should concede to Parliament concerning internal and external affairs. In general the wording adopted was a triumph for Adams and his supporters, especially in the fourth resolution, which was approved despite Galloway's arguments that it was dangerously close to declaring independence.

Within the next few months, assemblies, conventions, and town or county meetings of eleven colonies had approved or ratified the proceedings of the Congress. No vote was held in Georgia, and the New York Assembly rejected ratification. The Congress determined to meet again in May 1775 if their grievances expressed here were not addressed.

Whereas, since the close of the last war, the British Parliament, claiming a power of right to bind the people of America by statutes in all cases whatsoever, has in some acts expressly imposed taxes on them, and in others, under various pretenses but in fact for the purpose of raising a revenue, has imposed rates and duties payable in these colonies; established a Board of Commissioners with unconstitutional powers; and extended the jurisdiction of Courts of Admiralty, not only for collecting the said duties but for the trial of causes merely arising within the body of a county.

And whereas, in consequence of other statutes, judges, who before held only estates at will in their offices, have been made dependent on the Crown alone for their salaries, and standing armies kept in times of peace. *And whereas* it has lately been resolved in Parliament that, by force of a statute made in the thirty-fifth year of the reign of King Henry the Eighth, colonists may be transported to England and tried there upon accusations for treasons, and misprisions, or concealments of treasons committed in the colonies; and by a late statute, such trials have been directed in cases therein mentioned.

Unjust Laws

And whereas, in the last session of Parliament, three statutes were made; one, entitled "An act to discontinue, in such manner and for such time as are therein mentioned, the landing and discharging, lading, or shipping of goods, wares, and merchandise at the town, and within the harbor of Boston, in the province of Massachusetts Bay, in North America"; another, entitled "An act for the better regulating the government of the province of Massachusetts Bay in New England"; and another, entitled "An act for the impartial administration of justice in the cases of persons questioned for any act done by them in the execution of the law, or for the suppression of riots and tumults in the province of the Massachusetts Bay in New England"; and another statute was then made, "for making more effectual provision for the government of the province of Quebec, etc."; all which statutes are impolitic, unjust, and cruel, as well as unconstitutional, and most dangerous and destructive of American rights.

And whereas, assemblies have been frequently dissolved, contrary to the rights of the people, when they attempted to deliberate on grievances; and their dutiful, humble, loyal, and reasonable petitions to the Crown for redress have been repeatedly treated with contempt by His Majesty's ministers of state:

The good people of the several colonies of New Hampshire; Massachusetts Bay; Rhode Island and Providence Plantations; Connecticut; New York; New Jersey; Pennsylvania; Newcastle, Kent, and Sussex on Delaware; Maryland; Virginia; North Carolina; and South Carolina, justly alarmed at these arbitrary proceedings of Parliament and administration, have severally elected, constituted, and appointed deputies to meet and sit in General Congress in the city of Philadelphia in order to obtain such establishment as that their religion, laws, and liberties may not be subverted:

American Rights

Whereupon the deputies so appointed being now assembled, in a full and free representation of these colonies, taking into their most serious consideration the best means of attaining the ends aforesaid, do, in the first place, as Englishmen, their ancestors in like cases have usually done, for affecting and vindicating their rights and liberties, declare,

That the inhabitants of the English colonies in North America, by the immutable laws of nature, the principles of the English constitution, and the several charters or compacts, have the following rights:

Resolved:

1. That they are entitled to life, liberty, and property, and they have never ceded to any sovereign power whatever a right to dispose of either without their consent.

2. That our ancestors, who first settled these colonies, were at the time of their emigration from the mother country entitled to

A Corrupt British Government

Benjamin Franklin served in London as an agent for Pennsylvania and as an unofficial ambassador representing all the American colonies before Great Britain from 1765 to 1775. At first a strong believer in the colonies remaining in the British Empire, he later came to regard the British government as hopelessly corrupt and American independence as inevitable. In a February 25, 1775, letter to Joseph Galloway, a Pennsylvania delegate in the Continental Congress who had sent Franklin his plan of union between Britain and the colonies, Franklin expresses his objections to such a prospect.

I have not heard what objections were made to the plan in the Congress, nor would I make more than this one, that, when I consider the extreme corruption prevalent among all orders of men in this old, rotten state, and the glorious public virtue so predominant in our rising country, I cannot but apprehend more mischief than benefit from a closer union. I fear they will drag us after them in all the plundering wars which their desperate circumstances, injustice, and rapacity may prompt them to undertake; and their wide-wasting prodigality and profusion is a gulf that will swallow up every aid we may distress ourselves to afford them.

Here numberless and needless places, enormous salaries, pensions, perquisites, bribes, groundless quarrels, foolish expeditions, false accounts or no accounts, contracts and jobs, devour all revenue, and produce continual necessity in the midst of natural plenty. I apprehend, therefore, that to unite us intimately will only be to corrupt and poison us also.

all the rights, liberties, and immunities of free and natural-born subjects, within the Realm of England.

3. That by such emigration they by no means forfeited, surrendered, or lost any of those rights, but that they were, and their descendants now are, entitled to the exercise and enjoyment of all such of them as their local and other circumstances enable them to exercise and enjoy.

The Foundation of Liberty

4. That the foundation of English liberty, and of all free government, is a right in the people to participate in their legislative council; and as the English colonists are not represented, and from their local and other circumstances cannot properly be represented in the British Parliament, they are entitled to a free and exclusive power of legislation in their several provincial legislatures, where their right of representation can alone be preserved, in all cases of taxation and internal polity, subject only to the neg-

ative of their sovereign, in such manner as has been heretofore used and accustomed. But, from the necessity of the case and a regard to the mutual interest of both countries, we cheerfully consent to the operation of such acts of the British Parliament as are bona fide, restrained to the regulation of our external commerce, for the purpose of securing the commercial advantages of the whole empire to the mother country, and the commercial benefits of its respective members; excluding every idea of taxation, internal or external, for raising a revenue on the subjects in America without their consent.

5. That the respective colonies are entitled to the common law of England, and more especially to the great and inestimable privilege of being tried by their peers of the vicinage according to the course of that law.

6. That they are entitled to the benefit of such of the English statutes as existed at the time of their colonization; and which they have, by experience, respectively found to be applicable to their several local and other circumstances.

7. That these, His Majesty's colonies, are likewise entitled to all the immunities and privileges granted and confirmed to them by royal charters, or secured by their several codes of provincial laws.

8. That they have a right peaceably to assemble, consider of their grievances, and petition the King; and that all prosecutions, prohibitory proclamations, and commitments for the same are illegal.

9. That the keeping of a standing army in these colonies, in times of peace, without the consent of the legislature of that colony in which such army is kept is against law.

10. It is indispensably necessary to good government, and rendered essential by the English constitution, that the constituent branches of the legislature be independent of each other; that, therefore, the exercise of legislative power in several colonies, by a council appointed during pleasure by the Crown, is unconstitutional, dangerous, and destructive to the freedom of American legislation.

Liberties Threatened

All and each of which the aforesaid deputies, in behalf of themselves and their constituents, do claim, demand, and insist on as their indubitable rights and liberties; which cannot be legally taken from them, altered or abridged by any power whatever, without their own consent, by their representatives in their several provincial legislatures.

In the course of our inquiry, we find many infringements and violations of the foregoing rights, which, from an ardent desire that harmony and mutual intercourse of affection and interest may be restored, we pass over for the present, and proceed to state such acts and measures as have been adopted since the last war, which demonstrate a system formed to enslave America.

Resolved, that the following acts of Parliament are infringements and violations of the rights of the colonists; and that the repeal of them is essentially necessary in order to restore harmony between Great Britain and the American colonies, viz.:

The several acts . . . which impose duties for the purpose of raising a revenue in America, extend the powers of the Admiralty Courts beyond their ancient limits, deprive the American subject of trial by jury, authorize the judge's certificate to indemnify the prosecutor from damages that he might otherwise be liable to, requiring oppressive security from a claimant of ships and goods seized, before he shall be allowed to defend his property, and are subversive of American rights. . . .

Also the three acts passed in the last session of Parliament for stopping the port and blocking up the harbor of Boston, for altering the charter and government of Massachusetts Bay, and that which is entitled "An act for the better administration of justice, etc."

Also the act passed the same session for establishing the Roman Catholic religion in the province of Quebec, abolishing the equitable system of English laws, and erecting a tyranny there to the great danger, from so total a dissimilarity of religion, law, and government of the neighboring British colonies, by the assistance of whose blood and treasure the said country was conquered from France.

Also the act passed the same session for the better providing suitable quarters for officers and soldiers in His Majesty's service in North America.

Also, that the keeping a standing army in several of these colonies, in time of peace, without the consent of the legislature of that colony in which the army is kept, is against law.

To these grievous acts and measures Americans cannot submit, but in hopes that their fellow subjects in Great Britain will, on a revision of them, restore us to that state in which both countries found happiness and prosperity, we have for the present only resolved to pursue the following peaceable measures:

1. To enter into a nonimportation, nonconsumption, and nonexportation agreement or association.

2. To prepare an address to the people of Great Britain and a memorial to the inhabitants of British America.

3. To prepare a loyal address to His Majesty, agreeable to resolutions already entered into.

VIEWPOINT 3

*"To obtain redress of these grievances . . . we are
of opinion that a nonimportation, nonconsumption,
and nonexportation agreement, faithfully adhered to,
will prove the most speedy, effectual, and peaceable
measure."*

The Colonies Should
Break Off Trade with
Great Britain

The First Continental Congress (1774)

The First Continental Congress, after several weeks of debate, voted on September 27, 1774, to protest Great Britain's policies toward the colonies by refusing to trade with England. A congressional committee drafted a plan for carrying this resolution into effect, which was approved October 18. While individual colonies previously had engaged in nonimportation and nonexportation agreements, this marked the first such unified action by the colonies.

The plan, called the Continental Association and taken from the *Journals of the American Congress*, volume 1, (Washington, DC, 1823) is excerpted in the following viewpoint. It cut off all imports from Great Britain after December 1774 and all exports to Great Britain after September 1775. The latter date was a concession to southern tobacco planters who wanted to sell their current crop, and the exception of rice was a concession to planters in South Carolina. Other provisions of the agreement prohibited the importation of slaves and called for colonial committees of correspondence to enforce the rules of the association. While the association failed in its stated objectives of changing Britain's policies, it did succeed in creating a sense of unity among the colonies.

We, His Majesty's most loyal subjects, the delegates of the several colonies of New Hampshire, Massachusetts Bay, Rhode Island, Connecticut, New York, New Jersey, Pennsylvania, the three lower counties of Newcastle, Kent, and Sussex on Delaware, Maryland, Virginia, North Carolina, and South Carolina, deputed to represent them in a Continental Congress, held in the city of Philadelphia, on the 5th day of September, 1774, avowing our allegiance to His Majesty, our affection and regard for our fellow subjects in Great Britain and elsewhere, affected with the deepest anxiety and most alarming apprehensions at those grievances and distresses, with which His Majesty's American subjects are oppressed; and having taken under our most serious deliberation the state of the whole continent, find that the present unhappy situation of our affairs is occasioned by a ruinous system of colony administration, adopted by the British Ministry about the year 1763, evidently calculated for enslaving these colonies and with them, the British empire.

Cruel Acts

In prosecution of which system, various acts of Parliament have been passed for raising a revenue in America; for depriving the American subjects, in many instances, of the constitutional trial by jury; exposing their lives to danger by directing a new and illegal trial beyond the seas for crimes alleged to have been committed in America. And in prosecution of the same system, several late, cruel, and oppressive acts have been passed respecting the town of Boston and the Massachusetts Bay, and also an act for extending the province of Quebec, so as to border on the western frontiers of these colonies, establishing an arbitrary government therein, and discouraging the settlement of British subjects in that wide-extended country; thus, by the influence of civil principles and ancient prejudices to dispose the inhabitants to act with hostility against the free Protestant colonies, whenever a wicked Ministry shall choose to direct them.

To obtain redress of these grievances which threaten destruction to the lives, liberty, and property of His Majesty's subjects in North America, we are of opinion that a nonimportation, nonconsumption, and nonexportation agreement, faithfully adhered to, will prove the most speedy, effectual, and peaceable measure. And, therefore, we do, for ourselves and the inhabitants of the several colonies whom we represent, firmly agree and associate, under the sacred ties of virtue, honor, and love of our country, as follows:

1. That from and after the 1st day of December next, we will not import into British America from Great Britain or Ireland any goods, wares, or merchandise whatsoever, or from any other place, any such goods, wares, or merchandise, as shall have been exported from Great Britain or Ireland. Nor will we, after that day, import any East India tea from any part of the world; nor any molasses, syrups, paneles, coffee, or pimento from the British plantations or from Dominica; nor wines from Madeira or the Western Islands; nor foreign indigo.

2. We will neither import nor purchase any slave imported after the 1st day of December next; after which time, we will wholly discontinue the slave trade and will neither be concerned in it ourselves, nor will we hire our vessels, nor sell our commodities or manufactures to those who are concerned in it.

3. As a nonconsumption agreement, strictly adhered to, will be an effectual security for the observation of the nonimportation, we, as above, solemnly agree and associate that from this day we will not purchase or use any tea imported on account of the East India Company, or any on which a duty has been or shall be paid. And from and after the 1st day of March next, we will not purchase or use any East India tea whatever; nor will we, nor shall any person for or under us, purchase or use any of those goods, wares, or merchandise we have agreed not to import, which we shall know or have cause to suspect, were imported after the 1st day of December, except such as come under the rules and directions of the 10th Article hereafter mentioned.

Suspending Exports

4. The earnest desire we have not to injure our fellow subjects in Great Britain, Ireland, or the West Indies induces us to suspend a nonexportation [agreement] until the 10th day of September, 1775; at which time, if the said acts and parts of acts of the British Parliament hereinafter mentioned are not repealed, we will not directly or indirectly export any merchandise or commodity whatsoever to Great Britain, Ireland, or the West Indies, except rice to Europe.

5. Such as are merchants and use the British and Irish trade will give orders, as soon as possible, to their factors, agents, and correspondents in Great Britain and Ireland not to ship any goods to them, on any pretense whatsoever, as they cannot be received in

America; and if any merchant residing in Great Britain or Ireland shall directly or indirectly ship any goods, wares, or merchandise for America in order to break the said nonimportation agreement or in any manner contravene the same, on such unworthy conduct being well attested, it ought to be made public; and, on the same being so done, we will not, from thenceforth, have any commercial connection with such merchant.

6. That such as are owners of vessels will give positive orders to their captains or masters not to receive on board their vessels any goods prohibited by the said nonimportation agreement, on pain of immediate dismission from their service.

The First Continental Congress met in Carpenter's Hall in Philadelphia, Pennsylvania, from September 5 to October 26, 1774.

7. We will use our utmost endeavors to improve the breed of sheep and increase their number to the greatest extent; and to that end, we will kill them as seldom as may be, especially those of the most profitable kind; nor will we export any to the West Indies or elsewhere; and those of us who are or may become overstocked with, or can conveniently spare any, sheep will dispose of them to our neighbors, especially to the poorer sort, on moderate terms.

8. We will, in our several stations, encourage frugality, economy, and industry, and promote agriculture, arts, and the manufactures of this country, especially that of wool; and will discountenance and discourage every species of extravagance and dissipa-

tion, especially all horse racing, and all kinds of gaming, cock-fighting, exhibitions of shows, plays, and other expensive diversions and entertainments. And on the death of any relation or friend, none of us, or any of our families, will go into any further mourning dress than a black crape or ribbon on the arm or hat for gentlemen, and a black ribbon and necklace for ladies, and we will discontinue the giving of gloves and scarves at funerals.

9. Such as are vendors of goods or merchandise will not take advantage of the scarcity of goods that may be occasioned by this association, but will sell the same at the rates we have been respectively accustomed to do for twelve months last past. And if any vendor of goods or merchandise shall sell such goods on higher terms, or shall, in any manner or by any device whatsoever, violate or depart from this agreement, no person ought nor will any of us deal with any such person, or his or her factor or agent, at any time thereafter, for any commodity whatever.

10. In case any merchant, trader, or other person shall import any goods or merchandise after the 1st day of December and before the 1st day of February next, the same ought forthwith, at the election of the owner, to be either reshipped or delivered up to the committee of the country or town wherein they shall be imported, to be stored at the risk of the importer until the nonimportation agreement shall cease or be sold under the direction of the committee aforesaid. And in the last-mentioned case, the owner or owners of such goods shall be reimbursed out of the sales the first cost and charges, the profit, if any, to be applied toward relieving and employing such poor inhabitants of the town of Boston as are immediate sufferers by the Boston port bill; and a particular account of all goods so returned, stored, or sold to be inserted in the public papers. And if any goods or merchandises shall be imported after the said 1st day of February, the same ought forthwith to be sent back again, without breaking any of the packages thereof.

Enemies of Liberty

11. That a committee be chosen in every county, city, and town by those who are qualified to vote for representatives in the legislature, whose business it shall be attentively to observe the conduct of all persons touching this association. And when it shall be made to appear, to the satisfaction of a majority of any such committee, that any person within the limits of their appointment has violated this association, that such majority do forthwith cause the truth of the case to be published in the gazette; to the end that all such foes to the rights of British America may be publicly known and universally contemned as the enemies of American liberty; and thenceforth we respectively will break off all dealings

with him or her.

12. That the Committee of Correspondence, in the respective colonies, do frequently inspect the entries of their custom-houses, and inform each other, from time to time, of the true state thereof, and of every other material circumstance that may occur relative to this association.

13. That all manufactures of this country be sold at reasonable prices, so that no undue advantage be taken of a future scarcity of goods.

14. And we do further agree and resolve that we will have no trade, commerce, dealings, or intercourse whatsoever with any colony or province in North America which shall not accede to, or which shall hereafter violate, this association, but will hold them as unworthy of the rights of freemen and as inimical to the liberties of their country.

And we do solemnly bind ourselves and our constituents, under the ties aforesaid, to adhere to this association until such parts of the several acts of Parliament passed since the close of the last war, as impose or continue duties on tea, wine, molasses, syrups, paneles, coffee, sugar, pimento, indigo, foreign paper, glass, and painters' colors imported into America, and extend the powers of the Admiralty Courts beyond their ancient limits, deprive the American subject of trial by jury, authorize the judge's certificate to indemnify the prosecutor from damages, that he might otherwise be liable to from a trial by his peers, require oppressive security from a claimant of ships or goods seized, before he shall be allowed to defend his property, are repealed.

And until that part of the act . . . entitled "An act for the better securing His Majesty's dockyards, magazines, ships, ammunition, and stores," by which any persons charged with committing any of the offenses therein described, in America, may be tried in any shire or county within the Realm, is repealed; and until the four acts, passed the last session of Parliament, viz.: that for stopping the port and blocking up the harbor of Boston; that for altering the charter and government of the Massachusetts Bay; that which is entitled "An act for the better administration of justice, etc."; and that "for extending the limits of Quebec, etc.," are repealed. And we recommend it to the provincial conventions, and to the committees in the respective colonies, to establish such further regulations as they may think proper, for carrying into execution this association.

VIEWPOINT 4

"Can we think to threaten, and bully, and frighten the supreme government of the nation into a compliance with our demands?"

The Colonies Should Not Break Off Trade with Great Britain

Samuel Seabury (1729-1796)

Samuel Seabury was a doctor and Episcopalian minister in Westchester, New York. He wrote numerous pamphlets and tracts in support of the loyalist cause. One of his noteworthy pamphlets was *Letters of a Westchester Farmer*, published in 1774, and excerpted here, in which he strongly criticized the economic boycott organized by the First Continental Congress. Seabury asserts that a trade boycott will harm people in the colonies more than Great Britain, and that Americans are being led by dangerous radicals down a ruinous path of separation from the mother country.

Seabury remained a loyalist through the revolutionary war and was consequently forced to abandon his parish. After the war he remained in the new country, however. He was elected the first Episcopal bishop in America and had a strong influence in the creation of the Protestant Episcopal Church of the United States.

My Friends and Countrymen,
Permit me to address you upon a subject, which, next to your

eternal welfare in a future world, demands your most serious and dispassionate consideration. The American Colonies are unhappily involved in a scene of confusion and discord. The bands of civil society are broken; the authority of government weakened, and in some instances taken away: Individuals are deprived of their liberty; their property is frequently invaded by violence, and not a single Magistrate has had courage or virtue enough to interpose. From this distressed situation it was hoped, that the wisdom and prudence of the Congress lately assembled at Philadelphia, would have delivered us. The eyes of all men were turned to them. We ardently expected that some prudent scheme of accommodating our unhappy disputes with the Mother-Country, would have been adopted and pursued. But alas! they are broken up without even attempting it: they have taken no one step that tended to peace: they have gone on from bad to worse, and have either ignorantly misunderstood, carelessly neglected, or basely betrayed the interests of all the Colonies.

I shall in this, and some future publication, support this charge against the Congress, by incontestible facts: But my first business shall be to point out to you some of the consequences that will probably follow from the Non-importation, Non-exportation, and Non-consumption Agreements, which they have adopted, and which they have ordered to be enforced in the most arbitrary manner, and under the severest penalties. On this subject, I choose to address myself to You the *Farmers* of the Province of New-York, because I am most nearly connected with you, being one of your number, and having no interest in the country but in common with you; and also, because the interest of the farmers in general will be more sensibly affected, and more deeply injured by these agreements, than the interest of any other body of people on the continent. Another reason why I choose to address myself to you is, because the Farmers are of the greatest benefit to the state, of any people in it: They furnish food for the merchant, and mechanic; the raw materials for most manufacturers, the staple exports of the country, are the produce of their industry: be then convinced of your own importance, and think and act accordingly.

The Non-importation Agreement adopted by the Congress is to take place the first day of December next; after which no goods, wares, or merchandize, are to be imported from Great-Britain or Ireland; no East-India Tea from any part of the world; no molasses, syrups, paneles, coffee, or pimento, from our islands in the West-Indies; no wine from Madeira, or the Western-Islands; no foreign indigo.

The Non-exportation Agreement is to take effect on the tenth day of September next; after which we are not to export, directly or indirectly, any merchandize or commodity whatsoever to Great-Britain, Ireland, or the West-Indies, except RICE to Europe,—unless the several acts and parts of acts of the British Parliament, referred to by the fourth article of Association, be repealed.

The Non-consumption Agreement is to be in force the first day of March next; after which we are not to purchase or use any East-India Tea whatsoever; nor any goods, wares, or merchandize from Great-Britain or Ireland, imported after the first of December, nor molasses, &c. from the West-Indies; nor wine from Madeira, or the Western Islands, nor foreign indigo.

Dire Consequences

Let us now consider the probable consequences of these agreements, supposing they should take place, and be exactly adhered to. The first I shall mention is, clamours, discord, confusion, mobs, riots, insurrections, rebellions, in Great-Britain, Ireland, and the West-Indies. This consequence does not indeed immediately affect You, the Farmers of New-York; nor do I think it a probable one: But the Congress certainly intended it should happen in some degree, or to the effect they propose from these agreements cannot possibly take place. They intend to distress the manufacturers in Great-Britain, by depriving them of employment—to distress the inhabitants of Ireland, by depriving them of flaxseed, and of a vent for their linens,—to distress the West-India people, by with-holding provisions and lumber from them, and by stopping the market for their produce. And they hope, by these means, to force them all to join their clamours with ours, to get the acts complained of, repealed. This was the undoubted design of the Congress when these agreements were framed; and this is the avowed design of their warm supporters and partizans, in common conversation.

But where is the justice, where is the policy of this proceedure? The manufacturers of Great-Britain, the inhabitants of Ireland, and of the West-Indies, have done us no injury. They have been no ways instrumental in bringing our distresses upon us. Shall we then revenge ourselves upon them? Shall we endeavour to starve them into a compliance with our humours? Shall we, without any provocation, tempt or force them into riots and insurrections, which must be attended with the ruin of many—probably with the death of some of them? Shall we attempt to unsettle the whole British Government—to throw all into confusion, because our self-will is not complied with? Because the ill-projected, ill-conducted, abominable scheme of some of the colonists, to form a republican government independent of Great-Britain, cannot otherwise succeed?—Good God! can we look forward to the ruin, destruction, and desolation of the whole British Empire, without one relenting thought? Can we contemplate it with pleasure; and promote it with all our might and vigour, and at the same time call ourselves *his Majesty's most dutiful and loyal subjects?* Whatever the Gentlemen of the Congress may think of the matter, the spirit that dictated such a measure, was not the spirit of humanity.

Next let us consider the policy, or rather impolicy of this measure. Instead of conciliating, it will alienate the affections of the people of Great-Britain. Of friends it will make them our enemies; it will excite the resentment of the government at home against us; and their resentment will do us no good, but, on the contrary, much harm.

Can we think to threaten, and bully, and frighten the supreme government of the nation into a compliance with our demands? Can we expect to force a submission to our peevish and petulant humours, by exciting clamours and riots in England? We ought to know the temper and spirit, the power and strength of the nation better. A single campaign, should she exert her force, would ruin us effectually. But should she choose less violent means, she has it in her power to humble us without hurting herself. She might raise immense revenues, by laying duties in England, Ireland and the West-Indies, and we could have no remedy left; for this non-importation scheme cannot last forever. She can embarrass our trade in the Mediterranean with Spain, Holland, &c. nor can we help ourselves; for whatever regulations she should make, would effectually be enforced, by the same Navy that she keeps in readiness to protect her own trade. . . .

Hurting Ourselves

[Moreover we will not succeed in this attempt, for the people of Great-Britain, Ireland and the West-Indies will not be sufficiently distressed.] The first distress will fall on ourselves: it will be more severely felt by us, than by any part of all his Majesty's dominions; and it will affect us the longest. The fleets of Great-Britain command respect throughout the globe. Her influence extends to every part of the earth. Her manufactures are equal to any, superior to most in the world. Her wealth is great. Her people enterprizing, and persevering in their attempts to extend and enlarge and protect her trade. The total loss of our trade would be felt only for a time. Her merchants would turn their attention another way. New sources of trade and wealth would be opened: New schemes pursued. She would soon find a vent for all her manufactures in spite of all we could do. Our malice would hurt ourselves only. Should our schemes distress some branches of her trade, it could be only for a time; and there is ability and humanity enough in the nation to relieve those that are distressed by us,

Samuel Seabury wrote numerous articles and pamphlets in support of the loyalist cause.

and to put them in some other way of getting their living.

The case is very different with *us*. We have no trade but under the protection of Great-Britain. We can trade no where but where she pleases. We have no influence abroad, no ambassadors, no consuls, no fleet to protect our ships in passing the seas, nor our merchants and people in foreign countries. Should our mad schemes take place, our sailors, ship-carpenters, carmen, sail-makers, riggers, miners, smelters, forge-men, and workers in bar-iron, &c. would be immediately out of employ; and we should have twenty mobs and riots in our own country, before one would happen in Britain or Ireland. Want of food will make these people mad, and they will come in troops upon our farms, and take that by force which they have not money to purchase. And who could blame them? Justice, indeed, might hang them; but the sympathetic eye would drop the tear of humanity on their grave.

The next thing I shall take notice of, is the advanced prices of goods, which will, not only probably, but necessarily, follow, as soon as the non-importation from Great-Britain, &c. shall take effect. This is a consequence that most nearly concerns you; nor can you prevent it. You are obliged to buy many articles of clothing. You cannot make them yourselves; or you cannot make them so cheap as you can buy them. You want Woollens for your winter clothing. Few of you have wool enough to answer the purpose. For notwithstanding the boasts of some ignorant, hot-headed men, there is not wool enough on the continent, taking all the colonies together, to supply the inhabitants with stockings. Notwithstanding all the home-spun you can make, many of you find it difficult, at the year's end, to pay the shop-keeper for what the necessities of your families have obliged you to take up. What will you do when the prices of goods are advanced a quarter, for instance, or an half? To say that the prices of goods will not be raised, betrays your ignorance and folly. The price of any commodity always rises in proportion to the demand for it; and the demand always increases in proportion to its scarcity. As soon as the importation ceases in New-York, the quantity of goods will be daily lessened, by daily consumption; and the prices will gradually rise in proportion. "But the merchants of New-York have declared that, they will demand only a reasonable profit." Who is to judge what a reasonable profit is? Why, the merchants. Will they expose their invoices, and the secrets of their trade to you, that you may judge whether their profits are reasonable or not? Certainly they will not, and if they did, you cannot understand them; and consequently, can form no judgment about them. You have therefore nothing to trust to in this case but the honour of the merchants. Let us then consider how far we have reason to trust to their honour.

Not to raise the price of a commodity when it is scarce, and in demand, is contrary to the principles and practice of merchants. Their maxim is, to buy as cheap, and sell as dear, as they can. Will they let you have a piece of goods for twenty shillings, which will fetch twenty-five? When the stores and shops are full, and a price is demanded which you think unreasonable, you will ask an abatement. If you are refused, you will look elsewhere. But when there are few goods and many buyers, no abatement can be expected. If you won't give the price, your neighbor perhaps is in greater necessity, and *must* give it. Besides, the merchant knows that no more goods can be imported. He knows that the necessities of the country are increasing, and that what you refuse now at twenty shillings, you will be obliged to take, by and by, at twenty-five. . . .

Provoking England

I come now to the consideration of another probable consequence of a Non-importation Agreement, which is, That it will excite the resentment of the government at home against us, and induce the Parliament to block up our ports and prevent our trade intirely. It would certainly be good policy in the government to do so. Few Colonies are settled but by a trading people, and by them chiefly for the benefit of trade. The grand design of England in settling the American Colonies, was to extend her trade—to open a new vent for her manufacturers. If then we stop our imports, the benefit of our trade is in a manner lost to her, and she would find but little additional disadvantage, should she stop our trade with all the world.

But should the government pursue milder measures—though we indeed have no right to expect it will—yet the Congress have determined the expediency of our stopping our own trade, after a limited time, viz. ten months. In either case the consequence will be much the same; and it matters but little whether the government blocks up our ports, or whether we ourselves voluntarily put an end to our exports, as well as imports; after the 10th of September next we are to have but little trade except with our neighbouring colonies.

Consider the consequence, Should the government interpose, we shall have no trade at all, and consequently no vent for the produce of our farms. Such part of our wheat, flaxseed, corn, beef, pork, butter, cheese, as was not consumed in the province, must be left to rot and stink upon our hands. . . .

Look well to yourselves, I beseech you. From the day that the exports from this province are stopped, the farmers may date the commencement of their ruin. Can you live without money? Will the shop-keeper *give* you his goods? Will the weaver, shoemaker, blacksmith, carpenter, work for you without pay? If they will, it is far more than they will do for me. And unless you can sell your produce, how are you to get money? Nor will the case be better, if you are obliged to sell your produce at an under-rate; for then it will not pay you for the labour and expence of raising it. But this is the least part of the distress that will come upon you.

Unhappily, many of you are in debt, and obliged to pay the enormous interest of seven pounds on the hundred, for considerable sums. It matters not whether your debts have been contracted through necessity, or carelessness: You must pay them, at *least* the interest, punctually; the usurer will not wait long; indeed you cannot expect he should: You have had his money, and are obliged, in justice, to pay him the principal and interest, according to agreement. But without selling your produce, you can neither pay the one, nor the other; the consequence will be that after a while, a process of law will be commenced against you, and your farms must be sold by execution; and then you will have to pay not only principal and interest, but Sheriffs fees, Lawyers fees, and a long list of *et caeteras*. . . .

Consider now the situation you will be in, if Great-Britain, provoked by your Non-importation Agreement, should shut up our ports; or should the Non-exportation agreed to by the Congress, take effect. In that case you will not be able to sell your produce: you cannot pay even the interest of the money you are indebted for; your farms must be sold, and you and your families turned out, to beggary and wretchedness. Blessed fruits of Non-importation and Non-exportation! The farmer that is in debt, will be ruined: the farmer that is clear in the world, will be obliged to run in debt, to support his family: and while the proud merchant, and the forsworn smuggler, riot in their ill-gotten wealth; the laborious farmers, the grand support of every well-regulated country, must go to the dogs together.—Vile! Shamefull! Diabolical Device!

Let us now attend a little to the Non-consumption Agreement, which the Congress, in their Association, have imposed upon us. After the first of March we are not to purchase or use any East-India Tea whatsoever; nor any goods, wares, or merchandize from Great-Britain or Ireland, imported after the first day of December next: nor any molasses, syrups, &c. from the British plantations in the West-Indies, or from Dominica; nor wine from Madeira, or the Western Islands; nor foreign indigo.

Tyrannical Committees

Will you submit to this slavish regulation?—You must.—Our sovereign Lords and Masters, the High and Mighty Delegates, in Grand Continental Congress assembled, have ordered and directed it. They have directed the Committees in the respective Colonies, to establish such further regulations as they may think proper, for carrying their association, of which this Non-consumption Agreement is a part, into execution. . . . The Committee of New-York, hath issued his mandate, bearing date Nov. 7, 1774, recommending it to the freeholders and freemen of New-York, to assemble on the 18th of November, to choose eight persons out of every ward, to be a Committee, to carry the Association of the Congress into execution.—The business of the Committee so chosen is to be, to inspect the conduct of the inhabitants, and see whether they violate the Association.—Among other things, Whether they drink any Tea or wine in their families, after the first of March, or wear any British or Irish manufactures; or use any English molasses, &c. imported after the first day of December next. If they do, their names are to be published in the Gazette, that they might be *publickly known*, and *universally contemned*, as *foes to the Rights of British America, and enemies of American Liberty*.—And then *the parties of the said Association will respectively break off all dealings with him or her*.—In plain English,—They shall be considered as Out-laws, unworthy of the protection of civil society, and delivered over to the vengeance of a lawless, outrageous mob, to be *tarred, feathered, hanged, drawn, quartered, and burnt*.—O rare American Freedom! . . .

126

Will you be instrumental in bringing the most abject slavery on yourselves? Will you choose such Committees? Will you submit to them, should they be chosen by the weak, foolish, turbulent part of the country people?—Do as you please: but, by HIM that made me, I will not.—No, if I must be enslaved, let it be by a KING at least, and not by a parcel of upstart lawless Committee-men. If I must be devoured, let me be devoured by the jaws of a lion, and not *gnawed* to death by rats and vermin.

VIEWPOINT 5

"We ... renounce with disdain our connection with a kingdom of slaves; we bid a final adieu to Britain."

America Should Declare Independence from Great Britain

The Citizens of Malden, Massachusetts (1776)

On May 10, 1776, the Massachusetts House of Representatives passed a resolution that declared that the inhabitants of all towns in that colony "ought in full Meeting warned for that Purpose, to advise the Person or Persons who shall be chosen to Represent them in the next General Court, whether if the honorable Congress should, for the Safety of the said colonies, declare them Independent of the Kingdom of Great-Britain, they the said Inhabitants will solemnly engage with their Lives and Fortunes to Support the Congress in the Measure." Typical of many of the resolutions sent to the Second Continental Congress are the following declarations from the town of Malden, Massachusetts, approved in a May 27 town meeting and reprinted in *Principles and Acts of the Revolution in America* (Hezekiah Niles, ed., Baltimore, 1822). In justifying their plea for independence, the resolutions make special reference to the April 1775 battles of Lexington and Concord.

Sir—A resolution of the hon. house of representatives, calling upon the several towns in this colony to express their minds in respect to the important question of American independence, is the occasion of our now instructing you. The time was, sir, when we loved the king and the people of Great Britain with an affection truly filial; we felt ourselves interested in their glory; we shared in their joys and sorrows; we cheerfully poured the fruit of all our labours into the lap of our mother country, and without reluctance expended our blood and our treasure in their cause.

These were our sentiments toward Great Britain while she continued to act the part of a parent state; we felt ourselves happy in our connection with her, nor wished it to be dissolved; but our sentiments are altered, it is now the ardent wish of our soul that America may become a free and independent state.

Injuries from Britain

A sense of unprovoked injuries will arouse the resentment of the most peaceful. Such injuries these colonies have received from Britain. Unjustifiable claims have been made by the king and his minions to tax us without our consent; these claims have been prosecuted in a manner cruel and unjust to the highest degree. The frantic policy of administration hath induced them to send fleets and armies to America; that, by depriving us of our trade, and cutting the throats of our brethren, they might awe us into submission, and erect a system of despotism in America, which should so far enlarge the influence of the crown as to enable it to rivet their shackles upon the people of Great Britain.

This plan was brought to a crisis upon the ever memorable nineteenth of April. We remember the fatal day! the expiring groans of our countrymen yet vibrate on our ears! and we now behold the flames of their peaceful dwellings ascending to Heaven! we hear their blood crying to us from the ground for vengeance! charging us, as we value the peace of their names, to have no further connection with —, who can unfeelingly hear of the slaughter of —, and composedly sleep with their blood upon his soul. The manner in which the war has been prosecuted hath confirmed us in these sentiments; piracy and murder, robbery and breach of faith, have been conspicuous in the conduct of the king's troops: defenceless towns have been attacked and destroyed: the ruins of Charlestown, which are daily in our view, daily reminds of this: the cries of the widow and the orphan demand our attention; they demand that the hand of pity should wipe the tear from their eye, and that the sword of their country should avenge their wrongs. We long entertained hope that the spirit of the British nation would once more induce them to assert their own and our rights, and bring to condign punishment the elevated villains who have trampled upon the sacred rights of men and affronted the majesty of the people. We hoped in vain;

John Adams on Independence

John Adams was a leading advocate of independence in the Continental Congress and a member of the committee that helped draft the Declaration of Independence. His speech on July 1, 1776, rebutting John Dickinson, a Pennsylvania delegate who had argued before Congress against independence, was unfortunately not recorded. Several of Adams's arguments in favor of declaring independence, however, appear in his letter of June 23 to John Winthrop.

It is now universally acknowledged that we are and must be independent. But still, objections are made to a declaration of it. It is said that such a declaration will arouse and unite Great Britain. But are they not already aroused and united, as much as they will be? Will not such a declaration arouse and unite the friends of liberty, the few who are left, in opposition to the present system? It is also said that such a declaration will put us in the power of foreign States; that France will take advantage of us when they see we cannot recede, and demand severe terms of us; that she, and Spain too, will rejoice to see Britain and America wasting each other. But this reasoning has no weight with me, because I am not for soliciting any political connection, or military assistance, or indeed naval, from France. I wish for nothing but commerce, a mere marine treaty with them. And this they will never grant until we make the declaration, and this, I think, they cannot refuse, after we have made it.

The advantages which will result from such a declaration are, in my opinion, very numerous and very great. After that event the colonies will hesitate no longer to complete their governments. They will establish tests, and ascertain the criminality of toryism. The presses will produce no more seditious or traitorous speculations. Slanders upon public men and measures will be lessened. The legislatures of the colonies will exert themselves to manufacture saltpetre, sulphur, powder, arms, cannon, mortars, clothing, and every thing necessary for the support of life. Our civil governments will feel a vigor hitherto unknown. Our military operations by sea and land will be conducted with greater spirit. Privateers will swarm in vast numbers. Foreigners will then exert themselves to supply us with what we want. A foreign court will not disdain to treat with us upon equal terms. Nay farther, in my opinion, such a declaration, instead of uniting the people of Great Britain against us, will raise such a storm against the measures of administration as will obstruct the war, and throw the kingdom into confusion.

they have lost their love to freedom, they have lost their spirit of just resentment; we therefore renounce with disdain our connection with a kingdom of slaves; we bid a final adieu to Britain.

Could an accommodation now be effected, we have reason to think that it would be fatal to the liberties of America; we should soon catch the contagion of venality and dissipation, which hath Britains to lawless domination. Were we placed in the situation we were in 1763: were the powers of appointing to offices, and commanding the militia, in the hands of governors, our arts, trade and manufactures, would be cramped; nay, more than this, the life of every man who has been active in the cause of his country would be endangered.

An American Republic

For these reasons, as well as many others which might be produced, we are confirmed in the opinion, that the present age would be deficient in their duty to God, their posterity and themselves, if they do not establish an American republic. This is the only form of government which we wish to see established; for we can never be willingly subject to any other King than he who, being possessed of infinite wisdom, goodness and rectitude, is alone fit to possess unlimited power.

We have freely spoken our sentiments upon this important subject, but we mean not to dictate; we have unbounded confidence in the wisdom and uprightness of the continental congress: with pleasure we recollect that this affair is under their direction; and we now instruct you, sir, to give them the strongest assurance, that, if they should declare America to be a free and independent republic, your constituents will support and defend the measure, to the last drop of their blood, and the last farthing of their treasure.

VIEWPOINT 6

"Independence, I am aware, has attractions for all mankind; but I maintain that, in the present quarrel, the friends of independence are the promoters of slavery."

America Should Not Declare Independence from Great Britain

John Dickinson (1732-1808)

On June 7, 1776, Virginia delegate Richard Henry Lee made the following resolution to the Second Continental Congress, which had been assembling in Philadelphia since May 1775:

> *Resolved*, That these United Colonies are, and of right ought to be, free and independent states, that they are absolved from all allegiance to the British Crown, and that all political connection between them and the state of Great Britain is, and ought to be, totally dissolved.

After several days of debate, vote on the motion was delayed while a committee was appointed to draft a declaration justifying independence. Opponents of independence, following the repeated failures of attempting reconciliation with Great Britain, were in a dwindling minority. One of the most noteworthy was Pennsylvania delegate John Dickinson. A lawyer and member of the Pennsylvania Assembly, Dickinson had been one of the important leaders of the colonies' cause, and his pamphlets denouncing British tax policy had gained him wide renown in the colonies. Despite his opposition to much of Great Britain's stance toward America, Dickinson was opposed to total independence.

The following viewpoint is taken from Dickinson's speech on July 1, 1776, arguing against Lee's resolution. (The speech was not recorded at the time, but was reconstructed and published some years later.) It was reprinted in *Principles and Acts of the Revolution in America* (Hezekiah Niles, ed., Baltimore, 1822). Dickinson argues that the liberties he and other colonists seek are best found within a union with Great Britain. He also asserts that independence would lead to defeat against British armed forces and to anarchy and loss of liberty at home. He urges the delegates to resist emotional appeals for independence. Despite his efforts, the colonies unanimously voted the next day to adopt the independence resolution, Dickinson having arranged to be absent. Despite his misgivings about independence, Dickinson served in the American army during the Revolution. He later served as governor of Pennsylvania and as a delegate to the 1787 Constitutional Convention.

It too often happens, fellow citizens, that men, heated by the spirit of party, give more importance in their discourses, to the surface and appearance of objects, than either to reason or justice; thus evincing that their aim is not to appease tumults but to excite them; not to repress the passions but to inflame them; not to compose ferocious discords but to exasperate and embitter them more and more. They aspire but to please the powerful, to gratify their own ambition, to flatter the caprices of the multitude in order to captivate their favor. Accordingly, in popular commotions, the party of wisdom and of equity is commonly found in the minority; and, perhaps, it would be safer, in difficult circumstances, to consult the smaller instead of the greater number. Upon this principle I invite the attention of those who hear me, since my opinion may differ from that of the majority; but I dare believe it will be shared by all impartial and moderate citizens who condemn this tumultuous proceeding, this attempt to coerce our opinions, and to drag us, with so much precipitation, to the most serious and important of decisions.

Two Hundred Years of Happiness

But, coming to the subject in controversy, I affirm that prudent men do not abandon objects which are certain to go in pursuit of those which offer only uncertainty. Now, it is an established fact that America can be well and happily governed by the English laws, under the same king and the same Parliament. Two hun-

133

dred years of happiness furnish the proof of it; and we find it also in the present prosperity, which is the result of these venerable laws and of this ancient union. It is not as independent, but as subjects; not as republic, but as monarchy, that we have arrived at this degree of power and of greatness. What then is the object of these chimeras, hatched in the days of discord and war? Shall the transports of fury have more power over us than the experience of ages? Shall we destroy, in a moment of anger, the work cemented and tested by time?

Unity Must Come Before Independence

Carter Braxton, a congressional delegate from Virginia, wrote a letter dated April 14, 1776, to fellow Virginian Landon Carter, expressing doubts on the wisdom of declaring independence at that time. Braxton argued that the colonies were too divided over territorial disputes and other issues and that independence would worsen such divisions. Braxton believed in the ultimate goal of separation from Great Britain, however, and ultimately was a signer of the Declaration of Independence.

The Province of New York is not without her Fears and apprehensions from the Temper of her Neighbors, their great swarms and small Territory. Even Virginia is not free from Claim on Pennsylvania nor Maryland from those on Virginia. Some of the Delegates from our Colony carry their Ideas of right to lands so far to the Eastward that the middle Colonies dread their being swallowed up between the Claims of them and those from the East. And yet without any Adjustment of those disputes and a variety of other matters, some are for Lugging us into Independence. But so long as these remain unsettled and men act upon the Principles they ever have done, you may rely, no such thing will be generally agreed on. Upon reviewing the secret movements of Men and things I am convinced the Assertion of Independence is far off. If it was to be now asserted, the Continent would be torn in pieces by Intestine Wars and Convulsions. Previous to Independence all disputes must be healed and Harmony prevail. A grand Continental league must be formed and a superintending Power also. When these necessary Steps are taken and I see a Coalition formed sufficient to withstand the Power of Britain, or any other, then am I for an independent State and all its Consequences, as then I think they will produce Happiness to America. It is a true saying of a Wit—We must hang together or separately.

I know the name of liberty is dear to each one of us; but have we not enjoyed liberty even under the English monarchy? Shall we this day renounce that to go and seek it in I know not what form of republic, which will soon change into a licentious anarchy and popular tyranny? In the human body the head only sustains and governs all the members, directing them, with admirable harmony, to the same object, which is self-preservation and happiness; so the head of the body politic, that is the king, in concert with the Parliament, can alone maintain the union of the members of this Empire, lately so flourishing, and prevent civil war by obviating all the evils produced by variety of opinions and diversity of interests. And so firm is my persuasion of this that I fully believe the most cruel war which Great Britain could make upon us would be that of not making any; and that the surest means of bringing us back to her obedience would be that of employing none. For the dread of the English arms, once removed, provinces would rise up against provinces and cities against cities; and we shall be seen to turn against ourselves the arms we have taken up to combat the common enemy.

Insurmountable necessity would then compel us to resort to the tutelary authority which we should have rashly abjured, and, if it consented to receive us again under its aegis, it would be no longer as free citizens but as slaves. Still inexperienced and in our infancy, what proof have we given of our ability to walk without a guide? None, and, if we judge the future by the past, we must conclude that our concord will continue as long as the danger, and no longer.

Even when the powerful hand of England supported us, for the paltry motives of territorial limits and distant jurisdictions, have we not abandoned ourselves to discords, and sometimes even to violence? And what must we not expect, now that minds are heated, ambitions roused, and arms in the hands of all?

Foreign Considerations

If, therefore, our union with England offers us so many advantages for the maintenance of internal peace, it is no less necessary to procure us, with foreign powers, that condescension and respect which is so essential to the prosperity of our commerce, to the enjoyment of any consideration, and to the accomplishment of any enterprise. Hitherto in our intercourse with the different nations of the world, England has lent us the support of her name and of her arms. We have presented ourselves in all the ports and in all the cities of the globe, not as Americans, a people scarcely heard of, but as English. Under shadow of this respected name, every port was open to us, every way was smooth, every demand was heard with favor. From the moment when our separation shall take place, everything will assume a contrary direction. The nations will accustom themselves to look upon us with disdain; even the pirates of Africa and Europe will fall upon our vessels, will massacre our seamen, or lead them into a cruel and perpet-

135

ual slavery.

There is in the human species, often so inexplicable in their affections, a manifest propensity to oppress the feeble as well as to flatter the powerful. Fear always carries it against reason, pride against moderation, and cruelty against clemency.

Real Independence

Independence, I am aware, has attractions for all mankind; but I maintain that, in the present quarrel, the friends of independence are the promoters of slavery, and that those who desire to separate us would but render us more dependent, if independence means the right of commanding and not the necessity of obeying, and if being dependent is to obey and not command. If, in rendering ourselves independent of England, supposing, however, that we should be able to effect it, we might be so, at the same time, of all other nations, I should applaud the project; but to change the condition of English subjects for that of slaves to the whole world is a step that could only be counseled by insanity. If you would reduce yourselves to the necessity of obeying, in all things, the mandates of supercilious France, who is now kindling fire under our feet, declare yourselves independent. If, to British liberty, you prefer the liberty of Holland, of Venice, of Genoa, or of Ragusa, declare yourselves independent. But, if we would not change the signification of words, let us preserve and carefully maintain this dependence which has been, down to this very hour, the principle and source of our prosperity, of our liberty, of our real independence.

But here I am interrupted and told that no one questions the advantages which America derived at first from her conjunction with England; but that the new pretensions of the ministers have changed all, have subverted all. If I should deny that, for the last twelve years, the English government has given the most fatal direction to the affairs of the colonies, and that its measures toward us savor of tyranny, I should deny not only what is the manifest truth but even what I have so often advanced and supported. But is there any doubt that it already feels a secret repentance? These arms, these soldiers it prepares against us are not designed to establish tyranny upon our shores but to vanquish our obstinacy, and to compel us to subscribe to conditions of accommodation.

In vain is it asserted that the Ministry will employ all means to make themselves quite sure of us in order to exercise upon us, with impunity, all the rigor of their power; for to pretend to reduce us to an absolute impossibility of resistance, in cases of oppression, would be, on their part, a chimerical project. The distance of the seat of government, the vast extent of intervening seas, the continual increase of our population, our warlike spirit, our experience in arms, the lakes, the rivers, the forests, the defiles which abound in our territory, are our pledges that England will always prefer to found her power upon moderation and liberty rather than upon rigor and oppression. An uninterrupted succession of victories and of triumphs could alone constrain England to acknowledge American independence; which, whether we can expect, whoever knows the instability of fortune can easily judge.

If we have combated successfully at Lexington and at Boston, Quebec and all Canada have witnessed our reverses. Everyone sees the necessity of opposing the extraordinary pretensions of the ministers; but does everybody see also that of fighting for independence?

It is to be feared that, by changing the object of the war, the present harmony will be interrupted, that the ardor of the people will be chilled by apprehensions for their new situation. By substituting a total dismemberment to the revocation of the laws we complain of, we should fully justify the ministers; we should merit the infamous name of rebels, and all the British nation would arm, with an unanimous impulse, against those who, from oppressed and complaining subjects, should have become all at once irreconcilable enemies. The English cherish the liberty we defend; they respect the dignity of our cause; but they will blame, they will detest our recourse to independence, and will unite with one consent to combat us.

European Treachery

The propagators of the new doctrine are pleased to assure us that, out of jealousy toward England, foreign sovereigns will lavish their succors upon us, as if these sovereigns could sincerely applaud rebellion; as if they had not colonies, even here in America, in which it is important for them to maintain obedience and tranquility. Let us suppose, however, that jealousy, ambition, or vengeance should triumph over the fear of insurrection; do you think these princes will not make you pay dear for the assistance with which they flatter you? Who has not learned, to his cost, the perfidy and the cupidity of Europeans? They will disguise their avarice under pompous words; under the most benevolent pretexts they will despoil us of our territories, they will invade our fisheries and obstruct our navigation, they will attempt our liberty and our privileges. We shall learn too late what it costs to trust to those European flatteries, and to place that confidence in inveterate enemies which has been withdrawn from long tried friends.

There are many persons who, to gain their ends, extol the advantages of a republic over monarchy. I will not here undertake to examine which of these two forms of government merits the preference. I know, however, that the English nation, after having tried them both, has never found repose except in monarchy. I know, also, that in popular republics themselves, so necessary is monarchy to cement human society, it has been requisite to institute monarchical powers, more or less extensive, under the names of *archons*, of *consuls*, of *doges*, of *gonfaloniers*, and finally of *kings*. Nor should I here omit an observation, the truth of which appears to me incontestable—the English constitution seems to be the fruit of the experience of all anterior time, in which monarchy is so tempered that the monarch finds himself checked in his efforts to seize absolute power; and the authority of the people is so regulated that anarchy is not to be feared. But for us it is to be apprehended that, when the counterpoise of monarchy shall no longer exist, the democratic power may carry all before it and involve the whole state in confusion and ruin. Then an ambitious citizen may arise, seize the reins of power, and annihilate liberty forever; for such is the ordinary career of ill-balanced democracies, they fall into anarchy, and thence under despotism.

Such are the opinions which might have been offered you with more eloquence, but assuredly not with more zeal or sincerity. May heaven grant that such sinister forebodings be not one day accomplished! May it not permit that, in this solemn concourse of the friends of country, the impassioned language of presumptuous and ardent men should have more influence than the pacific exhortations of good and sober citizens; prudence and moderation found and preserve empires; temerity and presumption occasion their downfall.

VIEWPOINT 7

"'Tis repugnant to reason, to the universal order of things; to all examples from former ages, to suppose, that this Continent can long remain subject to any external power."

America Must Be Independent of Britain

Thomas Paine (1737-1809)

By the end of 1775 King George III had declared the colonies to be in a state of rebellion, and British and American forces had already engaged in violent clashes in New England and in Canada. The Continental Congress in Philadelphia was adopting measures indicative of an independent government, including the issuing of paper money, the establishment of a committee for foreign relations, and the appointment of George Washington as the commander of the Continental army. Yet many colonists, including influential members of the Congress, were not ready to contemplate the final step of full independence from Great Britain. Many people still professed loyalty to the king, maintaining that they were merely seeking their rights as English citizens denied by corrupt British ministers.

Perhaps the single document most influential in convincing the American colonists that independence was necessary was a pamphlet first published in Philadelphia on January 10, 1776. It was quickly reprinted throughout the colonies and sold an estimated 120,000 copies over the next three months. The pamphlet was *Common Sense*, and its author was Thomas Paine, an impoverished writer who had recently moved from Great Britain to America in 1774 after a checkered career as a corset maker, customs inspector, and schoolmaster.

Paine brought with him from England a dislike for the British aristocracy. Following the battles of Lexington and Concord in April 1775, he became an advocate for total independence from Great Britain. In *Common Sense*, Paine argues the case for independence in plain and forthright language. He attacks the monarchy in Great Britain and advocates a democratic government for America. The arguments presented in *Common Sense* were widely discussed throughout the colonies and greatly contributed to America's ultimate decision for independence.

In the following pages I offer nothing more than simple facts, plain arguments, and common sense: and have no other preliminaries to settle with the reader, than that he will divest himself of prejudice and prepossession, and suffer his reason and his feelings to determine for themselves: that he will put on, or rather that he will not put off the true character of a man, and generously enlarge his views beyond the present day.

Volumes have been written on the subject of the struggle between England and America. Men of all ranks have embarked in the controversy, from different motives, and with various designs; but all have been ineffectual, and the period of debate is closed. Arms as the last resource decide the contest; the appeal was the choice of the King, and the Continent has accepted the challenge. . . .

A Worthy Cause

The Sun never shined on a cause of greater worth. 'Tis not the affair of a City, a County, a Province or a Kingdom; but of a Continent—of at least one eighth part of the habitable Globe. 'Tis not the concern of a day, a year, or an age; posterity are virtually involved in the contest, and will be more or less affected even to the end of time by the proceedings now. Now is the seed time of Continental union, faith, and honour. The least fracture now, will be like a name engraved with the point of a pin on the tender rind of a young oak; the wound will enlarge with the tree, and posterity read it in full grown characters.

By referring the matter from argument to arms, a new era for politics is struck—a new method of thinking hath arisen. All plans, proposals, &c. prior to the 19th of April, i.e. to the commencement of hostilities, are like the almanacks of the last year; which tho' proper then, are superceded and useless now. Whatever was advanced by the advocates on either side of the question then, terminated in one and the same point, viz. a union with Great Britain; the only difference between the parties, was the method of effecting it; the one proposing force, the other friendship; but it hath so far happened that the first hath failed, and the second hath withdrawn her influence.

As much hath been said of the advantages of reconciliation, which like an agreeable dream, hath passed away and left us as we were, it is but right, that we should examine the contrary side of the argument, and enquire into some of the many material injuries which these Colonies sustain, and always will sustain, by being connected with and dependant on Great Britain. To examine that connection and dependance on the principles of nature and common sense, to see what we have to trust to if separated, and what we are to expect if dependant.

I have heard it asserted by some, that as America hath flourished under her former connection with Great Britain, that the same connection is necessary towards her future happiness and will always have the same effect—Nothing can be more fallacious than this kind of argument:—we may as well assert that because a child hath thrived upon milk, that it is never to have meat, or that the first twenty years of our lives is to become a precedent for the next twenty. But even this is admitting more than is true, for I answer, roundly, that America would have flourished as much, and probably much more had no European power taken any notice of her. The commerce by which she hath enriched herself are the necessaries of life, and will always have a market while eating is the custom of Europe.

But she has protected us say some. That she hath engrossed us is true, and defended the Continent at our expence as well as her own is admitted; and she would have defended Turkey from the same motive viz. the sake of trade and dominion.

Ancient Prejudices

Alas! we have been long led away by ancient prejudices and made large sacrifices to superstition. We have boasted the protection of Great Britain, without considering, that her motive was *interest* not *attachment*; that she did not protect us from *our enemies* on *our account*, but from *her enemies* on *her own account*, from those who had no quarrel with us on any *other account*, and who will always be our enemies on the *same account*. Let Britain wave her pretensions to the Continent, or the Continent throw off the dependance, and we should be at peace with France and Spain were they at war with Britain. The miseries of Hanover last war ought to warn us against connections.

It hath lately been asserted in parliament, that the Colonies have no relation to each other but through the Parent Country, i.e.

that Pennsylvania and the Jerseys and so on for the rest, are sister Colonies by the way of England; this is certainly a very round-about way of proving relationship, but it is the nearest and only true way of proving enmity (or enemyship, if I may so call it). France and Spain never were, nor perhaps ever will be our enemies as *Americans* but as our being the *subjects of Great Britain.*

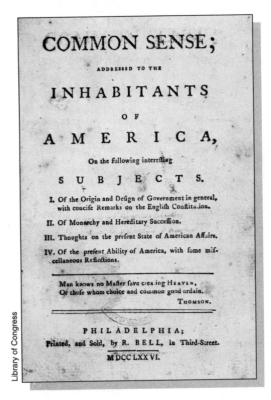

The pamphlet Common Sense *sold more than a half million copies in the colonies in 1776.*

But Britain is the parent country say some. Then the more shame upon her conduct. Even brutes do not devour their young, nor savages make war upon their families; wherefore the assertion if true, turns to her reproach; but it happens not to be true, or only partly so, and the phrase, *parent* or *mother country*, hath been jesuitically adopted by the King and his parasites, with a low papistical design of gaining an unfair bias on the credulous weakness of our minds. Europe and not England is the parent country of America. This new World hath been the asylum for the persecuted lovers of civil and religious liberty from *every part* of Europe. Hither have they fled, not from the tender embraces of the mother, but from the cruelty of the monster; and it is so far true of

England, that the same tyranny which drove the first emigrants from home, pursues their descendants still.

In this extensive quarter of the Globe, we forget the narrow limits of three hundred and sixty miles (the extent of England) and carry our friendship on a larger scale; we claim brotherhood with every European Christian, and triumph in the generosity of the sentiment. . . .

The Strength of Britain

Much hath been said of the united strength of Britain and the Colonies, that in conjunction they might bid defiance to the world: But this is mere presumption, the fate of war is uncertain, neither do the expressions mean any thing, for this Continent would never suffer itself to be drained of inhabitants, to support the British Arms in either Asia, Africa, or Europe.

Besides, what have we to do with setting the world at defiance? Our plan is commerce, and that well attended to, will secure us the peace and friendship of all Europe, because it is the interest of all Europe to have America a free port. Her trade will always be a protection, and her barrenness of gold and silver will secure her from invaders.

I challenge the warmest advocate for reconciliation, to shew, a single advantage that this Continent can reap, by being connected with Great Britain. I repeat the challenge, not a single advantage is derived. Our corn will fetch its price in any market in Europe and our imported goods must be paid for buy them where we will.

But the injuries and disadvantages we sustain by that connection, are without number, and our duty to mankind at large, as well as to ourselves, instruct us to renounce the alliance: because any submission to, or dependance on Great Britain, tends directly to involve this Continent in European wars and quarrels. As Europe is our market for trade, we ought to form no political connection with any part of it. 'Tis the true interest of America, to steer clear of European contentions, which she never can do, while by her dependance on Britain, she is made the make-weight in the scale of British politics.

Europe is too thickly planted with Kingdoms, to be long at peace, and whenever a war breaks out between England and any foreign power, the trade of America goes to ruin, *because of her connection with Britain*. The next war may not turn out like the last, and should it not, the advocates for reconciliation now, will be wishing for separation then, because neutrality in that case, would be a safer convoy than a man of war. Every thing that is right or reasonable pleads for separation. The blood of the slain, the weeping voice of nature cries, 'TIS TIME TO PART. Even the distance at which the Almighty hath placed England and America, is a strong and natural proof, that the authority of the one over the other, was never the design of Heaven. The time likewise at which the Continent was discovered, adds weight to the argument, and the manner in which it was peopled encreases the force of it. The Reformation was preceded by the discovery of America as if the Almighty graciously meant to open a sanctuary to the persecuted in future years, when home should afford neither friendship nor safety.

The authority of Great Britain over this Continent is a form of Government which sooner or later must have an end: And a serious mind can draw no true pleasure by looking forward, under the painful and positive conviction, that what he calls "the present constitution," is merely temporary. As parents, we can have no joy, knowing that this government is not sufficiently lasting to ensure any thing which we may bequeath to posterity: And by a plain method of argument, as we are running the next generation into debt, we ought to do the work of it, otherwise we use them meanly and pitifully. . . .

Those Who Advocate Reconciliation

Though I would carefully avoid giving unnecessary offence, yet I am inclined to believe, that all those who espouse the doctrine of reconciliation, may be included within the following descriptions. Interested men who are not to be trusted, weak men who cannot see, prejudiced men who will not see, and a certain set of moderate men who think better of the European world than it deserves; and this last class, by an ill-judged deliberation, will be the cause of more calamities to this Continent, than all the other three.

It is the good fortune of many to live distant from the scene of present sorrow; the evil is not sufficiently brought to their doors to make them feel the precariousness with which all American property is possessed. But let our imaginations transport us for a few moments to Boston; that seat of wretchedness will teach us wisdom, and instruct us for ever to renounce a power in whom we can have no trust. The inhabitants of that unfortunate city who but a few months ago were in ease and affluence, have now no other alternative than to stay and starve, or turn out to beg. Endangered by the fire of their friends if they continue within the city, and plundered by government if they leave it. In their present condition they are prisoners without the hope of redemption, and in a general attack for their relief, they would be exposed to the fury of both armies.

Men of passive tempers look somewhat lightly over the offences of Britain, and still hoping for the best, are apt to call out: *Come, come, we shall be friends again for all this.* But examine the passions and feelings of mankind: bring the doctrine of reconciliation to the touchstone of nature, and then tell me, whether you can hereafter love, honour, and faithfully serve the power that hath carried fire and sword into your land? If you cannot do all these, then are you only deceiving yourselves, and by your delay bringing ruin upon posterity. Your future connection with Britain whom you can neither love nor honour, will be forced and unnatural, and being formed only on the plan of present convenience, will in a little time, fall into a relapse more wretched than the first. But if you say, you can still pass the violations over, then I ask, hath your house been burnt? Hath your property been destroyed before your face? Are your wife and children destitute of a bed to lie on, or bread to live on? Have you lost a parent or a child by their hands, and yourself the ruined and wretched survivor? If you have not, then are you not a judge of those who have. But if you have and still can shake hands with the murderers, then are you unworthy the name of husband, father, friend, or lover, and whatever may be your rank or title in life, you have the heart of a coward, and the spirit of a sycophant.

This is not inflaming or exaggerating matters, but trying them by those feelings and affections which nature justifies, and without which, we should be incapable of discharging the social duties of life, or enjoying the felicities of it. I mean not to exhibit horror for the purpose of provoking revenge, but to awaken us from fatal and unmanly slumbers, that we may pursue determinately some fixed object. 'Tis not in the power of England or of Europe to conquer America, if she doth not conquer herself by delay and timidity. The present winter is worth an age if rightly employed, but if lost or neglected, the whole Continent will partake of the misfortune; and there is no punishment which that man doth not deserve, be he who, or what, or where he will, that may be the means of sacrificing a season so precious and useful.

Independence Is Inevitable

'Tis repugnant to reason, to the universal order of things; to all examples from former ages, to suppose, that this Continent can long remain subject to any external power. The most sanguine in Britain doth not think so. The utmost stretch of human wisdom cannot at this time compass a plan, short of separation, which can promise the Continent even a year's security. Reconciliation is *now* a fallacious dream. Nature hath deserted the connection, and art cannot supply her place. For as Milton wisely expresses "never can true reconcilement grow where wounds of deadly hate have pierced so deep."

Every quiet method for peace hath been ineffectual. Our prayers have been rejected with disdain; and hath tended to convince us that nothing flatters vanity or confirms obstinacy in Kings more than repeated petitioning—and nothing hath contributed more, than that very measure, to make the Kings of Europe absolute. Witness Denmark and Sweden. Wherefore since nothing but blows will do, for God's sake let us come to a final separation, and not leave the next generation to be cutting throats under the violated unmeaning names of parent and child.

To say they will never attempt it again is idle and visionary, we thought so at the repeal of the stamp-act, yet a year or two undeceived us; as well may we suppose that nations which have been once defeated will never renew the quarrel.

The Blessings of Independence

Jacob Green, a Congregationalist minister from New Jersey, was the author of the 1776 pamphlet Observations on the Reconciliation of Great-Britain and the Colonies, *in which he gave several arguments for American independence.*

If we are independent, this land of liberty will be glorious on many accounts: Population will abundantly increase, agriculture will be promoted, trade will flourish, religion unrestrained by human laws, will have free course to run and prevail, and America be an asylum for all noble spirits and sons of liberty from all parts of the world. Hither they may retire from every land of oppression; here they may expand and exult; here they may enjoy all the blessings which this terraqueous globe can afford to fallen men.

As to government matters 'tis not in the power of Britain to do this Continent justice: the business of it will soon be too weighty and intricate to be managed with any tolerable degree of convenience, by a power so distant from us, and so very ignorant of us; for if they cannot conquer us, they cannot govern us. To be always running three or four thousand miles with a tale or a petition, waiting four or five months for an answer, which when obtained requires five or six more to explain it in, will in a few years be looked upon as folly and childishness—There was a time when it was proper, and there is a proper time for it to cease.

Small islands not capable of protecting themselves are the proper objects for government to take under their care: but there is something very absurd, in supposing a Continent to be perpetually governed by an island. In no instance hath nature made the satellite larger than its primary planet, and as England and America with respect to each other reverse the common order of nature, it is evident they belong to different systems. England to Europe: America to itself.

I am not induced by motives of pride, party or resentment to espouse the doctrine of separation and independance; I am clearly, positively, and conscientiously persuaded that 'tis the true interest of this Continent to be so; that every thing short of that is mere patchwork, that it can afford no lasting felicity,—that it is leaving the sword to our children, and shrinking back at a time, when a little more, a little farther, would have rendered this Continent the glory of the earth.

As Britain hath not manifested the least inclination towards a compromise, we may be assured that no terms can be obtained worthy the acceptance of the Continent, or any ways equal to the expence of blood and treasure we have been already put to.

The object contended for, ought always to bear some just proportion to the expence. The removal of North, or the whole detestable junto, is a matter unworthy the millions we have expended. A temporary stoppage of trade was an inconvenience, which would have sufficiently ballanced the repeal of all the acts complained of, had such repeals been obtained; but if the whole Continent must take up arms, if every man must be a soldier, 'tis scarcely worth our while to fight against a contemptible ministry only. Dearly, dearly, do we pay for the repeal of the acts, if that is all we fight for; for in a just estimation, 'tis as great a folly to pay a Bunker-hill price for law as for land. As I have always considered the independancy of this Continent, as an event which sooner or later must arrive, so from the late rapid progress of the Continent to maturity, the event could not be far off. Wherefore on the breaking out of hostilities, it was not worth the while to have disputed a matter, which time would have finally redressed, unless we meant to be in earnest; otherwise it is like wasting an estate on a suit at law, to regulate the trespasses of a tenant, whose lease is just expiring. No man was a warmer wisher for reconciliation than myself, before the fatal 19th of April 1775, but the moment the event of that day was made known, I rejected the hardened, sullen tempered Pharoah of England for ever; and disdain the wretch, that with the pretended title of FATHER OF HIS PEOPLE can unfeelingly hear of their slaughter, and composedly sleep with their blood upon his soul.

If Reconciliation Were to Happen

But admitting that matters were now made up, what would be the event? I answer, the ruin of the Continent. And that for several reasons.

First. The powers of governing still remaining in the hands of the King, he will have a negative over the whole legislation of this Continent: and as he hath shewn himself such an inveterate enemy to liberty, and discovered such a thirst for arbitrary power; is he, or is he not, a proper man to say to these Colonies, *You shall make no laws but what I please.* And is there any inhabitant in America so ignorant, as not to know, that according to what is called the *present constitution*, that this Continent can make no laws but what the King gives leave to; and is there any man so unwise, as not to see, that (considering what has happened) he will suffer no laws to be made here, but such as suit his purpose. We may be as effectually enslaved by the want of laws in America, as by submitting to laws made for us in England. After matters are made up (as it is called) can there be any doubt, but the whole power of the crown will be exerted to keep this Continent as low and humble as possible? instead of going forward, we shall go backward, or be perpetually quarrelling or ridiculously petitioning.—We are already greater than the King wishes us to be, and will he not hereafter endeavour to make us less. To bring the matter to one point, is the power who is jealous of our prosperity, a proper power to govern us? Whoever says *no* to this question is an *Independant*, for independancy means no more than whether we shall make our own laws, or, whether the King, the greatest enemy this Continent hath, or can have, shall tell us, *there shall be no laws but such as I like. . . .*

Secondly—That as even the best terms which we can expect to obtain, can amount to no more than a temporary expedient, or a kind of government by guardianship, which can last no longer than till the Colonies come of age, so the general face and state of things in the interim will be unsettled and unpromising. Emigrants of property will not choose to come to a country whose form of government hangs but by a thread, and who is every day tottering on the brink of commotion and disturbance. And numbers of the present inhabitants would lay hold of the interval to dispose of their effects, and quit the Continent.

But the most powerful of all arguments is, that nothing but independance i.e. a Continental form of government, can keep the peace of the Continent and preserve it inviolate from civil wars. I dread the event of a reconciliation with Britain now, as it is more than probable, that it will be followed by a revolt some where or other, the consequences of which may be far more fatal than all the malice of Britain. . . .

I have heard some men say, many of whom I believe spoke without thinking, that they dreaded an independance, fearing that it would produce civil wars. It is but seldom that our first thoughts are truly correct, and that is the case here; for there are ten times more to dread from a patched up connection, than from independance. I make the sufferers, case my own, and I protest, that were I driven from house and home, my property destroyed, and my circumstances ruined, that as a man sensible of injuries, I could never relish the doctrine of reconciliation, or consider myself bound thereby. . . .

A government of our own is our natural right: and when a man seriously reflects on the precariousness of human affairs, he will become convinced, that it is infinitely wiser and safer, to form a constitution of our own, in a cool deliberate manner, while we have it in our power, than to trust such an interesting event to time and chance. . . .

Ye that tell us of harmony and reconciliation, can ye restore to us the time that is past? can ye give to prostitution its former innocence? neither can ye reconcile Britain and America. The last cord now is broken, the people of England are presenting addresses against us. There are injuries which nature cannot forgive; she would cease to be nature if she did. As well can the lover forgive the ravisher of his mistress, as the Continent forgive the murders of Britain. The Almighty hath implanted in us these unextinguishable feelings for good and wise purposes. They are the Guardians of his Image in our hearts. They distinguish us from the herd of common animals. The social compact would dissolve, and justice be extirpated from the earth, or have only a casual existence were we callous to the touches of affection. The robber and the murderer would often escape unpunished, did not the injuries which our tempers sustain, provoke us into justice.

O ye that love mankind! Ye that dare oppose not only the tyranny but the tyrant, stand forth! Every spot of the old world is over-run with oppression. Freedom hath been hunted round the Globe. Asia and Africa have long expelled her. Europe regards her like a stranger, and England hath given her warning to depart. O! receive the fugitive, and prepare in time an asylum for mankind.

VIEWPOINT 8

"Suppose we were to revolt from Great Britain, declare ourselves independent, and set up a republic of our own. . . . I stand aghast at the prospect; my blood runs chill when I think of . . . the complicated evils that must ensue."

America Must Seek Reconciliation with Britain

Charles Inglis (1734-1816)

The phenomenal success of Thomas Paine's *Common Sense* inspired several pamphlets rebutting its arguments. One of the most cogent of these pamphlets was written by Charles Inglis. Born in Ireland, Inglis first arrived in Pennsylvania in 1755 as a missionary for the Society for the Propagation of the Gospel in Foreign Parts, working especially among the Mohawk Indians. Ordained an Anglican clergyman in 1758 and assigned to Trinity Church in New York City in 1764, Inglis was a prolific writer of essays who consistently opposed American independence.

Inglis's pamphlet *The True Interest of America Impartially Stated, in Certain Strictures on a Pamphlet Intitled Common Sense* was published in 1776 in Philadelphia. It was reprinted in vol. 2 of *The Annals of America* (Encyclopædia Britannica, 1968). It begins by listing the advantages Inglis believes the colonies would derive from reconciling with Great Britain and goes on to list the disadvantages and calamities Inglis states would result from declaring independence.

Inglis was banished to England in 1783 by the American revolutionaries. He left, stating, "I do not leave behind me an individual against whom I have the smallest degree of resentment or ill-will." He later became an Anglican bishop presiding over Nova Scotia, Canada.

I think it no difficult matter to point out many advantages which will certainly attend our reconciliation and connection with Great Britain on a firm, constitutional plan. I shall select a few of these; and, that their importance may be more clearly discerned, I shall afterward point out some of the evils which inevitably must attend our separating from Britain and declaring for independency. On each article I shall study brevity.

Preventing War

1. By a reconciliation with Britain, a period would be put to the present calamitous war, by which so many lives have been lost, and so many more must be lost if it continues. This alone is an advantage devoutly to be wished for. This author [Paine] says: "The blood of the slain, the weeping voice of nature cries, 'Tis time to part." I think they cry just the reverse. The blood of the slain, the weeping voice of nature cries: It is time to be reconciled; it is time to lay aside those animosities which have pushed on Britons to shed the blood of Britons; it is high time that those who are connected by the endearing ties of religion, kindred, and country should resume their former friendship and be united in the bond of mutual affection, as their interests are inseparably united.

2. By a reconciliation with Great Britain, peace—that fairest offspring and gift of heaven—will be restored. In one respect peace is like health—we do not sufficiently know its value but by its absence. What uneasiness and anxiety, what evils has this short interruption of peace with the parent state brought on the whole British Empire! Let every man only consult his feelings—I except my antagonist—and it will require no great force of rhetoric to convince him that a removal of those evils and a restoration of peace would be a singular advantage and blessing.

3. Agriculture, commerce, and industry would resume their wonted vigor. At present, they languish and droop, both here and in Britain; and must continue to do so while this unhappy contest remains unsettled.

4. By a connection with Great Britain, our trade would still have the protection of the greatest naval power in the world. England

has the advantage, in this respect, of every other state, whether of ancient or modern times. Her insular situation, her nurseries for seamen, the superiority of those seamen above others—these circumstances, to mention no other, combine to make her the first maritime power in the universe—such exactly is the power whose protection we want for our commerce. To suppose, with our author, that we should have no war were we to revolt from England is too absurd to deserve a confutation. I could just as soon set about refuting the reveries of some brainsick enthusiast. Past experience shows that Britain is able to defend our commerce and our coasts; and we have no reason to doubt of her being able to do so for the future.

Reconciliation Better than Independence

Anglican clergyman and educator William Smith wrote a series of public letters in 1776 under the name "Cato" in reply to Thomas Paine's Common Sense.

We have already declared ourselves independent, as to all useful purposes, by resisting our oppressors upon our own foundation. And while we keep upon this ground, without connecting ourselves with any foreign nations, to involve us in fresh difficulties and endanger our liberties still further, we are able, in our own element (upon the shore), to continue this resistance; and it is our duty to continue it till Great Britain is convinced (as she must soon be) of her fatal policy, and open her arms to reconciliation, upon the permanent and sure footing of mutual interests and safety.

Upon such a footing, we may again be happy. Our trade will be revived. Our husbandmen, our mechanics, our artificers will flourish. Our language, our laws, and manners being the same with those of the nation with which we are again to be connected, that connection will be natural; and we shall the more easily guard against future innovations. Pennsylvania has much to lose in this contest and much to hope from a proper settlement of it. We have long flourished under our charter government. What may be the consequences of another form we cannot pronounce with certainty; but this we know, that it is a road we have not traveled and may be worse than it is described.

5. The protection of our trade, while connected with Britain, will not cost us a *fiftieth* part of what it must cost were we ourselves to raise a naval force sufficient for the purpose.

6. While connected with Great Britain, we have a bounty on almost every article of exportation; and we may be better supplied with goods by her than we could elsewhere. What our author says is true, "that our imported goods must be paid for, buy them

where we will"; but we may buy them dearer, and of worse quality, in one place than another. The manufactures of Great Britain confessedly surpass any in the world, particularly those in every kind of metal, which we want most; and no country can afford linens and woolens of equal quality cheaper.

7. When a reconciliation is effected, and things return into the old channel, a few years of peace will restore everything to its pristine state. Emigrants will flow in as usual from the different parts of Europe. Population will advance with the same rapid progress as formerly, and our lands will rise in value.

These advantages are not imaginary but real. They are such as we have already experienced; and such as we may derive from a connection with Great Britain for ages to come. Each of these might easily be enlarged on, and others added to them; but I only mean to suggest a few hints. . . .

Consequences of Independence

Let us now, if you please, take a view of the other side of the question. Suppose we were to revolt from Great Britain, declare ourselves independent, and set up a republic of our own—what would be the consequence? I stand aghast at the prospect; my blood runs chill when I think of the calamities, the complicated evils that must ensue, and may be clearly foreseen—it is impossible for any man to foresee them all.

Our author cautiously avoids saying anything of the inconveniences that would attend a separation. He does not even suppose that any inconvenience would attend it. Let us only declare ourselves independent, break loose from Great Britain, and, according to him, a paradisiacal state will follow! But a prudent man will consider and weigh matters well before he consents to such a measure—when on the brink of such a dreadful precipice, he must necessarily recoil and think of the consequences before he advances a step forward. Supposing then we declared for independency, what would follow? I answer:

1. All our property throughout the continent would be unhinged; the greatest confusion and most violent convulsions would take place. It would not be here as it was in England at the Revolution in 1688. That Revolution was not brought about by a defeasance or disannulling the right of succession. James II, by abdicating the throne, left it vacant for the next in succession; accordingly, his eldest daughter and her husband stepped in. Every other matter went on in the usual, regular way; and the constitution, instead of being dissolved, was strengthened. But in case of our revolt, the old constitution would be totally subverted. The common bond that tied us together, and by which our property was secured, would be snapped asunder. It is not to be doubted

but our Congress would endeavor to apply some remedy for those evils; but, with all deference to that respectable body, I do not apprehend that any remedy in their power would be adequate, at least for some time. I do not choose to be more explicit; but I am able to support my opinion.

2. What a horrid situation would thousands be reduced to who have taken the oath of allegiance to the King; yet, contrary to their oath as well as inclination, must be compelled to renounce that allegiance or abandon all their property in America! How many thousands more would be reduced to a similar situation, who, although they took not that oath, yet would think it inconsistent with their duty and a good conscience to renounce their sovereign. I dare say these will appear trifling difficulties to our author; but, whatever he may think, there are thousands and thousands who would sooner lose all they had in the world, nay, life itself, than thus wound their conscience. A declaration of independency would infallibly disunite and divide the colonists.

War Will Lead to Ruin

3. By a declaration for independency, every avenue to an accommodation with Great Britain would be closed; the sword only could then decide the quarrel; and the sword would not be sheathed till one had conquered the other.

The importance of these colonies to Britain need not be enlarged on—it is a thing so universally known. The greater their importance is to her, so much the more obstinate will her struggle be not to lose them. The independency of America would, in the end, deprive her of the West Indies, shake her empire to the foundation, and reduce her to a state of the most mortifying insignificance. Great Britain, therefore, must, for her own preservation, risk everything, and exert her whole strength to prevent such an event from taking place. This being the case,

4. Devastation and ruin must mark the progress of this war along the seacoast of America. Hitherto, Britain has not exerted her power. Her number of troops and ships of war here at present is very little more than she judged expedient in time of peace—the former does not amount to 12,000 men—nor the latter to 40 ships, including frigates. Both she and the colonies hoped for and expected an accommodation; neither of them has lost sight of that desirable object. The seas have been open to our ships; and, although some skirmishes have unfortunately happened, yet a ray of hope still cheered both sides that peace was not distant. But, as soon as we declare for independency, every prospect of this kind must vanish. Ruthless war, with all its aggravated horrors, will ravage our once happy land; our seacoasts and ports will be ruined, and our ships taken. Torrents of blood

will be spilled, and thousands reduced to beggary and wretchedness.

This melancholy contest would last till one side conquered. Supposing Britain to be victorious; however high my opinion is of British generosity, I should be exceedingly sorry to receive terms from her in the haughty tone of a conqueror. Or supposing such a failure of her manufactures, commerce, and strength, that victory should incline to the side of America; yet, who can say, in that case, what extremities her sense of resentment and self-preservation will drive Great Britain to? For my part, I should not in the least be surprised if, on such a prospect as the independency of America, she would parcel out this continent to the different European powers. Canada might be restored to France, Florida to Spain, with additions to each; other states also might come in for a portion. Let no man think this chimerical or improbable. The independency of America would be so fatal to Britain that she would leave nothing in her power undone to prevent it. I believe as firmly as I do my own existence that, if every other method failed, she would try some such expedient as this to disconcert our scheme of independency; and let any man figure to himself the situation of these British colonies, if only Canada were restored to France!

5. But supposing once more that we were able to cut off every regiment that Britain can spare or hire, and to destroy every ship she can send, that we could beat off any other European power that would presume to intrude upon this continent; yet, a republican form of government would neither suit the genius of the people nor the extent of America.

In nothing is the wisdom of a legislator more conspicuous than in adapting his government to the genius, manners, disposition, and other circumstances of the people with whom he is concerned. If this important point is overlooked, confusion will ensue; his system will sink into neglect and ruin. Whatever check or barriers may be interposed, nature will always surmount them and finally prevail. . . .

We Are Britons

The Americans are properly Britons. They have the manners, habits, and ideas of Britons; and have been accustomed to a similar form of government. But Britons never could bear the extremes, either of monarchy or republicanism. Some of their kings have aimed at despotism, but always failed. Repeated efforts have been made toward democracy, and they equally failed. Once, indeed, republicanism triumphed over the constitution; the despotism of one person ensued; both were finally expelled. The inhabitants of Great Britain were quite anxious for the restoration of royalty in 1660, as they were for its expulsion in 1642, and for some succeeding years. If we may judge of future events by past transactions, in similar circumstances, this would most probably be the case of America were a republican form of government adopted in our present ferment. After much blood was shed, those confusions would terminate in the despotism of some one successful adventurer; and should the Americans be so fortunate as to emancipate themselves from that thralldom, perhaps the whole would end in a limited monarchy, after shedding as much more blood. Limited monarchy is the form of government which is most favorable to liberty, which is best adapted to the genius and temper of Britons; although here and there among us a crack-brained zealot for democracy or absolute monarchy may be sometimes found.

Great Britain Not Intimidated

In a December 24, 1774, installment of Letters of a Westchester Farmer, *Episcopalian minister and loyalist Samuel Seabury writes on the folly of resistance to the powerful Great Britain. The tract was reprinted in a 1930 volume of* Letters *edited by Clarence H. Vance and published by the Westchester County Historical Society.*

Do you think, Sir, that Great Britain is like an old, wrinkled, withered, worn-out hag, whom every jackanapes that truants along the streets may insult with impunity? You will find her a vigorous matron, just approaching a green old age; and with spirit and strength sufficient to chastise her undutiful and rebellious children. Your measures have as yet produced none of the effects you looked for: Great Britain is not as yet intimidated; she has already a considerable fleet and army in America; more ships and troops are expected in the spring; every appearance indicates a design in her to support her claim with vigour. You may call it *infatuation, madness, frantic extravagance,* to hazard so small a number of troops as she can spare against the thousands of New England. Should the dreadful contest once begin—But God forbid! Save, heavenly Father! O save my country from perdition!

Besides the unsuitableness of the republican form to the genius of the people, America is too extensive for it. That form may do well enough for a single city or small territory, but would be utterly improper for such a continent as this. America is too unwieldy for the feeble, dilatory administration of democracy. . . .

It is well known that wages and the price of labor, in general, are much higher in America than in England. Labor must necessarily be dear in every country where land is cheap and large tracts of it unsettled, as is the case here. Hence an American regiment costs us *double* what a British regiment, of equal number, costs Britain. Were it proper to be explicit and descend to particulars, I could evince this past all possibility of doubt; and I appeal for the truth of it to those gentlemen among us who are acquainted with these matters.

The Costs of Revolution

Where the money is to come from which will defray this enormous annual expense of *three millions* sterling, and all those other debts, I know not; unless the author of *Common Sense*, or some other ingenious projector, can discover the Philosopher's Stone, by which iron and other base metals may be transmuted into gold. Certain I am that our commerce and agriculture, the two principal sources of our wealth, will not support such an expense. The whole of our exports from the Thirteen United Colonies, in the year 1769, amounted only to £2,887,898 sterling; which is not so much, by near half a million, as our annual expense would be were we independent of Great Britain. Those exports, with no inconsiderable part of the profits arising from them, it is well known, centered finally in Britain to pay the merchants and manufacturers there for goods we had imported thence—and yet left us still in debt! What then must our situation be, or what the state of our trade, when oppressed with such a burden of annual expense! When every article of commerce, every necessary of life, together with our lands, must be heavily taxed to defray that expense! . . .

Possible Alternatives

But here it may be said *that all the evils above specified are more tolerable than slavery*. With this sentiment I sincerely agree—any hardships, however great, are preferable to slavery. But then I ask—Is there no other alternative in the present case? Is there no choice left us but slavery, or those evils? I am confident there is; and that both may be equally avoided. Let us only show a disposition to treat or negotiate in earnest—let us fall upon some method to set a treaty or negotiation with Great Britain on foot; and, if once properly begun, there is moral certainty that this unhappy dispute will be settled to the mutual satisfaction and interest of both countries. For my part, I have not the least doubt about it.

It would be improper and needless for me to enlarge on the particulars that should be adjusted at such a treaty. The maturest deliberation will be necessary on the occasion, as well as a generous regard to every part of the Empire. I shall just beg leave to suggest my opinion on a few points—I think America should insist that the claim of parliamentary taxation be either explicitly relinquished, or else such security given as the case will admit, and may be equivalent to a formal relinquishment, that this claim shall not be exerted. When this most important point is gained, America should consider that there is a great difference between having her money wrested from her by others and not giving any of it herself when it is proper to give. While she is protected and shares in the advantages resulting from being a part of the British Empire, she should contribute something for that protection and those advantages; and I never heard a sensible American deny this. Moreover, she should stipulate for such a freedom of trade as is consistent with the general welfare of the State; and that this interesting object be settled in such a manner as to preclude, as much as possible, any impolitic or injurious infringements hereafter. All this may be easily done if both sides are only disposed for peace; and there are many other particulars which would be exceedingly beneficial to America, and might be obtained, as they could not interfere with the interest of Great Britain or any other part of the Empire. We have abundant proof of this, as well as several good hints to proceed on, in the late concessions to Nova Scotia from government. . . .

But a declaration for independency on the part of America would preclude treaty entirely and could answer no good purpose. We actually have already every advantage of independency, without its inconveniences. By a declaration of independency, we should instantly lose all assistance from our friends in England. It would stop their mouths; for, were they to say anything in our favor, they would be deemed rebels and treated accordingly.

No Help from Other Nations

Our author is much elated with the prospect of foreign succor, if we once declare ourselves independent, and from thence promises us mighty matters. This, no doubt, is intended to spirit up the desponding—all who might shrink at the thought of America encountering, singly and unsupported, the whole strength of Great Britain. I believe, in my conscience, that he is as much mistaken in this as in anything else; and that this expectation is delusive, vain, and fallacious. My reasons are these, and I submit them to the reader's judgement:

The only European power from which we can possibly receive assistance is France. But France is now at peace with Great Britain; and is it probable that France would interrupt that peace and hazard a war with the power which lately reduced her so low, from a disinterested motive of aiding and protecting these colonies? . . .

It is well known that some of the French and Spanish colonists, not long since, offered to put themselves under the protection of England and declare themselves independent of France and Spain; but England rejected both offers. The example would be rather dangerous to states that have colonies—to none could it be more so than to France and Spain, who have so many and such extensive colonies. "The practice of courts are as much against us" in this as in the instance our author mentions. Can anyone imagine that, because we declared ourselves independent of England, France would *therefore* consider us as really independent! And before England had acquiesced, or made any effort worth mentioning to reduce us? Or can anyone be so weak as to think that France would run the risk of a war with England, unless she (France) were sure of some extraordinary advantage by it, in having the colonies under her *immediate jurisdiction?* If England will not protect us for our trade, surely France will not. . . .

A Blessed Country

America is far from being yet in a desperate situation. I am confident she may obtain honorable and advantageous terms from Great Britain. A few years of peace will soon retrieve all her losses. She will rapidly advance to a state of maturity whereby she may not only repay the parent state amply for all past benefits but also lay under the greatest obligations.

America, till very lately, has been the happiest country in the universe. Blessed with all that nature could bestow with the profusest bounty, she enjoyed, besides, more liberty, greater privileges than any other land. How painful is it to reflect on these things, and to look forward to the gloomy prospects now before us! But it is not too late to hope that matters may mend. By prudent management her former happiness may again return; and continue to increase for ages to come, in a union with the parent state.

However distant humanity may wish the period, yet, in the rotation of human affairs, a period may arrive when (both countries being prepared for it) some terrible disaster, some dreadful convulsion in Great Britain may transfer the seat of empire to this Western Hemisphere—where the British constitution, like the Phoenix from its parent's ashes, shall rise with youthful vigor and shine with redoubled splendor.

But if America should now mistake her real interest—if her sons, infatuated with romantic notions of conquest and empire, ere things are ripe, should adopt this republican's scheme—they will infallibly destroy this smiling prospect. They will dismember this happy country, make it a scene of blood and slaughter, and entail wretchedness and misery on millions yet unborn.

CHAPTER 4

The War

Chapter Preface

The Declaration of Independence in many ways was the culmination of debates that had occurred within the American colonies over the previous thirteen years. However, the colonies faced great obstacles in actually achieving their goal. They faced a military confrontation with what was then the world's greatest military power. They faced the task of convincing France and other European nations to recognize the new nation and to lend critical support to their cause. Soldiers in the American army faced low pay, insufficient munitions, and bad living conditions. The new nation faced internal division as well. The War for Independence was in many respects a civil war in which the American population was divided between people who fought for independence and loyalists who were against it.

Estimates of the number of loyalists during the American Revolution vary. John Adams speculated that perhaps one-third of the American population supported independence, one-third remained loyal to Britain, and one-third stayed neutral or apathetic. Historians have estimated that perhaps a half million, about one-fifth of the total colonial population, sided with Great Britain. Loyalists came from a variety of social classes and situations, ranging from African-American slaves, white indentured servants, and poor farmers to wealthy landowners and merchants. Thousands of loyalists fought openly for the British, while others served as propagandists, guides, and spies.

During the War for Independence the new states passed a variety of laws treating loyalists as traitors. These included banishment and confiscation of property. An estimated eighty thousand loyalists fled or were banished from America. Loyalists were denied freedom of speech, the right to vote, and access to the courts. Local "committees of safety" targeted people suspected of pro-British views who refused to leave and subjected them to social ostracism, tarring and feathering, and sometimes fatal violence.

The divisions between rebels and loyalists continued after the war, even though in the 1783 peace treaty Congress had made allowances for the loyalists to return to their homes and obtain restitution for their losses. Within a few years anti-loyalist legislation was a thing of the past as people concentrated on maintaining the gains made during the American Revolution.

VIEWPOINT 1

"We cannot but, with distressed minds, beseech all such
... to consider that, if by their acting and persisting in
a proud, selfish spirit ... such measures are pursued as
tend to the shedding of innocent blood."

War Against the British Is Not Justified

The Ancient Testimony and Principles of the People Called Quakers (1776)

The start of the war against Great Britain predated America's Declaration of Independence. Most historians date the beginning of the war with the clashes between British troops and American militia in Lexington and Concord, Massachusetts, on April 19, 1775. By the end of that year the bloodiest battle of the entire war, Breed's Hill, had been fought; George Washington had taken command of the Continental army; and Americans under Benedict Arnold and Richard Montgomery had launched an ultimately failed invasion of Canada.

The commencement of war did not stop debate on its utility or justification. On January 20, 1776, an address arising from a meeting of Quakers was published in Philadelphia. The full title of the tract was *The Ancient Testimony and Principles of the People Called Quakers, Renewed with Respect to the King and Government; and Touching the Commotions now prevailing in these and other Parts of America*. With its expressions of abhorrence of violent measures, the pamphlet reflected the Quaker tradition of pacifism. The pamphlet calls on the colonists to maintain what it describes as a happy connection to Great Britain. John Pemberton (1727-1795), who as clerk to the meeting signed his name to the pamphlet, was later imprisoned in Philadelphia, in September 1777, because

162

of his suspected loyalist views. He was pardoned by George Washington in April 1778.

A religious concern for our friends and fellow subjects of every denomination, and more especially for those of all ranks, who, in the present commotions, are engaged in publick employments and stations, induces us earnestly to beseech every individual in the most solemn manner, to consider the end and tendency of the measures they are promoting; and on the most impartial enquiry into the state of their minds, carefully to examine whether they are acting in the fear of God, and in conformity to the precepts and doctrine of our Lord Jesus Christ, whom we profess to believe in, and that by him alone we expect to be saved from our sins.

The calamities and afflictions which now surround us should, as we apprehend, affect every mind with the most awful considerations of the dispensations of Divine Providence to mankind in general in former ages, and that as the sins and iniquities of the people subjected them to grievous sufferings, the same causes still produce the like effects.

Peace and Plenty

The inhabitants of these provinces were long signally favoured with peace and plenty: Have the returns of true thankfulness been generally manifest? Have integrity and godly simplicity been maintained, and religiously regarded? Hath a religious care to do justly, love mercy, and walk humbly, been evident? Hath the precept of Christ, to do unto others as we would they should do unto us, been the governing rule of our conduct? Hath an upright impartial desire to prevent the slavery and oppression of our fellow-men, and to restore them to their natural right, to true christian liberty, been cherished and encouraged? Or have pride, wantonness, luxury, profaneness, a partial spirit, and forgetfulness of the goodness and mercies of God, become lamentably prevalent? Have we not, therefore, abundant occasion to break off from our sins by righteousness, and our iniquities by shewing mercy to the poor; and with true contrition and abasement of soul, to humble ourselves, and supplicate the Almighty Preserver of men, to shew favour, and to renew unto us a state of tranquillity and peace?

It is our fervent desire that this may soon appear to be the pious resolution of the people in general, of all ranks and denomina-

163

tions: then may we have a well grounded hope, that wisdom from above, which is pure, peaceable, and full of mercy and good fruits, will preside and govern in the deliberations of those who, in these perilous times, undertake the transaction of the most important public affairs; and that by their steady care and endeavours, constantly to act under the influences of this wisdom, those of inferior stations will be incited diligently to pursue those measures which make for peace, and tend to the reconciliation of contending parties, on principles dictated by the spirit of Christ, who "came not to destroy men's lives, but to save them." Luke ix. 56.

We Should Seek Peace

The same group of people who produced The Ancient Testimony and Principles of the People Called Quakers *had produced a similar statement on January 24, 1775, outlining their pacifist objections to violent rebellion.*

The Divine Principle of grace and truth which we profess, leads all who attend to its dictates, to demean themselves as peaceable subjects, and to discountenance and avoid every measure tending to excite disaffection to the king, as supreme magistrate, or to the legal authority of his government; to which purpose many of the late political writings and addresses to the people appearing to be calculated, we are led by a sense of duty to declare our entire disapprobation of them—their spirit and temper being not only contrary to the nature and precepts of the gospel, but destructive of the peace and harmony of civil society, disqualify men in these times of difficulty, for the wise and judicious consideration and promoting of such measures as would be most effectual for reconciling differences, or obtaining the redress of grievances.

From our past experience of the clemency of the king and his royal ancestors, we have grounds to hope and believe, that decent and respectful addresses from those who are vested with legal authority, representing the prevailing dissatisfactions and the cause of them, would avail towards obtaining relief, ascertaining and establishing the just rights of the people and restoring the public tranquillity; and we deeply lament that contrary modes of proceeding have been pursued, which have involved the colonies in confusion, appear likely to produce violence and bloodshed.

We are so fully assured that these principles are the most certain and effectual means of preventing the extreme misery and desolations of wars and bloodshed, that we are constrained to intreat all who profess faith in Christ, to manifest that they really believe in him, and desire to obtain the blessings he pronounced to the makers of peace, Mat. v. 9.

His spirit ever leads to seek for and improve every opportunity of promoting peace and reconciliation; and constantly to remember, that as we really confide in him, he can, in his own time, change the hearts of all men in such manner, that the way to obtain it hath been often opened, contrary to every human prospect or expectation.

May we, therefore, heartily and sincerely unite in supplications to the Father of Mercies, to grant the plentiful effusions of his Spirit to all, and in an especial manner to those in superior stations, that they may, with sincerity, guard against and reject all such measures and councils, as may increase and perpetuate the discord, animosities, and unhappy contentions which now sorrowfully abound.

We cannot but, with distressed minds, beseech all such, in the most solemn and awful manner, to consider that, if by their acting and persisting in a proud, selfish spirit, and not regarding the dictates of true wisdom, such measures are pursued as tend to the shedding of innocent blood; in the day when they and all men shall appear at the judgment-seat of Christ, to receive a reward according to their works, they will be excluded from his favour, and their portion will be in everlasting misery. See Mat. xxv. 41. 2 Cor. v. 10.

The peculiar evidence of divine regard manifested to our ancestors, in the founding and settlement of these provinces, we have often commemorated, and desire ever to remember with true thankfulness and reverent admiration.

Making Peace

When we consider—That at the time they were persecuted and subjected to severe sufferings, as a people unworthy of the benefits of religious or civil society, the hearts of the king and rulers, under whom they thus suffered, were inclined to grant them these fruitful countries, and entrust them with charters of very extensive powers and privileges.—That on their arrival here, the minds of the natives were inclined to receive them with great hospitality and friendship, and to cede to them the most valuable part of their land on very easy terms.—That while the principles of justice and mercy continued to preside, they were preserved in tranquility and peace, free from the desolating calamities of war; and their endeavours were wonderfully blessed and prospered; so that the saying of the wisest of kings was signally verified to them, "When a man's ways please the Lord, he maketh even his enemies to be at peace with him." Prov. xvi. 7.

The benefits, advantages, and favour, we have experienced by our dependence on, and connection with, the kings and government, under which we have enjoyed this happy state, appear to demand from us the greatest circumspection, care, and constant endeavours, to guard against every attempt to alter, or subvert, that dependence and connection.

The scenes lately presented to our view, and the prospect before us, we are sensible, are very distressing and discouraging. And though we lament that such amicable measures, as have been proposed, both here and in England, for the adjustment of the unhappy contests subsisting, have not yet been effectual; nevertheless, we should rejoice to observe the continuance of mutual peaceable endeavours for effecting a reconciliation; having grounds to hope that the divine favour and blessing will attend them.

> It hath ever been our judgment and principle, since we were called to profess the Light of Christ Jesus, manifested in our consciences, unto this day, that the setting up, and putting down kings and governments, is God's peculiar prerogative; for causes best known to himself: and that it is not our business to have any hand or contrivance therein: nor to be busy-bodies above our station, much less to plot and contrive the ruin, or overturn any of them; but to pray for the king, and safety of our nation, and good of all men; that we may live a peaceable and quiet life, in all godliness and honesty, under the government which God is pleased to set over us. Ancient Testimony, 1696, in Sewell's History.

May we therefore firmly unite in the abhorrence of all such writings and measures, as evidence a desire and design to break off the happy connection we have heretofore enjoyed with the kingdom of Great Britain, and our just and necessary subordination to the king, and those who are lawfully placed in authority under him; that thus the repeated solemn declarations made on this subject, in the addresses sent to the king on behalf of the people of America in general, may be confirmed, and remain to be our firm and sincere intentions to observe and fulfil.

VIEWPOINT 2

"[I]f God is on our side we need not fear what man can do unto us."

War Against the British Is Justified

John Carmichael (1728-1785)

John Carmichael was a Presbyterian minister serving in Chester County, Pennsylvania. In the late 1760s he began preaching and writing against British actions in the colonies.

On June 4, 1775, he preached a sermon to a company of Chester County militia in Lancaster, Pennsylvania. The sermon was later reprinted in a pamphlet titled *A Self-Defensive War Lawful* (Philadelphia, 1775) and was widely circulated. Speaking after the battles of Lexington and Concord in April 1775, Carmichael argues that wars against oppressors are sometimes justified and that British actions against the colonies make violent resistance necessary. Carmichael adds a plea for the nonpersecution of those who in conscience oppose war and violence, unless they are actively helping the British.

Carmichael's writings and sermons persuaded most members of his congregation to join the American cause. He later addressed the Continental Congress and was a frequent visitor to George Washington's Continental army.

At a time when the unjust storm of ministerial wrath is discharging itself, in a cruel and ignominious manner, on the noble, patriotic, brave people of the ancient, loyal, important colony of the Massachusetts-Bay, in New-England;—at a time when all the other colonies in North-America, like the true children of *a free-born family*, are roused to some just resentment of such insults, on their natural and legal rights, taking each other as by the hand, and uniting by the invincible chains of love, friendship, and interest, are determined to support this their elder sister colony, now suffering so gloriously in the common cause, or *sink* together;—at a time when the alarm is sounding from east to west, over this vast continent of North-America, to arms! to arms!—in short, at a time when the minds of *all* are in such a ferment, that they can be scarce composed to hear any subject, but what may have some reference to the present times;—it is but reasonable to suppose, that even the Minister of *the Prince of Peace*, whose business for ordinary is neither *war* or *politicks*, in such a situation, being member of civil society, and interested like other men would improve the times, by adopting their public instructions, to the best service of the people, and not offensive or displeasing to God; whose holy word is a blessed directory in every emergency.

It is also but reasonable to suppose, that every judicious, sober American, being now reduced to the dreadful alternative, either to take up arms, apparently against that very government, which he was wont to revere, and under which he expected protection for both life and property; or submit tamely to the galling yoke of *perpetual slavery*; I say, it is supposable, that every such Christian American soldier will be all ear to wholesome instructions, relative to his present duty. . . .

Discerning the Circumstances That Justify War

Although war is in itself a very great evil, and one of those sore judgments, by which a holy God punishes the world for sin, therefore to be deprecated, and avoided as much as possible; yet is, at times, by reason of certain circumstances, so unavoidable, that it is our duty to enter into it—The method I design to pursue, in opening up the doctrine, for improvement, is the following:—

I. Humbly attempt to shew (with submission to better judgment) when a war is so unavoidable and necessary, that it is our duty to enter into it.

II. Shew how we should enter into, and prosecute even a just war.

III. Improve the subject, by the deduction of a few natural inferences from the whole.

You are sensible, my hearers, that there are some Christian people in the world, and some of them in these parts, who merit the regard of the public, by their general character of industry, inoffensiveness and sobriety; yet do maintain it, as a sacred conscientious tenet, not to be dispensed with, *not to go to war, or take up arms on any occasion whatsoever*; and charity, the leading grace of the Christian system, will lead us to deal tenderly with such, as far as we have grounds to believe they are sincere in their profession: We ought to pity such for their mistake, and, if possible, to convince them; but not by any means to urge them against their avowed sentiments, lest we come under the odious appellations of *persecutors*.

As far as these sober people make use of the Bible, to found their principles on, they rely on such passages as these, Gen. ix, 6. *He that sheddeth man's blood, by man shall his blood be shed*; and Exod. xx, 13. *Thou shalt not kill*; and in the New-Testament, *But I say unto you, love your enemies;—if any smite thee on the one cheek turn to him the other also;—for all they that take the sword shall perish by the sword*: Matth. v. 39, 44 and xxvi, 52. and hence conclude, though I think falsely, that all war is unlawful, except the spiritual, with our own corruptions, by the sword of the spirit, in Christ's spiritual kingdom, which is not of this world, else would his children fight.

But if I mistake not, these people regard only such passages of holy scripture, as seem to favour their favourite opinion, let the language of other passages be what they will;—and hence their own imagination is substituted instead of divine revelation, so that when people are determined to keep by a sentiment, be it right or wrong, there is an end of all disputation.

We readily allow, that it would be happy for us all, if there was no moral or natural evil in the world. But how plausible soever such opinions may appear, to the weal of society, they are rather calculated to the condition of innocent, than depraved nature; which now is, and ever has been such, since the fall of our first parents, that there is need of some remedy to curb its evil tendencies, or mankind would scarce be able to subsist in the world; and this our alwise righteous Creator knows; and has therefore set up civil government to keep men from destroying each other: But civil government has no power, if it has not the sword, to be a terror to evil-doers, and a praise to them that do well.—Hence it will follow, that men are under a necessity to part with some of their natural rights, to secure the rest; they must give part of their earnings to such as are chosen by themselves to rule the whole; and then again, they must help the rulers to execute the good and wholesome laws of government, against their violators. Suppose, for instance, a great banditti rise to rescue murderers; if these are not quelled, government is overthrown, if the people do not assist good government, and here then arises a necessity to go to war.

And suppose again, on the other hand, which is very supposable, that the rulers of the people should give way to the many temptations their high stations will lead them to; to indulge the inclinations of a lust for absolute dominion, independent of the people, so that all the barrier of oaths and covenants are broke through, to effect the plan; and the people have no security, for either life or property, but the mere sovereign pleasure of the absolute rulers;—then the people are under a disagreeable, but pressing necessity, rather than be crushed by an iron rod, to re-ascertain their own just rights; and stand forth all of them to oppose such tyranny:—Here then is another instance of self-defence—in which a war is both unavoidable and necessary, and therefore lawful, if self-preservation is lawful; which is the point I shall next, in order, endeavour to prove indisputably, both from the light of nature, and divine revelation; and first from the light of nature.

It is certainly evident, wherever we turn our eyes, on any part of the whole creation of God, that the principle of self-love or self-preservation, or the desire of existence, is deeply engraved on the nature of every creature. . . .

Why We Fight

In 1776 Thomas Paine published an Epistle to Quakers, *a direct rebuttal to* The Ancient Testimony and Principles of the People Called Quakers, *in which he defended war against the British.*

We fight neither for revenge nor conquest; neither from pride nor passion; we are not insulting the world with our fleets and armies, nor ravaging the globe for plunder. Beneath the shade of our own vines are we attacked; in our own houses and on our own lands is the violence committed against us. We view our enemies in the characters of highwaymen and housebreakers, and having no defense for ourselves in the civil law, are obliged to punish them by the military one, and apply the sword, in the very case where you have before now applied the halter. Perhaps we feel for the ruined and insulted sufferers in all and every part of the continent with a degree of tenderness which has not yet made its way into some of your bosoms. But be ye sure that ye mistake not the cause and ground of your testimony. Call not coldness of soul religion; nor put the bigot in the place of the Christian.

The little industrious bee is furnished by her Creator with a sting, to preserve for her own use her sweet honey, the fruit of her toil and industry.

The ox has his horns; and the horse his teeth and hoofs.—The deer her feet for flight, and the fowls their wings to escape danger and preserve themselves. And shall man, the noblest creature in his lower world, be destitute of this necessary principle! which we see engraved by instinct on the irrational creation: Man is blest with reason to direct his enquiries, in search of happiness. His maker God allows him to seek to be as happy as he possibly can, both in this life and the life to come. But since man is a fallen, sinful creature, he has lost his true road to happiness—and can never find it, until his Maker points it out to him in the Holy Bible. Here we are taught how to conduct both in the civil and religious life: We are certain the scriptures allow us to defend ourselves in the best manner we can against an enemy.

Therefore, such passages, as would seem to speak a different language; such as those already quoted, must be understood, in a consistency with this great law of nature; as well as consistent with other parts of scripture. For Christ came not to make void, or destroy the law, but to fulfil—when therefore we are forbid to shed blood, or to kill; it is innocent blood is meant—but this doth not forbid to execute a murderer. The divine law requires, that a murderer should be executed, and forbids to take a ransom for his life.

Also, when a body of wicked people join together, or a nation unite, to fall upon and destroy without any just cause an innocent people: The insulted, or invaded people, are then to unite together, to oppose, expel and punish the guilty invaders—as in Judges v, 23. *Curse ye Meroz, (said the Angel of the Lord) curse ye bitterly the inhabitants thereof: Because they came not to the help of the Lord, against the mighty:* And Jeremiah xlviii, 10. *Cursed be he that doth the work of the Lord deceitfully; and cursed be he that keepeth back his sword from blood:* And in Luke xxii, 36. Jesus Christ told his Disciples to arm themselves against approaching danger.—*And he that hath no sword let him sell his garment and buy one. . . .*

Self-Preservation

Also, it must of course follow, that where our blessed Lord enjoins us, when smote on the one cheek, to turn the other also, he does not mean to forbid us to use lawful and proper means of self-preservation. But the meaning must be as the phrase is proverbial, that we should at no time discover a revengeful or unforgiving disposition; but should be ready to put up with a good deal of ill-usage, before we would create disturbance,—yea that we should do any thing consistent with our own safety. Again, where our Lord enjoins us to love our enemies—he can't possibly mean that we should love them better than ourselves—that we should put it in the enemy's power to kill us, when we had it in our power to save our own life, by killing the enemy. I say, this cannot be the meaning; for that exposition will thwart the original first great law of self-preservation. The meaning therefore must be, that we do not cherish a spirit of hatred towards the enemies, and would be willing to be reconciled again—and would be desirous, the enemy would be convinced of his evil sentiment against us, that we might be again on friendly terms,—that we can be sincere in our prayer to God, to bring such a desirable event to pass. Again,

That a self-defensive war is lawful, I will prove from the conduct of Jesus Christ himself. If civil government is necessary to self-preservation, and war is necessary, at times, in government, as has been already proved; then it will follow, that those who support civil government, do support war, and so of consequence approve of war. But Jesus Christ did pay his tribute money, to the Emperor Tiberius, Matthew xvii, 27. And those who are acquainted with the life of Tiberius Caesar know that he had frequent wars. . . .

I think I have now proved, from the light of nature, from the reason of things—from the Old and New-Testament, as well as from the example of Christ and his Apostles, that a self-defensive war is lawful. . . .

It is also equally unfair, to say, *Let us stand still and see the salvation of God*; for if this proves any thing, it proves too much, it proves that we are to use no means at all, for why to use lawful means in our power one time, and not another; we must therefore neither plow or sow; build, raise stock, or do any thing in the use of means, *but stand still and see the salvation of God*: But our reason is given us to use it in a proper manner, to preserve our own lives and the lives of others, as God's servants, in a state of probation in this world; and God will reward every one finally, according to his works; when we have no means in our power, we honor God to trust him, as Israel at the Red-Sea, and in the wilderness;—but when means are in our power, and we do not use them, we then tempt God, and rebel against his government, which he exercises over the world, in the way of free and moral agency.

Do Not Persecute Pacifists

Therefore for these people, to argue as they do now, when they are among other societies,—who they know will preserve the state from slaughter or slavery, in the use of lawful means, as has been now proved, is vastly disingenuous, and will undoubtedly subject their opinions to this censure, that it is a sanctuary of sloth—for greed—cowardice, &c.—*for it is easy to stay at home and earn money, to what it is to spend money and expose life, to protect and defend the worldling coward;—it is easy to pay money, to what it is to be slain in battle*, &c. But after all that has been said, I am myself so warm an advocate for the sacred rights of conscience, that if these people will not be convinced of their duty; can not get their eyes open; they are to be pitied, but not persecuted. I beg of all, for God and conscience sake, to let them alone, if they will not in these terrible times, draw the sword *for* Liberty and their Country; surely they will not *against* Liberty and their Country; and if we can do with them, we can without them: O then, let there be no disturbance on that head! But should any of these inoffensive guiltless anti-warriors be detected in assisting Gage or his army with provisions, &c. for lucre or any other motive whatever conscience could not apologize for them but ought to be dealt with accordingly. . . .

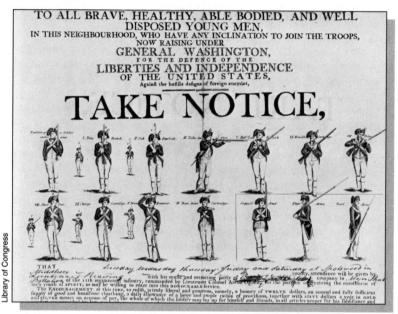

A recruiting poster for the Continental army offers would-be soldiers a signing bonus of twelve dollars and the "opportunity of spending a few happy years in viewing the different parts of this beautiful continent, in the . . . truly respectable character of a soldier, after which, he may, if he pleases return home to his friends, with his pockets full of money and his head covered with laurels."

I am happy, that I can with a good conscience, congratulate you and myself this day, on the certainty we have, for the justice and goodness of our cause: The angry tools of power who mislead government, may call us American "rebels, who would throw off all government,—would be independent and what not."—But we can now, with great confidence, appeal to God that that is false—we desire no such things—we desire to be as we were in the beginning of the present unhappy reign—we have tried every lawful, peaceable mean in our power—but all in vain!—we would love them if they would suffer us—we would be peaceable, obedient, loving subjects if they would let us; but it would seem as if the present ministry were determined to cram disloyalty, and disobedience down our throats—and then call us all rebels—then confiscate our country and sell it, to pay their 140,000,000 of debt, or else we know not what they would be at. We do in America all declare ourselves the subjects of King George the third, but we never swore allegiance to the Parliament of Great-Britain—or else we would have above 500 Kings—they are our fellow-subjects, chosen by the freeholders of that island to legislate for them, as our Assembly doth for Pennsylvania; but if their present claims are admitted, we may give up our Assemblies—and our Charters are cyphers!—

In the close of the last war, the King had not in all his dominions so many more affectionate subjects than the Americans—and in every valuable enterprize which would exhaust both treasure and blood the brave New-Englanders took the lead—and by our industry and trade with England, the nation rose to her present eminence; and now the very power we helped to give her, is retorted on us with redoubled vengeance and unheard of cruelty—but if they beat down our trading Cities and oppress us all they can, we will have our woods and liberty; for as we are the descendants of Britons, *we scorn to be slaves.*—We are now come to our *ne plus ultra*—the sword, the last argument must decide the controversy. Therefore, you can, Gentlemen Soldiers, appeal to G O D, for the justice of your cause, he is the judge of all the earth, and will do right, the final determination of all matters is in his righteous, holy, powerful hand. When England went to war with France and Spain in the time of last reign, they invoked the aids of the God of heaven by fasting and prayer—and then government discovered no leanings to popery—But now, when they are going to murder and butcher their own children in America, that have been so obedient, useful and affectionate—we do not hear that they ask counsel of God—but if they do not let us ask counsel and assistance from the God of heaven—he is on our side, we hope, and if God is on our side we need not fear what man can do unto us.

VIEWPOINT 3

"Under so many discourageing circumstances, can virtue, can honour, can the love of your country prompt you to persevere? Humanity itself . . . calls upon you to desist."

The American Cause Is Hopeless

Jacob Duché (1738-1798)

Jacob Duché was an Anglican clergyman in Philadelphia. He served as chaplain to the Continental Congress and was sympathetic to the American cause. However, in 1776 when the British under Gen. William Howe captured Philadelphia and imprisoned Duché, he came to believe that fighting a war for independence was a mistake. On October 8, 1777, Duché wrote the following letter to George Washington, who as commander in chief of the American armed forces was soon to be encamped for the winter in Valley Forge. The letter was reprinted in *The Spirit of 'Seventy Six* (Henry Steele Commager, ed. New York: Bobbs Merrill, 1958).

Duché argues in his letter to Washington that the Americans have no hope of victory against the British. He writes that both the Continental Congress and Washington's military forces have greatly deteriorated and that hopes for an alliance with France are illusory. Duché implores Washington to use his prestige and influence to convince the Americans to give up their dreams of independence and to reach an accommodation with the British.

Duché's letter was written shortly before the American victory at Saratoga, which did inspire France to provide aid to the rebelling colonies, and which was later seen as a turning point in the war. Duché moved to England in 1777 because of his loyalist views. He was not allowed to return to Pennsylvania until 1792.

And now, my dear Sir, suffer me in the language of truth and real affection to address myself to you. All the world must be convinced that you are engaged in the service of your country from motives perfectly disinterested. You risked every thing that was dear to you. You abandoned all those sweets of domestic life of which your affluent fortune gave you the uninterrupted enjoyment. But had you? could you have had the least idea of matters being carried to such a dangerous extremity as they are now? Your most intimate friends at that time shuddered at the thoughts of a separation from the mother country; and I took it for granted that your sentiments coincided with theirs. What have been the consequences of this rash and violent measure? A degeneracy of representation—confusion of counsels—blunders without number. The most respectable characters have withdrawn themselves, and are succeeded by a great majority of illiberal and violent men.

Take an impartial view of the present Congress, and what can you expect from them? Your feelings must be greatly hurt by the representation from your native province. You have no longer a Randolph, a Bland, or a Braxton; . . . Characters now present themselves whose minds can never mingle with your own. Your Harrison alone remains, and he disgusted with his unworthy associates. As to those of my own province, some of them are so obscure that their very names never met my ears before, and others have only been distinguished for the weakness of their understandings and the violence of their tempers. One alone I except from the general charge. . . .

From the New England Provinces can you find one that as a gentleman you could wish to associate with? unless the soft and mild address of Mr. Hancock can atone for his want of every other qualification necessary for the station he fills. Bankrupts, attorneys, and men of desperate fortunes are his colleagues. . . .

Are the dregs of a Congress then still to influence a mind like yours? These are not the men you engaged to serve. These are not the men that America has chosen to represent her now. Most of them were elected by a little low faction, and the few gentlemen that are among them now well known to be upon the balance and looking up to your hand alone to move the beam. 'Tis you, Sir, and you alone that supports the present Congress. Of this you must be fully sensible. Long before they left Philadelphia, their dignity and consequence was gone. What must it be now, since their precipitate retreat? . . .

After this view of Congress, turn to your army. The whole world knows that its very existence depends upon you, that your death or captivity disperses it in a moment, and that there is not a man on that side of the question in America, capable of succeeding you. As to the army itself, what have you to expect from them? Have they not frequently abandoned even yourself in the hour of extremity? Have you, can you have, the least confidence in a set of undisciplined men and officers, many of whom have been taken from the lowest of the people, without principle and without courage? Take away those that surround your person, how few are there that you can ask to sit at your table?

Turn to your little navy—of *that little*, what is *left?* Of the Delaware fleet, part are taken, the rest must soon surrender. Of those in the other Provinces, some taken, one or two at sea, and others lying unmanned and unrigged in their harbours.

Washington's troops in Valley Forge, Pennsylvania, had to survive the winter of 1777-1778 with inadequate food, clothing, and shelter.

And now where are your resources? O, my dear Sir! how sadly have you been abused by a faction void of truth and void of tenderness to you and your country! They have amused you with hopes of a declaration of war on the part of France. Believe me from the best authority, it was a fiction from the first. . . .

From your friends in England, you have nothing to expect. Their numbers are diminished to a cipher. The spirit of the whole nation is in full activity against you. A few sounding names among the nobility, though perpetually rung in your ears, are said to be without character, without influence. Disappointed ambition, I am told, has made them desperate, and they only wish to make the deluded Americans instruments of their revenge. All orders and ranks of men in Great Britain are now unanimous, and determined to risk their all on the contest. Trade and manufactures are found to flourish; and new channels are continually opening, that will, perhaps, more than supply the old. In a word, your harbours are blocked up, your cities fall one after another, fortress after fortress, battle after battle is lost. A British army, after having passed almost unmolested through a vast extent of country, have possessed themselves with ease of the capital of America. How unequal the contest now! How fruitless the expense of blood!

A Call to Desist

Under so many discourageing circumstances, can virtue, can honour, can the love of your country prompt you to persevere? Humanity itself (and sure I am humanity is no stranger to your breast) calls upon you to desist. Your army must perish for want of common necessaries, or thousands of innocent families must perish to support them. Wherever they encamp the country must be impoverished. Wherever they march the troops of Britain will pursue, and must complete the devastation which America herself has begun.

Perhaps it may be said that "it is better to die than to be slaves." This, indeed, is a splendid maxim in theory; and, perhaps, in some instances, may be found experimentally true. But where there is the least probability of any happy accommodation, surely wisdom and humanity call for some sacrifices to be made to prevent inevitable destruction. You will know that there is but one invincible bar to such an accommodation; could this be removed, other obstacles might readily be overcome. 'Tis to you, and you alone, your bleeding country looks, and calls aloud for this sacrifice. Your arm alone has strength sufficient to remove this bar. May Heaven inspire you with the glorious resolution of exerting this strength at so interesting a crisis, and thus immortalizing yourself as a friend and guardian of your country.

Your penetrating eye needs not more explicit language to discern my meaning. With that prudence and delicacy, therefore, of which I know you to be possessed, represent to Congress the indispensable necessity of rescinding the hasty and ill-advised Declaration of Independency. Recommend, and you have an undoubted right to recommend, an immediate cessation of hostilities. Let the controversy be taken up where that Declaration left it, and where Lord Howe certainly expected to find it. Let men of clear and impartial characters, in or out of Congress, liberal in their sentiments, heretofore independent in their fortunes (and some such may surely be found in America), be appointed to confer with His Majesty's Commissioners. Let them, if they please, prepare some well-digested constitutional plan, to lay before them as the commencement of a negotiation. When they have gone thus far, I am confident that the most happy consequences will ensue. Unanimity will immediately take place through the different Provinces. Thousands who are now ardently wishing and praying for such a measure will step forth and declare themselves the zealous advocates of constitutional liberty, and millions will bless the Hero that left the field of war to decide this most important contest with the weapons of wisdom and humanity.

VIEWPOINT 4

"Add to this, that in a cause so just and righteous on our part, we have the highest reason to expect the blessing of Heaven upon our glorious conflict."

The Revolutionary Cause Will Be Victorious

William Livingston (1723-1790)

William Livingston, a wealthy merchant and landlord, served as the state of New Jersey's first governor from 1776 to his death in 1790. He also represented New Jersey in the first and second Continental Congresses and was commander to New Jersey's militia. New Jersey was the site of many important revolutionary battles, including the American victories at Trenton and Princeton. Livingston's administration was noted for its vigor in prosecuting the war.

The following viewpoint is taken from an address Livingston gave on February 25, 1777, to the New Jersey legislature. It was reprinted in *Principles and Acts of the Revolution in America* (Baltimore, 1822). Livingston, attempting to bolster the spirits of Americans, argues that Britain is not as powerful as some people claim, and he encourages the American people to continue to support the war effort.

GENTLEMEN . . . [There are some] who, terrified by the power of Britain, have persuaded themselves that she is not only formidable, but irresistible. That her power is great, is beyond question; that it is not to be despised, is the dictate of common prudence. But then we ought also to consider her, as weak in council, and ingulfed in debt—reduced in her trade—reduced in her revenue—immersed in pleasure—enervated with luxury—and, in dissipation and venality, surpassing all Europe. We ought to consider her as hated by a potent rival, her natural enemy and particularly exasperated by her imperious conduct in the last war, as well as her insolent manner of commencing it; and thence inflamed with resentment, and only watching a favorable juncture for open hostilities. We ought to consider the amazing expense and difficulty of transporting troops and provisions above three thousand miles, with the impossibility of recruiting their army at a less distance, save only with such recreants, whose conscious guilt must at the first approach of danger, appeal the stoutest heart. Those insuperable obstacles are known and acknowledged by every virtuous and impartial man in the nation. Even the author of this horrid war is incapable of concealing his own confusion and distress. Too great to be wholly suppressed, it frequently discovers itself in the course of his speech—a speech terrible in word, and fraught with contradiction—breathing threatenings, and betraying terror—a motley mixture of magnanimity and consternation—of grandeur and abasement.—With troops invincible he dreaded a defeat, and wants reinforcements. Victorious in America, and triumphant on the ocean, he is an humble dependent on a petty prince; and apprehends an attack upon his metropolis; and, with full confidence in the friendship and alliance of France, he trembles upon his throne, at her secret designs and open preparations.

The Hardy Americans

With all this, we ought to contrast the numerous and hardy sons of America, inured to toil—seasoned alike to heat and cold—hale—robust—patient of fatigue—and, from their ardent love of liberty, ready to face danger and death—the immense extent of continent, which our infatuated enemies have undertaken to subjugate—the remarkable unanimity of its inhabitants, notwithstanding the exception of a few apostates and deserters—their unshaken resolution to maintain their freedom, or perish in the attempt—the fertility of our soil in all kinds of provisions necessary for the support of war—our inexhaustible internal resources for military stores and naval armaments—our comparative economy in public expenses—and the millions we save by having reprobated the farther exchange of our valuable staples for the worthless baubles and finery of English manufacture. Add to this, that in a cause so just and righteous on our part, we have

181

the highest reason to expect the blessing of Heaven upon our glorious conflict. For who can doubt the interposition of the supremely just, in favor of a people forced to recur to arms in defence of every thing dear and precious. . . .

A Call for Resolve

Following the publication of his pamphlet Common Sense, *Thomas Paine joined the Continental army. Between 1776 and 1783 he wrote a series of patriotic tracts called* The Crisis. *The opening paragraphs of his first article call for American perseverance. George Washington ordered the article read to his troops before it was published in the* Pennsylvania Journal *on December 19, 1776.*

These are the times that try men's souls. The summer soldier and the sunshine patriot will, in this crisis, shrink from the service of their country; but he that stands it *now* deserves the love and thanks of man and woman. Tyranny, like hell, is not easily conquered; yet we have this consolation with us, that the harder the conflict, the more glorious the triumph. What we obtain too cheap, we esteem too lightly: it is dearness only that gives every thing its value. Heaven knows how to put a proper price upon its goods; and it would be strange indeed if so celestial an article as FREEDOM should not be highly rated. Britain, with an army to enforce her tyranny, has declared that she has a right (*not only to* TAX) but "to BIND us in ALL CASES WHATSOEVER," and if being *bound in that manner* is not slavery, then is there not such a thing as slavery upon earth. Even the expression is impious; for so unlimited a power can belong only to God. . . .

I have as little superstition in me as any man living, but my secret opinion has ever been, and still is, that God Almighty will not give up a people to military destruction, or leave them unsupportedly to perish, who have so earnestly and so repeatedly sought to avoid the calamities of war by every decent method which wisdom could invent. Neither have I so much of the infidel in me as to suppose that He has relinquished the government of the world and given us up to the care of devils; and as I do not, I cannot see on what grounds the king of Britain can look up to heaven for help against us: a common murderer, a highwayman or a house-breaker has as good a pretence as he.

Let us not, however, presumptuously rely on the interposition of Providence, without exerting those efforts which it is our duty to exert, and which our bountiful Creator has enabled us to exert. Let us do our part to open the next campaign with redoubled vigor; and until the United States have humbled the pride of Britain, and obtained an honorable peace, cheerfully furnish our proportion for continuing the war—a war, founded on our side of

the immutable obligation of self-defence and in support of freedom, of virtue, and everything tending to ennoble our nature,
and render a people happy—on their part, prompted by bound-
less avarice, and a thirst for absolute sway, and built on a claim
repugnant to every principle of reason and equity—a claim subversive of all liberty, natural, civil, moral, and religious; incompatible with human happiness, and usurping the attributes of deity, degrading man, and blaspheming God.

Keeping the Faith

Let us all, therefore, of every rank and degree, remember our
plighted faith and honor, to maintain the cause with our lives and
fortunes. Let us inflexibly persevere in prosecuting to a happy period, what has been so gloriously begun, and hitherto so prosper-
ously conducted. And let those in more distinguished stations
use all their influence and authority, to rouse the supine; to ani-
mate the irresolute; to confirm the wavering; and to draw from
his lurking hole, the skulking neutral, who leaving to others the
heat and burden of the day, means in the final result to reap the
fruits of that victory, for which he will not contend. Let us be pe-
culiarly assiduous in bringing to condign punishment, those detestable parricides who have been openly active against their native country. And may we, in all our deliberations and proceedings, be influenced and directed by the Great Arbiter of the fate of
nations, by whom empires rise and fall, and who will not always
suffer the sceptre of the wicked to rest on the lot of the righteous,
but in due time avenge an injured people on their unfeeling oppressor, and his bloody instruments.

VIEWPOINT 5

"Drive far from you every baneful wretch who wishes to see you fettered with the chains of tyranny."

Loyalists Should Be Treated Harshly

"A Whig" (1779)

An important issue facing the American colonies during the revolutionary war was what to do with Americans who remained loyal to Britain. Historian Wallace Brown estimates that a half-million colonists, about one-fifth of the total white population, were loyalists. Other historians have supposed that up to a third of all Americans could be considered loyalists. Over eighty thousand people were permanently exiled from the American colonies during or after the revolutionary war because of their loyalist views.

During the revolutionary war many loyalists (also called Tories) were victims of property confiscation, public humiliation, and violence. The following viewpoint, a newspaper editorial by an anonymous author published in the August 5, 1779, issue of the *Pennsylvania Packet* and reprinted in *Diary of the American Revolution: From Newspapers and Original Documents* (Frank Moore, ed. New York: Charles Scribner, 1860), calls the loyalists (Tories) a serious threat to the American cause of independence and advocates harsh measures toward them, including banishment from America.

Among the many errors America has been guilty of during her contest with Great Britain, few have been greater, or attended with more fatal consequences to these States, than her lenity to the Tories. At first it might have been right, or perhaps political; but is it not surprising that, after repeated proofs of the same evils resulting therefrom, it should still be continued? We are all crying out against the depreciation of our money, and entering into measures to restore it to its value; while the Tories, who are one principal cause of the depreciation, are taken no notice of, but suffered to live quietly among us. We can no longer be silent on this subject, and see the independence of the country, after standing every shock from without, endangered by internal enemies. Rouse, America! your danger is great—great from a quarter where you least expect it. The Tories, the Tories will yet be the ruin of you! 'Tis high time they were separated from among you. They are now busy engaged in undermining your liberties. They have a thousand ways of doing it, and they make use of them all. Who were the occasion of this war? The Tories! Who persuaded the tyrant of Britain to prosecute it in a manner before unknown to civilized nations, and shocking even to barbarians? The Tories! Who prevailed on the savages of the wilderness to join the standard of the enemy? The Tories! Who have assisted the Indians in taking the scalp from the aged matron, the blooming fair one, the helpless infant, and the dying hero? The Tories! Who advised and who assisted in burning your towns, ravaging your country, and violating the chastity of your women? The Tories! Who are the occasion that thousands of you now mourn the loss of your dearest connections? The Tories! Who have always counteracted the endeavors of Congress to secure the liberties of this country? The Tories! Who refused their money when as good as specie, though stamped with the image of his most sacred Majesty? The Tories! Who continue to refuse it? The Tories! Who do all in their power to depreciate it? The Tories! Who propagate lies among us to discourage the Whigs? The Tories! Who corrupt the minds of the good people of these States by every species of insidious counsel? The Tories! Who hold a traitorous correspondence with the enemy? The Tories! Who daily sends them intelligence? The Tories! Who take the oaths of allegiance to the States one day, and break them the next? The Tories! Who prevent your battalions from being filled? The Tories! Who dissuade men from entering the army? The Tories! Who persuade those who have enlisted to desert? The Tories! Who harbor those who do desert? The Tories! In short, who wish to see us conquered, to see us slaves, to see us hewers of wood and drawers of water? The Tories!

Banish the Tories

And is it possible that we should suffer men, who have been guilty of all these and a thousand other calamities which this

Loyalists in America had to endure the wrath of supporters of the American Revolution. Here, a loyalist is hoisted above a crowd. Note the bucket of tar and the gathering of goose feathers at the bottom of the picture.

country has experienced, to live among us! To live among us, did I say? Nay, do they not move in our Assemblies? Do they not insult us with their impudence? Do they not hold traitorous assemblies of their own? Do they not walk the streets at noon day, and taste the air of liberty? In short, do they not enjoy every privilege of the brave soldier who has spilt his blood, or the honest patriot who has sacrificed his all in our righteous cause? Yes—to our eternal shame be it spoken—they do. Those very men who wish to entail slavery on our country, are caressed and harbored among us. Posterity will not believe it; if they do, they will curse the memory of their forefathers for their shameful lenity. Can we ever expect any grateful return for our humanity, if it deserves that name? Believe not a spark of that or any other virtue is to be found in the Tory's breast; for what principle can that wretch have who would sell his soul to subject his country to the will of the greatest tyrant the world at present produces? 'Tis time to rid ourselves of these bosom vipers. An immediate separation is necessary. I dread to think of the evils every moment is big with, while a single Tory remains among us. May we not soon expect to hear of plots, assassinations, and every species of wickedness their malice and rancor can suggest? for what can restrain those who have already imbrued their hands in their country's blood? Did not that villain Matthews, when permitted to live among us at New York, plot the assassination of General Washington? He did; he was detected, and had he received his deserts, he would now have been in gibbets, instead of torturing our unfortunate friends, prisoners in New York, with every species of barbarity. Can we hear this, and still harbor a Tory among us? For my own part, whenever I meet one in the street, or at the coffee house, my blood boils within me. Their guilt is equalled only by their impudence. They strut, and seem to bid defiance to every one. In every place, and in every company, they spread their damnable doctrines, and then laugh at the pusillanimity of those who let them go unpunished. I flatter myself, however, with the hopes of soon seeing a period to their reign, and a total end to their existence in America. Awake, Americans, to a sense of your danger. No time to be lost. Instantly banish every Tory from among you. Let America be sacred alone to freemen.

Drive far from you every baneful wretch who wishes to see you fettered with the chains of tyranny. Send them where they may enjoy their beloved slavery to perfection—send them to the island of Britain; there let them drink the cup of slavery and eat the bread of bitterness all the days of their existence—there let them drag out a painful life, despised and accursed by those very men whose cause they have had the wickedness to espouse. Never let them return to this happy land—never let them taste the sweets of that independence which they strove to prevent. Banishment, perpetual banishment, should be their lot.

VIEWPOINT 6

"Where a community splits into a faction, and has recourse to arms, and one finally gets the better, a law to bury in oblivion past transactions is absolutely necessary to restore tranquillity."

Loyalists Should Be Treated Charitably

Aedanus Burke (1743-1802)

Following the war, the government of South Carolina in 1783 passed harsh laws confiscating the property of and otherwise treating as traitors people they suspected of being loyalists. Aedanus Burke, the South Carolina chief justice who had served in the revolutionary militia and later became a member of the first United States Congress, spoke out against these laws. He argues in a 1783 pamphlet published in Philadelphia entitled *An Address to the Freemen of the State of South-Carolina* that the British occupation of South Carolina during the last years of the revolutionary war made it difficult to distinguish those who had cooperated out of principle from those who were forced to cooperate. Burke argues that the harsh laws jeopardized the freedoms that Americans had fought for and that the best course would be to proceed in the spirit of amnesty and forgiveness toward those who had supported the losing side of the American Revolution. This excerpt from Burke's pamphlet was taken from a reprint published in *Revolutionary vs. Loyalist*, Leslie F. S. Upton, ed. (Waltham, MA: Blaisdell Publishing Company, 1968).

Friends and fellow citizens,

The proceedings of the late Assembly held at Jacksonborough have already excited the attention not only of this but of other States; and some of the laws then enacted are of so serious a nature; that the memory of them will last, and their consequences operate, when the authors of the measures shall be no more. By one of those laws, upwards of two hundred men who have been citizens of this State before the reduction of Charlestown, have been stripped of all their property; innocent wives and children involved in the calamity of husbands and fathers, their widows are deprived of the right of dower, their children disinherited, and themselves banished forever from this country. And this *without process, trial, examination,* or *hearing;* and without allowing them the sacred right of proving their innocence on a future day. Under other acts of that assembly, a number of the inhabitants are subjected to heavy fines, some to near one third, others to one eighth and some to a tenth part of their estate, real and personal, without better proof of crime than report and suggestions. Another act excludes from the freedom of voting or being elected to a seat in the legislature, almost a majority of our citizens. The crimes of all consist in the part which they were said to have taken after the reduction of South Carolina by the British army.

One would imagine there is no free country upon earth, in which laws bringing such ruin on so many families, and so big with political mischief, would not have been publickly discussed before this day. But whether it be owing, that the measures have succeeded in breaking the spirit of the people, by filling every man with a sense of his own danger; or that the fear of the Governor's *extraordinary power,* awes men into silence; or that they are indifferent about public affairs; not a man has yet undertaken to inquire into the justice or injustice of it, or ask his neighbour how far the Legislature could effect the ruin and disgrace of so many of his fellow citizens, consistently with the laws, constitution, and happiness of his country. . . .

Conquered Territory

This State, soon after the reduction of Charlestown, may be strictly said to have been conquered. Not only the capital, but every post throughout the country was in the hands of the enemy. The Governor who represented the Sovereignty of the State, had provided for his safety by flight, and all the Continental troops in South Carolina were either killed, taken, or routed.

The enemy, thus masters of the country, resolved to reduce by military force the inhabitants to obedience. And Sir Henry Clinton accordingly in the month of June 1781, issued a proclamation,

> Commanding all persons whatever inhabitants of this province, (those who were in Charlestown and Fort Moultrie at the time of their capitulations and surrender, or were then in actual confinement excepted) who shall after the 20th of June next, neglect to return to his allegiance and to his Majesty's government, will be considered as enemies and rebels to the same, and treated accordingly.

Thus a military despotism was established throughout the settlements, and to compleat this miserable scene of woes, the army under General Gates, and a division under General Sumpter, to whom we looked up as our deliverers, were entirely defeated. The country thus abandoned to a cruel, unprincipled foe, the people had no idea but that our independence was lost irrecoverably. And indeed the advantages gained by the enemy were so rapid and decisive, it was for some time apprehended thro' the other States, and even by many members of Congress, that Carolina and Georgia must in the end revert to the domination of Great Britain.

Moderation, Not Violence

Revolutionary leader Alexander Hamilton argues in a 1784 New York pamphlet that fair treatment of former British loyalists will benefit the nation.

Nothing can be more ridiculous than the idea of expelling a few from this city and neighbourhood, while there are numbers in different parts of this and other states, who must necessarily partake in our governments, and who can never expect to be the objects of animadversion or exclusion. It is confirming *many* in their enmity and prejudices against the state, to indulge our enmity and prejudices against a few.

The idea of suffering the Tories to live among us under disqualifications, is equally mischievous and absurd. It is necessitating a large body of citizens in the state to continue enemies to the government, ready, at all times, in a moment of commotion, to throw their weight into that scale which meditates a change whether favourable or unfavourable to public liberty.

Viewing the subject in every possible light, there is not a single interest of the community but dictates moderation rather than violence.

In this situation *necessity*, whose domination triumphs over all human laws pointed out to our inhabitants, that as there were neither government, laws, nor army to protect them, they were at liberty to protect themselves, as well as they could. This is the law of Nature and of Nations: And all Statesmen, the best lawyers, and most eminent writers, agree, that when an invader overruns a country, defeats the standing forces, and subverts its government, the inhabitants of such a country are justifiable to take the conqueror's protection and obey his laws; and whether the government be a monarchy or a republick, it makes no difference, as the reason of the thing is the same. . . .

Every country of which we have any account from history, has had its day of woe and affliction, by foreign invasion, or civil discord, as we have had. But in every one of them as soon as the troubles were over, and the country regained; the government returned to its antient form, and the subjects were reinstated in the participation of their rights and privileges. And this is not only agreeable to justice, but the freedom and liberty of the country would be destroyed if it were otherwise. If in a republic a few could set up pretensions to superior political merit, over the whole aggregate body of the people, and deprive the latter of their rights and privileges, this would be nothing more nor less than overthrowing the constitution, seizing on the liberties of the people, and setting up an arbitrary government of the *few*. The laws of nations as well as the rights of nature therefore dictate, that when a country oppressed by a foreign power regains its liberty, the citizens should be restored to all the rights and liberties they before enjoyed.

Restoring Tranquillity

I shall now enter on the Confiscation Act; make a few remarks on the Amercement Law; and conclude with endeavouring to prove that an Act of Amnesty and Oblivion is the only means for restoring order, tranquillity and happiness to our common country.

The principal difficulty I meet with on a subject where so much may be said, is to confine myself within the narrow compass I proposed.

It is impossible not to feel distress when we reflect on the miseries that each party in a civil war, inflict on the other as they become uppermost. The cruel oppressions of the British, particularly the personal insults and outrage we suffered from their officers, after the fall of the country, is enough to make a man shudder.

Their treatment was so extravagantly outrageous, that no descriptions will even give a just idea of it; and to myself who was a witness and a sufferer, it appears like a dream, and almost incredible to me. Their cruelty to the garrison; their violation of the capitulation; their sequestration and plunder; their banishing the tender sex, our wives, and children, to a distant country, merely to gratify malice, as a day's journey would have set them down amidst their friends in their own country: During all this scene of violence and revenge, we ourselves never ceased to make the most tragical complaints, and calling heaven and earth to witness and avenge the injustice of our enemies; and yet no sooner did Providence turn things in our favour, and restore to us our country, then instead of thinking how to settle the peace and happiness of it, we took the quite contrary way, and looked about for means of doing vengeance in our turn, by way of retaliation. No sooner did we cease to fear and suffer, than our next endeavour was to make others fear and feel misery, as if it were necessary either to be suffering ruin or doing mischief. In thinking on these bitter calamities which men are so ingenious in contriving for each other, he must be more or less than man who cannot feel compassion and sorrow for the unhappy lot of human nature. . . .

The experience of all countries has shewn, that where a community splits into a faction, and has recourse to arms, and one finally gets the better, a law to bury in *oblivion* past transactions is absolutely necessary to restore tranquillity. For if after a civil war, and one party vanquished, persecution was to go on; if the fury of laws and the fierce rage of passions prevailed, while the minds of men were yet fired by deadly revenge against their fallen adversaries; this would be worse than keeping up the war: It would be carrying on hostility under the shape of justice, which is the most oppressive, and of all other injustice, excites the greatest detestation, in the most violent factions and division. . . .

The Need for Amnesty

It is a maxim in politics, that if a breach be made in the constitution of a government, and it be not healed, it will prove as fatal to its freedom, as a wound that is neglected and suffered to mortify, would be to the life of a man. I proved clearly that ours received a mortal one; and should the present assembly leave it *to inflame* without applying a cure, we cease to be a free people. The remedy I speak of is lenient, all healing. *Repeal at once the late election act, the amercement law, and the confiscation act, as far as it affects those who were our citizens.*—And in order that such proceedings may not be drawn into precedent hereafter, let there be a clause, *to obliterate those three acts* from the journals of both houses. *Pass an act of amnesty and oblivion, with as few exceptions as possible*; allowing such as may be excluded, a day to come in and be heard, either before the court of sessions, on a fair and public trial; or should they be men whose inveteracy, power or influence may be dangerous to the State, and are not liable to punishment by our laws; let them have a hearing before the legislature on articles of impeachment.—Provided that we mean that the word *Republic* should signify something more than mere *sound, pass an Act for dissolving the present Assembly.*

If every citizen cannot enjoy the rights of *election and representation* according to the constitution, I hope no body will be so idle as to talk of *Liberty. This, and the reversal of the three acts above mentioned,* is the measure, *and the only one* that can reconcile us to the friendship of each other; it will put an end to silly distinctions and faction: leave us at liberty to shake hands as brethren, whose fate it is to live together; and it will stand as a more lasting monument of our national wisdom, justice and magnanimity, than statues of brass or marble.

CHAPTER 5

Beyond Independence: Re-Forming the United States

Chapter Preface

The American colonies, in breaking from Great Britain, faced not only the military task of defeating the British army and navy, but also the political task of creating their own government. This undertaking and the debates that surrounded it took place on two levels. On the federal level, the Second Continental Congress drafted and adopted the Articles of Confederation in 1777. Ratified by all the states by 1781, the Articles established a relatively weak central government over the states. Much of the energy and thought in this period, including numerous pamphlet and newspaper editorials and debates, went to the establishment of individual state constitutions to replace the colonial governments. A great concern was the creation of political systems that could best preserve the "unalienable" rights of liberty and equality expressed in the Declaration of Independence. Many states called special constitutional conventions, and by 1777 all the new states except Massachusetts had adopted new constitutions.

The creators of these new constitutions, which included most of the influential political leaders of the American Revolution, drew upon several sources for ideas and inspiration. Many looked to aspects of the British government for guidance, especially its 1689 Bill of Rights, which listed specific limitations on government power against individuals, and its structure based on the division of powers between executive, legislative, and judicial branches, which sought to limit both government and popular power. Other colonial writers and leaders did not view England, with its monarchy, hereditary nobility, and corruption, as a model to be followed. They sought instead to create a brand new form of American government based on the ideas and experience developed in the previous thirteen years when the colonies were protesting British rule.

A related disagreement in the views of America's revolutionary leaders developed over how much power should be granted to popular majorities. Some revolutionary leaders and writers, including Thomas Paine, called for popular democracies and argued that the revolution was not only against the British, but against colonial elites. Others, such as John Adams, viewed popular democracies with alarm, believing they could lead to social anarchy and confusion, which in turn could lead to renewed tyranny. Langdon Carter of Virginia wrote to George Washington warning of some people wanting "a form of government that, by being independent of rich men, every man would then be able to do as he pleased." Carter and other conservatives sought to avoid such results by creating constitutional governments in which the popular vote of the majority alone would not dictate the direction of government.

The new state constitutions varied greatly. Some were little more than revisions of existing colonial constitutions minus references to English authority. Others, especially the Pennsylvania constitution adopted in 1776, were radically new in their extension of democracy to a greater selection of male voters and in the establishment of a powerful unicameral legislature. While many of the state constitutions were revised or replaced within a few years, the ideas expressed in them and the experience of creating them played important roles in the formation of the U. S. Constitution in 1787.

VIEWPOINT 1

"The natural liberty of man is to be free from any superior power on earth, and not to be under the will or legislative authority of man, but only to have the law of nature for his rule."

Natural Rights Should Form the Basis of Government

Samuel Adams (1722-1803)

Samuel Adams was an American political leader whose writings and speeches helped instigate the drive for American independence. Highlights of his political career include membership in the Continental Congress from 1774 to 1781, the signing of the Declaration of Independence in 1776, and the governorship of Massachusetts from 1794 to 1797. Adams's time of greatest influence was in the years immediately leading up to the Declaration of Independence.

The following viewpoint is a concise summary of Adams's views toward government and liberty. It is taken from a collection of documents, *Old South Leaflets* (Boston: Directors of the Old South Work, Old South Meeting House, n.d.). In 1772 the British announced that the Massachusetts governor and judges would be paid directly by the Crown, rather than by the colonial legislature—a development viewed with alarm by many colonists who believed the move was an attempt to take away local control of their government. On November 2, 1772, Adams made a motion at the Boston town meeting to establish "a committee of correspondence . . . to state the rights of the Colonists . . . and to communicate the same to the several towns and to the world." Adams was made a member of that committee and was the primary writer of the declaration it drafted and presented on November 20. The declaration states that all people have certain natural rights that the government cannot lawfully take away and that government exists to preserve these rights. The principles laid out in this declaration were influential when the colonies began forming their own state constitutions a few years later.

Among the natural rights of the colonists are these: first, a right to life; second, to liberty; third, to property; together with the right to support and defend them in the best manner they can. These are evident branches of, rather than deductions from, the duty of self-preservation, commonly called the first law of nature.

Natural Rights

All men have a right to remain in a state of nature as long as they please; and in case of intolerable oppression, civil or religious, to leave the society they belong to, and enter into another.

When men enter into society, it is by voluntary consent; and they have a right to demand and insist upon the performance of such conditions and previous limitations as form an equitable original compact.

Every natural right not expressly given up, or, from the nature of a social compact, necessarily ceded, remains.

All positive and civil laws should conform, as far as possible, to the law of natural reason and equity.

As neither reason requires nor religion permits the contrary, every man living in or out of a state of civil society has a right peaceably and quietly to worship God according to the dictates of his conscience.

"Just and true liberty, equal and impartial liberty," in matters spiritual and temporal, is a thing that all men are clearly entitled to by the eternal and immutable laws of God and nature, as well as by the law of nations and all well-grounded municipal laws, which must have their foundation in the former.

In regard to religion, mutual toleration in the different professions thereof is what all good and candid minds in all ages have ever practised, and, both by precept and example, inculcated on mankind. And it is now generally agreed among Christians that this spirit of toleration, in the fullest extent consistent with the being of civil society, is the chief characteristical mark of the church.

Virginia's Declaration of Rights

Virginia's Declaration of Rights was written by George Mason, a Virginia planter and statesman, and adopted by the Virginia Constitutional Convention on June 12, 1776. The ideals expressed here drew inspiration both from the English Bill of Rights of 1689 and from the experiences and grievances of the colonies toward Great Britain. Besides forming the basis for Virginia's new constitution, the ideas expressed in the declaration greatly influenced the Declaration of Independence, other state constitutions, and ultimately the Bill of Rights amended to the U.S. Constitution. The declaration contained sixteen sections, the first three of which are reprinted here.

A Declaration of Rights made by the representatives of the good people of Virginia, assembled in full and free convention: which rights do pertain to them and their posterity, as the basis and foundation of government.

Section 1. That all men are by nature equally free and independent and have certain inherent rights, of which, when they enter into a state of society, they cannot, by any compact, deprive or divest their posterity; namely, the enjoyment of life and liberty, with the means of acquiring and possessing property, and pursuing and obtaining happiness and safety.

Section 2. That all power is vested in, and consequently derived from, the people; that magistrates are their trustees and servants and at all times amenable to them.

Section 3. That government is, or ought to be, instituted for the common benefit, protection, and security of the people, nation, or community; of all the various modes and forms of government, that is best which is capable of producing the greatest degree of happiness and safety and is most effectually secured against the danger of maladministration. And that, when any government shall be found inadequate or contrary to these purposes, a majority of the community has an indubitable, inalienable, and indefeasible right to reform, alter, or abolish it, in such manner as shall be judged most conducive to the public weal.

Insomuch that Mr. Locke has asserted and proved, beyond the possibility of contradiction on any solid ground, that such toleration ought to be extended to all whose doctrines are not subversive of society. The only sects which he thinks ought to be, and which by all wise laws are excluded from such toleration, are those who teach doctrines subversive of the civil government under which they live. The Roman Catholics or Papists are excluded by reason of such doctrines as these: that princes excommunicated may be deposed, and those that they call heretics may be destroyed without mercy; besides their recognizing the pope in so absolute a manner, in subversion of government, by introducing, as far as possible into the states under whose protection they enjoy life, liberty, and property, that solecism in politics, *imperium in imperio*, leading directly to the worst anarchy and confusion, civil discord, war, and bloodshed.

The natural liberty of man, by entering into society, is abridged or restrained so far only as is necessary for the great end of society, the best good of the whole.

In the state of nature every man is, under God, judge and sole judge of his own rights and of the injuries done him. By entering into society he agrees to an arbiter or indifferent judge between him and his neighbors; but he no more renounces his original right than by taking a cause out of the ordinary course of law, and leaving the decision to referees or indifferent arbitrators. In the last case, he must pay the referees for time and trouble. He should also be willing to pay his just quota for the support of government, the law, and the constitution; the end of which is to furnish indifferent and impartial judges in all cases that may happen, whether civil, ecclesiastical, marine, or military.

The *natural* liberty of man is to be free from any superior power on earth, and not to be under the will or legislative authority of man, but only to have the law of nature for his rule.

The Role of Government

In the state of nature men may, as the patriarchs did, employ hired servants for the defense of their lives, liberties, and property; and they should pay them reasonable wages. Government was instituted for the purposes of common defense, and those who hold the reins of government have an equitable, natural right to an honorable support from the same principle that "the laborer is worthy of his hire." But then the same community which they serve ought to be the assessors of their pay. Governors have no right to seek and take what they please; by this, instead of being content with the station assigned them, that of honorable servants of the society, they would soon become absolute masters, despots, and tyrants. Hence, as a private man has a right to say what wages he will give in his private affairs, so has a community to determine what *they* will give and grant of their substance for the administration of public affairs. And, in both cases, more are ready to offer their service at the proposed and stipulated price than are able and willing to perform their duty.

In short, it is the greatest absurdity to suppose it in the power of one or any number of men, at the entering into society, to renounce their essential natural rights, or the means of preserving those rights, when the grand end of civil government, from the very nature of its institution, is for the support, protection, and defense of those very rights; the principal of which, as is before observed, are life, liberty, and property. If men, through fear, fraud, or mistake, should in terms renounce or give up any essential natural right, the eternal law of reason and the grand end of society would absolutely vacate such renunciation. The right to freedom being the gift of God Almighty, it is not in the power of man to alienate this gift and voluntarily become a slave. . . .

The State

A commonwealth or state is a body politic, or civil society of men, united together to promote their mutual safety and prosperity by means of their union.

The absolute rights of Englishmen and all freemen, in or out of civil society, are principally personal security, personal liberty, and private property.

All persons born in the British American colonies are, by the laws of God and nature and by the common law of England, exclusive of all charters from the Crown, well entitled, and by acts of the British Parliament are declared to be entitled, to all the natural, essential, inherent, and inseparable rights, liberties, and privileges of subjects born in Great Britain or within the Realm. Among those rights are the following, which no man, or body of men, consistently with their own rights as men and citizens, or members of society, can for themselves give up or take away from others.

First, "the first fundamental positive law of all commonwealths or states is the establishing the legislative power. As the first fundamental *natural* law, also, which is to govern even the legislative power itself, is the preservation of the society."

Second, the legislative has no right to absolute, arbitrary power over the lives and fortunes of the people; nor can mortals assume a prerogative not only too high for men, but for angels, and therefore reserved for the exercise of the Deity alone.

"The legislative cannot justly assume to itself a power to rule by extempore arbitrary decrees; but it is bound to see that justice is dispensed, and that the rights of the subjects be decided by promulgated, standing, and known laws, and authorized *independent judges*"; that is, independent, as far as possible, of prince and people. "There should be one rule of justice for rich and poor, for the favorite at court, and the countryman at the plough."

Third, the supreme power cannot justly take from any man any part of his property, without his consent in person or by his representative.

VIEWPOINT 2

"This ... notion ... that the whole human race is born equal; and that no man is naturally inferior or, in any respect, subjected to another ... is ... ill-founded and false both in its premises and conclusions."

Natural Rights Should Not Form the Basis of Government

Jonathan Boucher (1738-1804)

Jonathan Boucher was an Anglican minister who arrived in Virginia from England in 1759. His pro-British views grew increasingly unpopular as American desires for independence grew, and he preached his last sermons with loaded pistols in his pulpit for self-protection. The following viewpoint is taken from a sermon delivered in 1775, shortly before his return to England. It was later included in a collection of sermons, *A View of the Causes and Consequences of the American Revolution* (London), published by Boucher in 1797. Boucher questions the philosophic underpinnings of the American Revolution as expressed by Samuel Adams and later in the Declaration of Independence. He argues that governmental authority is derived from God, not from the consent of the governed, and that it requires obedience. Boucher also questions the doctrine that all people are created equal.

———————

It has ... been observed that the liberty inculcated in the Scriptures ... is wholly of the spiritual or religious kind. This liberty was the natural result of the new religion in which mankind were then instructed, which certainly gave them no new civil privileges. They remained subject to the governments under which they lived, just as they had been before they became Christians, and just as others were who never became Christians, with this difference only—that the duty of submission and obedience to government was enjoined on the converts to Christianity with new and stronger sanctions. The doctrines of the Gospel make no manner of alteration in the nature or form of civil government, but enforce afresh, upon all Christians, that obedience which is due to the respective constitutions of every nation in which they may happen to live. . . .

Obedience and Liberty

Obedience to government is every man's duty, because it is every man's interest; but it is particularly incumbent on Christians, because (in addition to its moral fitness) it is enjoined by the positive commands of God; and, therefore, when Christians are disobedient to human ordinances, they are also disobedient to God. If the form of government under which the good providence of God has been pleased to place us be mild and free, it is our duty to enjoy it with gratitude and with thankfulness and, in particular, to be careful not to abuse it by licentiousness. If it be less indulgent and less liberal than in reason it ought to be, still it is our duty not to disturb and destroy the peace of the community by becoming refractory and rebellious subjects and resisting the ordinances of God. However humiliating such acquiescence may seem to men of warm and eager minds, the wisdom of God in having made it our duty is manifest. For, as it is the natural temper and bias of the human mind to be impatient under restraint, it was wise and merciful in the Blessed Author of our religion not to add any new impulse to the natural force of this prevailing propensity, but, with the whole weight of His authority, altogether to discountenance every tendency to disobedience.

If it were necessary to vindicate the Scriptures for this their total unconcern about a principle which so many other writings seem to regard as the first of all human considerations, it might be observed that, avoiding the vague and declamatory manner of such writings, and avoiding also the useless and impracticable subtleties of metaphysical definitions, these Scriptures have better consulted the great general interests of mankind by summarily recommending and enjoining a conscientious reverence for law whether human or divine. To respect the laws is to respect liberty in the only rational sense in which the term can be used, for liberty consists in a subserviency to law. "Where there is no law," says Mr. [John] Locke, "there is no freedom." The mere man of nature (if such a one there ever was) has no freedom: all his life-time he is subject to bondage. It is by being included within the pale of civil polity and government that he takes his rank in society as a free man. . . .

True liberty, then, is a liberty to do everything that is right, and the being restrained from doing anything that is wrong. So far from our having a right to do everything that we please, under a notion of liberty, liberty itself is limited and confined; but limited and confined only by laws which are at the same time both its foundation and its support. It can, however, hardly be necessary to inform you that ideas and notions respecting liberty very different from these are daily suggested in the speeches and the writings of the times; and also that some opinions on the subject of government at large, which appear to me to be particularly loose and dangerous, are advanced in the sermon now under consideration; and that, therefore, you will acknowledge the propriety of my bestowing some further notice on them both.

It is laid down in this sermon as a settled maxim that the end of government is "the common good of mankind." I am not sure that the position itself is indisputable; but, if it were, it would by no means follow that "this common good being matter of common feeling, government must therefore have been instituted by common consent." There is an appearance of logical accuracy and precision in this statement; but it is only an appearance. The position is vague and loose; and the assertion is made without an attempt to prove it. If by men's "common feelings" we are to understand that principle in the human mind called common sense, the assertion is either unmeaning and insignificant, or it is false. In no instance have mankind ever yet agreed as to what is or is not "the common good."

A form or mode of government cannot be named which these "common feelings" and "common consent," the sole arbiters, as it seems, of "common good," have not, at one time or another, set up and established, and again pulled down and reprobated. What one people in one age have concurred in establishing as the "common good," another in another age have voted to be mischievous and big with ruin. The premises, therefore, that "the common good is matter of common feeling," being false, the consequence drawn from it, viz., that government was instituted by "common consent," is of course equally false.

This popular notion that government was originally formed by the consent or by a compact of the people rests on, and is supported by, another similar notion, not less popular nor better founded. This other notion is that the whole human race is born equal; and that no man is naturally inferior or, in any respect, subjected to another; and that he can be made subject to another only by his own consent. The position is equally ill-founded and false both in its premises and conclusions. In hardly any sense that can be imagined is the position strictly true; but, as applied to the case under consideration, it is demonstrably not true.

Man differs from man in everything that can be supposed to lead to supremacy and subjection, as one star differs from another star in glory. It was the purpose of the Creator that man should be social; but, without government, there can be no society; nor, without some relative inferiority and superiority, can there be any government. A musical instrument composed of chords, keys, or pipes, all perfectly equal in size and power, might as well be expected to produce harmony as a society composed of members all perfectly equal to be productive of order and peace.

If (according to the idea of the advocates of this chimerical scheme of equality) no man could rightfully be compelled to come in and be a member even of a government to be formed by a regular compact, but by his own individual consent, it clearly follows from the same principles that neither could he rightfully be made or compelled to submit to the ordinances of any government already formed to which he has not individually or actually consented. On the principle of equality, neither his parents, nor even the vote of a majority of the society (however virtuously and honorably that vote might be obtained), can have any such authority over any man. Neither can it be maintained that acquiescence implies consent; because acquiescence may have been extorted from impotence or incapacity. Even an explicit consent can bind a man no longer than he chooses to be bound. The same principle of equality that exempts him from being governed without his own consent clearly entitles him to recall and resume that consent whenever he sees fit; and he alone has a right to judge when and for what reasons it may be resumed.

Any attempt, therefore, to introduce this fantastic system into practice would reduce the whole business of social life to the wearisome, confused, and useless task of mankind's first expressing and then withdrawing their consent to an endless succession of schemes of government. Governments, though always forming, would never be completely formed; for the majority today might be the minority tomorrow, and, of course, that which is now fixed might and would be soon unfixed. . . .

False Theories of Government

Such theories of government seem to give something like plausibility to the notions of those other modern theorists who regard all governments as invasions of the natural rights of men, usurpations, and tyranny. On this principle it would follow, and could not be denied, that government was indeed fundamentally, as our people are sedulously taught it still is, an evil. Yet it is to government that mankind owe their having, after their fall and corruption, been again reclaimed from a state of barbarity and war to the conveniency and the safety of the social state; and it is by means of government that society is still preserved, the weak protected from the strong, and the artless and innocent from the wrongs of proud oppressors. It was not without reason, then, that Mr. Locke asserted that a greater wrong cannot be done to prince and people than is done by "propagating wrong notions concerning government."

VIEWPOINT 3

"It would ... be ... wise to consider whether, if the [English] Constitution was brought back to its original state, ... it would not afford more happiness than any other."

American Government Should Model the English Constitution

Carter Braxton (1736-1797)

The Declaration of Independence and the overthrow of the colonial governments left the American colonies with the task of constructing their own government. In 1776 a pamphlet addressed to the Virginia Convention, an association of Virginia's leaders that had become the de facto colonial government, was published. Historians attribute the pamphlet to Carter Braxton, a wealthy planter, Continental Congress delegate, and signer of the Declaration of Independence (with regret, according to John Adams). Braxton feared "the tumult and riot" of a "simple Democracy." He argued that the best way to preserve liberty and stability in Virginia would be to model its government after the British constitution. The British system divided governmental authority between the king or queen and the Parliament, which was made up of the House of Lords representing the aristocracy and the House of Commons representing the many. Braxton proposed for Virginia a governor appointed for life by the legislature (subject to recall) and a legislature divided in a way analogous to the division in the British Parliament. The constitution Virginia ultimately adopted in June 1776 included a bicameral legislature but rejected many of Braxton's other proposals. The pamphlet was later reprinted in *American Archives: Fourth Series* (Washington, 1837-1843), volume VI, edited by Peter Force.

Gentlemen: When despotism had displayed her banners, and with unremitting ardour and fury scattered here engines of oppression through this wide extended continent, the virtuous opposition of the people to its progress relaxed the tone of Government in almost every Colony, and occasioned in many instances a total suspension of law. These inconveniences, however, were natural, and the more readily submitted to, as there was then reason to hope that justice would be done to our injured country, the same laws, executed under the same authority, soon regain their former use and lustre, and peace, raised on a permanent foundation, bless this our native land.

But since these hopes have hitherto proved delusive, and time, instead of bringing us relief, daily brings forth new proofs of *British* tyranny, and thereby separates us farther from that reconciliation we so ardently wished; does it not become the duty of you, and every other Convention, to assume the reins of Government, and no longer suffer the people to live without the benefit of law, and order the protection it affords? Anarchy and riot will follow a continuance of its suspension, and render the enjoyment of our liberties and future quiet at least very precarious.

Presuming that this object will, ere long, engage your attention, and fully persuaded that when it does it will be considered with all the candour and deliberation due to its importance, I have ventured to collect my sentiments on the subject, and in a friendly manner offer them to your consideration. . . .

Forms of Government

Taking for granted, therefore, the necessity of instituting a Government capable of affording all the blessings of which the most cruel attempts have been made to deprive us, the first inquiry will be, which of the various forms is best adapted to our situation, and will in every respect most probably answer our purpose? . . .

Although all writers agree in the object of Government, and admit that it was designed to promote and secure the happiness of every member of society; yet their opinions as to the system most productive of this general benefit have been extremely contradictory. As all these systems are said to move on separate and dis-

208

Fear of the Mob

Many of America's revolutionary leaders were skeptical about extending democracy to most Americans. Such sentiments can be seen in this description by Gouveneur Morris, taken from a May 20, 1774, letter. Morris, a New York lawyer who later served in the Continental Congress and the 1787 Constitutional Convention, expresses fears of government falling into the hands of "a riotous mob."

[Y]esterday, I was present at a grand division of the city, and there I beheld my fellow citizens very accurately counting all their chickens, not only before any of them were hatched but before above one-half of the eggs were laid. In short, they fairly contended about the future forms of our government, whether it should be founded upon aristocratic or democratic principles.

I stood in the balcony, and on my right hand were ranged all the people of property, with some few poor dependents, and on the other all the tradesmen, etc., who thought it worth their while to leave daily labor for the good of the country. The spirit of the English constitution has yet a little influence left, and but a little. The remains of it, however, will give the wealthy people a superiority this time, but would they secure it they must banish all schoolmasters and confine all knowledge to themselves. This cannot be. The mob begin to think and to reason. Poor reptiles! it is with them a vernal morning; they are struggling to cast off their winter's slough, they bask in the sunshine, and ere noon they will bite, depend upon it.

The gentry begin to fear this. Their committee will be appointed; they will deceive the people and again forfeit a share of their confidence. And if these instances of what with one side is policy, with the other perfidy, shall continue to increase and become more frequent, farewell aristocracy. I see, and I see it with fear and trembling, that if the disputes with Great Britain continue, we shall be under the worst of all possible dominions; we shall be under the domination of a riotous mob.

tinct principles, it may not be improper to analyze them, and by that means show the manner of their operations.

Government is generally divided into two parts: *Its mode or form of Constitution*, and the *principle* intended to direct it.

The simple forms of Government are Despotism, Monarchy, Aristocracy, and Democracy. Out of these an infinite variety of combinations may be deduced. The absolute unlimited control of one man describes Despotism, whereas Monarchy compels the Sovereign to rule agreeable to certain fundamental laws. Aristocracy vests the sovereignty of a State in a few nobles; and Democracy allows it to reside in the body of the people, and is thence called a popular Government.

Each of these forms are actuated by different principles. The subjects of an unlimited despotick Prince, whose will is their only rule of conduct, are influenced by the principle of fear. In a Monarchy limited by laws, the people are insensibly led to the pursuit of honour; they feel an interest in the greatness of their Princes; and, inspired by a desire of glory, rank, and promotion, unite in giving strength and energy to the whole machine. Aristocracy and Democracy claim for their principle publick virtue, or a regard for the publick good independent of private interest.

Let us inquire from which of these several vines we should take a scion to ingraft on our wild one; see which is most congenial to our soil, and by the extent and strength of its branches best calculated to shelter the people from the rage of those tempests which often darken the political hemisphere. I will not deny, whatever others may do, that individuals have enjoyed a certain degree of happiness under all these forms. Content, and consequently happiness, depend more on the state of our minds than external circumstances, and some men are satisfied with fewer enjoyments than others. Upon these occasions the inclinations of men, which are often regulated by what they have seen and experienced, ought to be consulted. It cannot be wise to draw them further from their former institutions than obvious reasons and necessity will justify. Should a form of Government directly opposite to the ancient one under which they have been happy, be introduced and established, will they not, on the least disgust, repine at the change, and be disposed even to acts of violence in order to regain their former condition? Many examples in the history of almost every country prove the truth of this remark.

The English Constitution

What has been the Government of *Virginia*, and in a revolution how is its spirit to be preserved, are important questions. The better to discuss these points, we should take a view of the Constitution of *England*, because by that model ours was constructed, and under it we have enjoyed tranquillity and security. Our ancestors, the *English*, after contemplating the various forms of Government, and experiencing, as well as perceiving the defects of each, wisely refused to resign their liberties either to the single man, the few, or the many. They determined to make a compound of each the foundation of their Government, and of the most valuable parts of them all to build a superstructure that should surpass all others, and bid defiance to time to injure, or anything, except national degeneracy and corruption, to demolish.

In rearing this fabrick, and connecting its parts, much time, blood, and treasure, were expended. By the vigilance, persever-

210

ance, and activity, of innumerable martyrs, the happy edifice was at length completed, under the auspices of the renowned King *William* in the year 1688. They wisely united the hereditary succession of the Crown with the good behaviour of the Prince; they gave respect and stability to the Legislature, by the independence of the Lords, and security, as well as importance to the People, by being parties with their Sovereign in every act of legislation. Here, then, our ancestors rested from their long and laborious pursuit, and saw many good days in the peaceable enjoyment of the fruit of their labours. Content with having provided against the ills which had befallen them, they seemed to have forgotten that although the seeds of destruction might be excluded from their Constitution, they were, nevertheless, to be found in those by whom their affairs were administered.

Time, the improver as well as destroyer of all things, discovered to them that the very man who had wrought their deliverance was capable of pursuing measures leading to their destruction. Much is it to be lamented that this magnanimous Prince, ascending a throne beset with uncertainty and war, was induced, by the force of both, to invent and practice the art of funding to supply his wants, and create an interest that might support him in possession of his Crown. He succeeded to his wish, and thereby established a moneyed interest, which was followed by levying of taxes, by a host of tax-gatherers, and a long train of dependants on the Crown. The practice grew into system, till at length the Crown found means to break down those barriers which the Constitution had assigned to each branch of the Legislature, and effectually destroyed the independence of both Lords and Commons. These breaches, instead of being repaired as soon as discovered, were, by the supineness of the nation, permitted to widen by daily practice, till, finally, the influence of the Crown pervaded and overwhelmed the whole people, and gave birth to the many calamities which we now bewail, and for the removal of which the united efforts of *America* are at this time exerted.

Men are prone to condemn the whole because a part is objectionable; but certainly it would, in the present case, be more wise to consider whether, if the Constitution was brought back to its original state, and its present imperfections remedied, it would not afford more happiness than any other. If the independence of the Commons could be secured, and the dignity of the Lords preserved, how can a Government be better formed for the preservation of freedom? And is there anything more easy than this? If placemen and pensioners were excluded a seat in either House, and elections made triennial, what danger could be apprehended from prerogative? I have the best authority for asserting, that with these improvements, added to the suppression of boroughs, and giving the people an equal and adequate representation, *England* would have remained a land of liberty to the latest ages.

Judge of the *principle* of this Constitution by the great effects it has produced. Their code of laws, the boast of *Englishmen* and of freedom; the rapid progress they have made in trade, in arts and sciences; the respect they commanded from their neighbours; then gaining the empire of the sea; are all powerful arguments of the wisdom of that Constitution and Government which raised the people of that island to their late degree of greatness. But though I admire their perfections, I must mourn their faults; and though I would guard against, and cast off their oppression, yet would I retain all their wise maxims, and derive advantage from their mistakes and misfortunes. The testimony of the learned *Montesquieu* in favor of the *English* Constitution is very respectable: "There is (says he) one nation in the world that has for the direct end of its Constitution political liberty." Again he says, "It is not my business to examine whether the *English* actually enjoy this liberty or not; sufficient it is for my purpose to observe that it is established by their laws, and I inquire no further."

This Constitution and these laws have also been those of *Virginia*, and let it be remembered, that under them she flourished and was happy. The same principles which led the *English* to greatness animates us. To that principle our laws, our customs, and our manners, are adapted; and it would be perverting all order to oblige us, by a novel Government, to give up our laws, our customs, and our manners.

Adopting the English System

However necessary it may be to shake off the authority of arbitrary *British* dictators, we ought, nevertheless, to adopt and perfect that system which *England* has suffered to be grossly abused, and the experience of ages has taught us to venerate. This, like almost everything else, is perhaps liable to objections, and probably the difficulty of adopting a limited Monarchy will be largely insisted on. Admit this objection to have weight, and that we cannot in every instance assimilate a Government to that, yet no good reason can be assigned why the same principle, or spirit, may not in a great measure be preserved. But honourable as this spirit is, we daily see it calumniated by advocates for popular Governments, and rendered obnoxious to all whom their artifices can influence or delude. The systems recommended to the Colonies seem to accord with the temper of the times, and are fraught with all the tumult and riot incident to simple Democracy—systems which many think it their interest to support, and without doubt will be industriously propagated among you. The best of these systems exist only in theory, and were never confirmed by the experience even of those who recommend them. I flatter myself, therefore, that you will not quit a substance actually enjoyed, for a shadow or phantom, by which, instead of being benefited, many have been misled and perplexed.

Let us examine the principles they assign to their Government, and try its merits by the unerring standard of truth. In a late pamphlet it is thus stated: The happiness of man, as well as his dignity, consists in virtue: if there be a form of Government, then, whose principle is virtue, will not every sober man acknowledge it better calculated to promote the general happiness of society than any other form? Virtue is the principle of a Republick, therefore a Republick is the best form of Government.

The Dangers of a Unicameral Legislature

Many members of the colonial elite opposed a united or unicameral legislature as a basis for government. Among these opponents was William Hooper, a North Carolina delegate to the Continental Congress, who expressed his views in an October 26, 1776, letter.

A single branch of legislation is a many headed monster which without any check must soon defeat the very purposes for which it was created, and its members become a tyranny dreadful in proportion to the numbers which compose it; and, possessed of power uncontrolled, would soon exercise it to put themselves free from the restraint of those who made them, and to make their own political existence perpetual. The consultations of large bodies are likewise less correct and perfect than those where a few only are concerned. The people at large have generally just objects in their pursuit but often fall short in the means made use of to obtain them. A warmth of zeal may lead them into errors which a more cool, dispassionate enquiry may discover and rectify.

This points out the necessity of another branch of legislation at least, which may be a refinement of the first choice of the people at large, selected for their wisdom, remarkable integrity, or that weight which arises from property and gives independence and impartiality to the human mind.

The author, with what design I know not, seems to have cautiously blended private and publick virtue, as if for the purpose of confounding the two, and thereby recommending his plan under the amiable appearance of courting virtue. It is well known that private and publick virtue are materially different. The happiness and dignity of man, I admit, consists in the practice of private virtues, and to this he is stimulated by the rewards promised to such conduct. In this he acts for himself, and with a view of promoting his own particular welfare. Publick virtue, on the other hand, means a disinterested attachment to the publick good, exclusive and independent of all private and selfish interest, and which, though sometimes possessed by a few individuals, never characterized the mass of the people in any state. And this is said to be the principle of democratical Governments, and to influence every subject of it to pursue such measures as conduce to the prosperity of the whole. A man, therefore, to qualify himself for a member of such a community, must divest himself of all interested motives, and engage in no pursuits which do not ultimately redound to the benefit of society. He must not, through ambition, desire to be great, because it would destroy that equality on which the security of the Government depends; nor ought he to be rich, lest he be tempted to indulge himself in those luxuries which, though lawful, are not expedient, and might occasion envy and emulation. Should a person deserve the esteem of his fellow-citizens and become popular, he must be neglected, if not banished, lest his growing influence disturb the equilibrium. . . .

To this species of Government everything that looks like elegance and refinement is inimical, however necessary to the introduction of manufactures and the cultivation of arts and sciences. Hence, in some ancient Republicks, flowed those numberless sumptuary laws, which restrained men to plainness and familiarity in dress and diet, and all the mischiefs which attend agrarian laws, and unjust attempts to maintain their idol equality by an equal division of property.

Schemes like these may be practicable in countries so sterile by nature as to afford a scanty supply of the necessaries, and none of the conveniences of life; but they can never meet with a favourable reception from people who inhabit a country to which Providence has been more bountiful. They will always claim a right of using and enjoying the fruits of their honest industry, unrestrained by any ideal principles of Government, and will gather estates for themselves and children without regarding the whimsical impropriety of being richer than their neighbours. These are rights which freemen will never consent to relinquish; and after fighting for deliverance from one species of tyranny, it would be unreasonable to expect they should tamely acquiesce under another.

The truth is, that men will not be poor from choice or compulsion, and these Governments can exist only in countries where the people are so from necessity. In all others they have ceased almost as soon as erected, and in many instances been succeeded by despotism, and the arbitrary sway of some usurper, who had before perhaps gained the confidence of the people by eulogiums on liberty, and possessing no property of his own, by most disinterestedly proposing depredations on that of his neighbours.

The most considerable state in which the shadow of Democracy exists (for it is far from being purely so) is that of the United Provinces of *Holland*, &c. Their territories are confined within narrow limits, and the exports of their own produce very inconsiderable. Trade is the support of that people, and, however said to be considerable, will not admit of luxury. With the greatest parsimony and industry, they, as a people, can but barely support themselves, although individuals among them may amass estates. I own they have exhibited to mankind an example of perseverance and magnanimity that appeared like a prodigy. By the profits of their trade they maintained large armies, and supported a navy equal to the first in the day of warfare; but their military strength, as well as the form of their Government, have long since given way. Their navy has dwindled into a few ships of war, and their Government into an Aristocracy, as unhappy and despotick as the one of which we complain.

The State of *Venice*, once a Republick, is now governed by one of the worst of despotisms. In short, I do not recollect a single instance of a nation who supported this form of Government for any length of time, or with any degree of greatness; which convinces me, as it has many others, that the principle contended for is ideal, and a mere creature of a warm imagination. . . .

Dividing the Powers of Government

That I may not tire your patience, I will now proceed to delineate the method in which I would distribute the powers of Government, so as to devise the best code of laws, engage their due execution, preserve the strength of the Constitution, and secure the liberties of the people. It is agreed by most writers on this subject, that this power should be divided into three parts, each independent of, but having connection with each other. Let the people in the first place choose their usual number of Representatives, and let this right return to them every third year.

Let these Representatives, when convened, elect a Governour, to continue in authority during his good behaviour, of which the two Houses of Council of State and Assembly should jointly be the judges, and by majority of voices supply any vacancy in that office, which may happen by dismission, death, or resignation.

Let the Representatives also choose out of the Colony at large twenty-four proper persons to constitute a Council of State, who should form a distinct or intermediate branch of the Legislature, and hold their places for life, in order that they might possess all the weight, stability, and dignity, due to the importance of their office. Upon the death or resignation of any of the members, let the Assembly appoint another to succeed him.

Let no member of either House, except the Treasurer, hold a

post of profit in the Government.

Let the Governour have a Privy Council of seven to advise him, though they should not be members of either House.

Let the Judges of the Courts of Common Law and Chancery be appointed by the Governour, with the advice of his Privy Council, to hold their offices during their good behaviour, but should be excluded a seat in either House.

Let the Treasurer, Secretary, and other great officers of State, be chosen by the lower House, and proper salaries assigned to them, as well as to the Judges, &c.

Let all military officers be appointed by the Governour, and all other inferior civil ones.

Let the different Courts appoint their own Clerks. The Justices in each County should be paid for their services, and required to meet for the despatch of business every three months. Let five of them be authorized to form a Court to hear and determine causes, and the others empowered to keep the peace, &c.

These are the outlines of a Government which would, I think, preserve the principle of our Constitution, and secure the freedom and happiness of the people better than any other.

The Governour will have dignity to command necessary respect and authority, to enable him to execute the laws, without being deterred by the fear of giving offence; and yet be amenable to the other branches of the Legislature for every violation of the rights of the people. If this great officer was exposed to the uncertain issue of frequent elections, he would be induced to relax and abate the vigorous execution of the laws whenever such conduct would increase his popularity. Should he, by discharging his duty with impartiality, give offence to men of weight and influence, he would be liable to all the opposition, threats, and insults, which resentment could suggest, and which few men in such a dependent state would have sufficient resolution to neglect and despise; and hence it would follow, that the apprehensions of losing his election would frequently induce him to court the favour of the great, at the expense of the duties of his station and the publick good. For these, and a variety of other reasons, this office should be held during good behaviour.

The Council of State, who are to constitute the second branch of the Legislature, should be for life. They ought to be well informed of the policy and laws of other States, and therefore should be induced, by the permanence of their appointment, to devote their time to such studies as may best qualify them for that station. They will acquire firmness from their independency, and wisdom from their reflection and experience, and appropriate both to the good of the State. Upon any disagreement between the Governour and lower House, this body will mediate and adjust such difference; will investigate the propriety of laws, and often propose such as may be of publick utility for the adoption of the Legislature. Being secluded from offices of profit, they will not be seduced from their duty by pecuniary considerations.

The Representatives of the people will be under no temptation to swerve from the design of their institution by bribery or corruption, all lucrative posts being denied them. And should they, on any occasion, be influenced by improper motives, the short period of their duration will give their constituents an opportunity of depriving them of power to do injury. The Governour, and the members of the Council of State, should be restrained from intermeddling further in the elections of Representatives than merely by giving their votes.

VIEWPOINT 4

"If we suffer ourselves to examine the component parts of the English constitution, we shall find them to be the base remains of two ancient tyrannies."

American Government Should Not Model the English Constitution

Thomas Paine (1737-1809)

Thomas Paine was an influential pamphleteer of the American Revolution. His pamphlet *Common Sense*, first published in Philadelphia on January 10, 1776, sold an estimated 120,000 copies over the next three months. Paine, a recent emigré from England, attacks the English constitutional system, which he argues should be replaced by a more direct form of democracy. Paine's more radical ideas were reflected in the constitution adopted by Pennsylvania in September 1776.

Some writers have so confounded society with government, as to leave little or no distinction between them; whereas, they are not only different, but have different origins. Society is produced by our wants, and government by our wickedness; the former promotes our happiness *positively* by uniting our affections, the latter *negatively* by restraining our vices. The one encourages intercourse, the other creates distinctions. The first is a patron, the last a punisher.

218

Society in every state is a blessing, but Government even in its best state is but a necessary evil; in its worst state an intolerable one: for when we suffer, or are exposed to the same miseries by *a Government*, which we might expect in a country *without Government*, our calamity is heightened by reflecting that we furnish the means by which we suffer. Government like dress is the badge of lost innocence, the palaces of kings are built on the ruins of the bowers of paradise. For were the impulses of conscience clear, uniform, and irresistibly obeyed, man would need no other lawgiver; but that not being the case, he finds it necessary to surrender up a part of his property to furnish means for the protection of the rest; and this he is induced to do, by the same prudence which in every other case advises him, out of two evils to choose the least. *Wherefore*, security being the true design and end of government, it unanswerably follows, that whatever *form* thereof appears most likely to ensure it to us, with the least expence and greatest benefit, is preferable to all others.

Origins of Government

In order to gain a clear and just idea of the design and end of government, let us suppose a small number of persons settled in some sequestered part of the earth, unconnected with the rest; they will then represent the first peopling of any country, or of the world. In this state of natural liberty, society will be their first thought. A thousand motives will excite them thereto, the strength of one man is so unequal to his wants, and his mind so unfitted for perpetual solitude, that he is soon obliged to seek assistance and relief of another, who in his turn requires the same. Four or five united would be able to raise a tolerable dwelling in the midst of a wilderness, but *one* man might labour out the common period of life without accomplishing any thing; when he had felled his timber he could not remove it, nor erect it after it was removed; hunger in the mean time would urge him from his work, and every different want call him a different way. Disease, nay even misfortune would be death; for tho' neither might be mortal, yet either would disable him from living, and reduce him to a state in which he might rather be said to perish, than to die.

Thus necessity like a gravitating power would soon form out newly arrived emigrants into society, the reciprocal blessings of which, would supersede, and render the obligations of law and government unnecessary while they remained perfectly just to each other; but as nothing but Heaven is impregnable to vice, it will unavoidably happen that in proportion as they surmount the first difficulties of emigration, which bound them together in a common cause, they will begin to relax in their duty and attachment to each other: and this remissness will point out the necessity of establishing some form of government to supply the defect of moral virtue.

Some convenient Tree will afford them a State-House, under the branches of which the whole Colony may assemble to deliberate on public matters. It is more than probable that their first laws will have the title only of REGULATIONS and be enforced by no other penalty than public disesteem. In this first parliament every man by natural right will have a seat.

Defects of the English Constitution

An anonymous Pennsylvania tract published in 1776 and titled Four Letters on Interesting Subjects *argues that the English Constitution has defects and should not be the basis for the new Pennsylvania government.*

Among the many publications which have appeared on the subject of political Constitutions, none, that I have seen, have properly defined what is meant by *a Constitution*, that word having been bandied about without any determinate sense being affixed thereto. A Constitution, and a form of government, are frequently confounded together, and spoken of as synonimous things; whereas they are not only different, but are established for different purposes: All countries have some form of government, but few, or perhaps none, have truly a Constitution. The form of government in England is by a king, lords, and commons; but if you ask an Englishman what he means when he speaks of the English constitution, he is unable to give you any answer. The truth is, the English have no fixed Constitution. The prerogative of the crown, it is true, is under several restrictions; but the legislative power, which includes kings, lords, and commons, is under none; and whatever acts *they* pass, are laws, be they ever so oppressive or arbitrary. England is likewise defective in Constitution in three other material points, viz. The crown, by virtue of a patent from itself, can increase the number of the lords (one of the legislative branches) at his pleasure. . . . The crown can likewise, by a patent, incorporate any town or village, small or great, and empower it to send members to the house of commons, and fix what the precise number of the electors shall be. And an act of the legislative power, that is, an act of king, lords, and commons, can again diminish the house of commons to what number they please, by disfranchising any county, city or town.

But as the colony increases, the public concerns will increase likewise, and the distance at which the members may be separated, will render it too inconvenient for all of them to meet on every occasion as at first, when their number was small, their habitations near, and the public concerns few and trifling. This will point out the convenience of their consenting to leave the legislative part to be managed by a select number chosen from the whole body, who are supposed to have the same concerns at stake which those have who appointed them, and who will act in the same manner as the whole body would act were they present. If the colony continues increasing, it will become necessary to augment the number of the representatives, and that the interest of every part of the colony may be attended to, it will be found best to divide the whole into convenient parts, each part sending its proper number: and that the *elected* might never form to themselves an interest separate from the electors, prudence will point out the propriety of having elections often: because as the elected might by that means return and mix again with the general body of the electors in a few months, their fidelity to the public will be secured by the prudent reflexion of not making a rod for themselves. And as this frequent interchange will establish a common interest with every part of the community, they will mutually and naturally support each other, and on this (not on the unmeaning name of king), depends the *strength of government; and the happiness of the governed.*

Here then is the origin and rise of government; namely, a mode rendered necessary by the inability of moral virtue to govern the world; here too is the design and end of government, viz. Freedom and security. And however our eyes may be dazzled with show, or our ears deceived by sound; however prejudice may warp our wills, or interest darken our understanding, the simple voice of nature and of reason will say, 'tis right.

The English Constitution

I draw my idea of the form of government from a principle in nature which no art can overturn, viz. That the more simple any thing is, the less liable it is to be disordered, and the easier repaired when disordered; and with this maxim in view I offer a few remarks on the so much boasted constitution of England. That it was noble for the dark and slavish times in which it was erected, is granted. When the world was over-run with tyranny the least remove therefrom was a glorious rescue. But that it is imperfect, subject to convulsions, and incapable of producing what it seems to promise is easily demonstrated.

Absolute governments, (tho' the disgrace of human nature) have this advantage with them, that they are simple; if the people suffer, they know the head from which their suffering springs; know likewise the remedy; and are not bewildered by a variety of causes and cures. But the constitution of England is so exceedingly complex, that the nation may suffer for years together without being able to discover in which part the fault lies, some will say in one and some in another, and every political physician will advise a different medicine.

I know it is difficult to get over local or long standing prejudices, yet if we will suffer ourselves to examine the component parts of the English constitution, we shall find them to be the base remains of two ancient tyrannies, compounded with some new Republican materials.

Thomas Paine. John Adams wrote in 1805: "I know not whether any man in the world has had more influence on its inhabitants or affairs for the last thirty years than Tom Paine."

First. The remains of Monarchical tyranny in the person of the King.

Secondly. The remains of Aristocratical tyranny in the persons of the Peers.

Thirdly. The new Republican materials, in the persons of the Commons. on whose virtue depends the freedom of England.

The two first by being hereditary are independent of the People; wherefore in a *constitutional sense* they contribute nothing towards the freedom of the State.

To say that the constitution of England is a *union* of three powers reciprocally *checking* each other, is farcical, either the words have no meaning or they are flat contradictions.

To say that the Commons are a check upon the King, presupposes two things.

First. That the King is not to be trusted without being looked af-

222

ter; or in other words, that a thirst for absolute power is the natural disease of Monarchy.

Secondly. That the Commons by being appointed for that purpose, are either wiser or more worthy of confidence than the Crown.

But as the same constitution which gives the Commons a power to check the King by with-holding the supplies, gives afterwards the King a power to check the Commons by empowering him to reject their other bills; it again supposes that the King is wiser than those, whom it has already supposed to be wiser than him. A mere absurdity!

There is something exceedingly ridiculous in the composition of Monarchy; it first excludes a man from the means of information, yet empowers him to act in cases where the highest judgment is required. The state of a King shuts him from the World, yet the business of a King requires him to know it thoroughly: wherefore, the different parts by unnaturally opposing and destroying each other, prove the whole character to be absurd and useless.

The People and the King

Some writers have explained the English constitution thus; the King say they is one, the People another; the Peers are an house in behalf of the King; the Commons in behalf of the People; But this hath all the distinctions of an house divided against itself; and tho' the expressions be pleasantly arranged, yet when examined they appear idle and ambiguous: and it will always happen, that the nicest construction that words are capable of, when applied to the description of some thing which either cannot exist, or is too incomprehensible to be within the compass of description, will be words of sound only, and tho' they may amuse the ear, they cannot inform the mind: for this explanation includes a previous question, viz. *how came the King by a power which the People are afraid to trust and always obliged to check?* Such a power could not be the gift of a wise People, neither can any power which needs checking be from God: yet the provision which the constitution makes, supposes such a power to exist.

But the provision is unequal to the task, the means either cannot, or will not accomplish the end, and the whole affair is a *Felo de se:* for as the greater weight will always carry up the less, and as all the wheels of a machine are put in motion by one, it only remains to know which power in the constitution has the most weight, for that will govern: and tho' the others, or a part of them, may clog, or check the rapidity of its motion, yet so long as they cannot stop it, their endeavours will be ineffectual: the first moving power will at last have its way, and what it wants in speed will be supplied by time.

That the crown is this overbearing part in the English constitution needs not be mentioned, and that it derives its whole consequences merely from being the giver of places and pensions is self-evident, wherefore, tho' we have been wise enough to lock the door against absolute Monarchy, we at the same time have been foolish enough to put the Crown in possession of the key.

The prejudice of Englishmen in favour of their own government by King, Lords and Commons, arises as much or more from national pride than reason. Individuals are undoubtedly safer in England than in some other Countries: but the *will* of the King is as much the *law* of the land in Britain as in France, with this difference, that instead of proceeding directly from his mouth, it is handed to the People under the more formidable shape of an act of Parliament. For the fate of Charles the first, hath only made Kings more subtle—not more just.

Wherefore laying aside all national pride and prejudice in favour of modes and forms, the plain truth is, that *it is wholly owing to the constitution of the People, and not to the constitution of the Government* that the Crown is not as oppressive in England as in Turkey.

An inquiry into the *constitutional errors* in the English form of government, is at this time highly necessary; for as we are never in a proper condition of doing justice to others, while we continue under the influence of some leading partiality, so neither are we capable of doing it to ourselves while we remain fettered by any obstinate prejudice. And as a man who is attached to a prostitute is unfitted to choose or judge of a wife, so any prepossession in favour of a rotten constitution of government will disable us from discerning a good one.

VIEWPOINT 5

"There is no good government but what is republican."

Republics Are the Best Form of Government

John Adams (1735-1826)

John Adams was one of the most important figures in American history. A lawyer from Massachusetts, he first became identified with the revolutionary cause when he wrote a series of resolutions for the town of Braintree, Massachusetts, in 1765, condemning the Stamp Act. A delegate at both the first and second Continental Congresses, Adams became a forceful advocate for American independence. He later served the United States as a diplomat in France and Great Britain, as vice president under George Washington, and as the second president of the United States.

Adams, like many other revolutionary leaders, was distrustful of the extreme forms of democracy advocated by Thomas Paine and others, believing that popular power carried its own threat of tyranny by the majority. This was one reason he opposed unicameral legislatures such as the one adopted by Pennsylvania in 1777, believing instead in the separation of powers of government that would prevent one branch from gaining too much control. The following viewpoint is taken from *Thoughts on Government; in a Letter from a Gentleman to His Friend* (Boston, 1776). In it, Adams advocates a republican form of government in which the different branches of government check the powers of each other and in which true liberty could be preserved.

My dear Sir,—If I was equal to the task of forming a plan for the government of a colony, I should be flattered with your request, and very happy to comply with it; because, as the divine science of politics is the science of social happiness, and the blessings of society depend entirely on the constitutions of government, which are generally institutions that last for many generations, there can be no employment more agreeable to a benevolent mind than a research after the best.

Pope flattered tyrants too much when he said,

> For forms of government let fools contest,
> That which is best administered is best.

Nothing can be more fallacious than this. But poets read history to collect flowers, not fruits; they attend to fanciful images, not the effects of social institutions. Nothing is more certain, from the history of nations and nature of man, than that some forms of government are better fitted for being well administered than others.

We ought to consider what is the end of government, before we determine which is the best form. Upon this point all speculative politicians will agree, that the happiness of society is the end of government, as all divines and moral philosophers will agree that the happiness of the individual is the end of man. From this principle it will follow, that the form of government which communicates ease, comfort, security, or, in one word, happiness, to the greatest number of persons, and in the greatest degree, is the best.

All sober inquirers after truth, ancient and modern, pagan and Christian, have declared that the happiness of man, as well as his dignity, consists in virtue. Confucius, Zoroaster, Socrates, Mahomet, not to mention authorities really sacred, have agreed in this.

If there is a form of government, then, whose principle and foundation is virtue, will not every sober man acknowledge it better calculated to promote the general happiness than any other form?

Fear is the foundation of most governments; but it is so sordid and brutal a passion, and renders men in whose breasts it predominates so stupid and miserable, that Americans will not be likely to approve of any political institution which is founded on it.

Honor is truly sacred, but holds a lower rank in the scale of moral excellence than virtue. Indeed, the former is but a part of the latter, and consequently has not equal pretensions to support a frame of government productive of human happiness.

The foundation of every government is some principle or passion in the minds of people. The noblest principles and most generous affections in our nature, then, have the fairest chance to support the noblest and most generous models of government.

A man must be indifferent to the sneers of modern Englishmen, to mention in their company the names of Sidney, Harrington, Locke, Milton, Nedham, Neville, Burnet, and Hoadly. No small fortitude is necessary to confess that one has read them. The wretched condition of this country, however, for ten or fifteen years past, has frequently reminded me of their principles and reasonings. They will convince any candid mind, that there is no good government but what is republican. That the only valuable part of the British constitution is so; because the very definition of a republic is "an empire of laws, and not of men." That, as a republic is the best of governments, so that particular arrangement of the powers of society, or, in other words, that form of government which is best contrived to secure an impartial and exact execution of the laws, is the best of republics.

John Adams was the person most responsible for the creation and ratification of the 1780 Massachusetts constitution.

Of republics there is an inexhaustible variety, because the possible combinations of the powers of society are capable of innumerable variations.

As good government is an empire of laws, how shall your laws be made? In a large society, inhabiting an extensive country, it is impossible that the whole should assemble to make laws. The first necessary step, then, is to depute power from the many to a few of the most wise and good. But by what rules shall you choose your representatives? Agree upon the number and qualifications of persons who shall have the benefit of choosing, or annex this privilege to the inhabitants of a certain extent of ground.

The principal difficulty lies, and the greatest care should be employed, in constituting this representative assembly. It should be in miniature an exact portrait of the people at large. It should think, feel, reason, and act like them. That it may be the interest of this assembly to do strict justice at all times, it should be an equal representation, or, in other words, equal interests among the people should have equal interests in it. Great care should be taken to effect this, and to prevent unfair, partial, and corrupt elections. Such regulations, however, may be better made in times of greater tranquillity than the present; and they will spring up themselves naturally, when all the powers of government come to be in the hands of the people's friends. At present, it will be safest to proceed in all established modes, to which the people have been familiarized by habit.

Disadvantages of One Assembly

A representation of the people in one assembly being obtained, a question arises, whether all the powers of government, legislative, executive, and judicial, shall be left in this body? I think a people cannot be long free, nor ever happy, whose government is in one assembly. My reasons for this opinion are as follow:—

1. A single assembly is liable to all the vices, follies, and frailties of an individual; subject to fits of humor, starts of passion, flights of enthusiasm, partialities, or prejudice, and consequently productive of hasty results and absurd judgments. And all these errors ought to be corrected and defects supplied by some controlling power.

2. A single assembly is apt to be avaricious, and in time will not scruple to exempt itself from burdens, which it will lay, without compunction, on its constituents.

3. A single assembly is apt to grow ambitious, and after a time will not hesitate to vote itself perpetual. This was one fault of the Long Parliament; but more remarkably of Holland, whose assembly first voted themselves from annual to septennial, then for life, and after a course of years, that all vacancies happening by death or otherwise, should be filled by themselves, without any application to constituents at all.

4. A representative assembly, although extremely well qualified, and absolutely necessary, as a branch of the legislative, is unfit to exercise the executive power, for want of two essential properties, secrecy and despatch.

5. A representative assembly is still less qualified for the judicial power, because it is too numerous, too slow, and too little skilled in the laws.

6. Because a single assembly, possessed of all the powers of government, would make arbitrary laws for their own interest, execute all laws arbitrarily for their own interest, and adjudge all controversies in their own favor.

But shall the whole power of legislation rest in one assembly? Most of the foregoing reasons apply equally to prove that the legislative power ought to be more complex; to which we may add, that if the legislative power is wholly in one assembly, and the executive in another, or in a single person, these two powers will oppose and encroach upon each other, until the contest shall end in war, and the whole power, legislative and executive, be usurped by the strongest.

The judicial power, in such case, could not mediate, or hold the balance between the two contending powers, because the legislative would undermine it. And this shows the necessity, too, of giving the executive power a negative upon the legislative, otherwise this will be continually encroaching upon that.

To avoid these dangers, let a distinct assembly be constituted, as a mediator between the two extreme branches of the legislature, that which represents the people, and that which is vested with the executive power.

Let the representative assembly then elect by ballot, from among themselves or their constituents, or both, a distinct assembly, which, for the sake of perspicuity, we will call a council. It may consist of any number you please, say twenty or thirty, and should have a free and independent exercise of its judgment, and consequently a negative voice in the legislature.

The Governor

These two bodies, thus constituted, and made integral parts of the legislature, let them unite, and by joint ballot choose a governor, who, after being stripped of most of those badges of domination, called prerogatives, should have a free and independent exercise of his judgment, and be made also an integral part of the legislature. This, I know, is liable to objections; and, if you please, you may make him only president of the council, as in Connecticut. But as the governor is to be invested with the executive power, with consent of council, I think he ought to have a negative upon the legislative. If he is annually elective, as he ought to be, he will always have so much reverence and affection for the people, their representatives and counsellors, that, although you give him an independent exercise of his judgment, he will seldom use it in opposition to the two houses, except in cases the public utility of which would be conspicuous; and some such cases would happen.

In the present exigency of American affairs, when, by an act of

Parliament, we are put out of the royal protection, and consequently discharged from our allegiance, and it has become necessary to assume government for our immediate security, the governor, lieutenant-governor, secretary, treasurer, commissary, attorney-general, should be chosen by joint ballot of both houses. And these and all other elections, especially of representatives and counsellors, should be annual, there not being in the whole circle of the sciences a maxim more infallible than this, "where annual elections end, there slavery begins."

These great men, in this respect, should be, once a year,

> Like bubbles on the sea of matter borne,
> They rise, they break, and to that sea return.

This will teach them the great political virtues of humility, patience, and moderation, without which every man in power becomes a ravenous beast of prey.

This mode of constituting the great offices of state will answer very well for the present; but if by experiment it should be found inconvenient, the legislature may, at its leisure, devise other methods of creating them, by elections of the people at large, as in Connecticut, or it may enlarge the term for which they shall be

---

Who Should Vote

John Adams reveals some of his views on the limits of direct democracy in this May 26, 1776, letter to James Sullivan, a Massachusetts legislator who had written to Adams with some ideas on altering the legal qualifications for voters.

Your idea that those laws which affect the lives and personal liberty of all, or which inflict corporal punishment, affect those who are not qualified to vote, as well as those who are, is just. But so they do women as well as men; children as well as adults. What reason should there be for excluding a man of twenty years eleven months and twenty-seven days old from a vote, when you admit one who is twenty-one? The reason is you must fix upon some period in life when the understanding and will of men in general is fit to be trusted by the public. Will not the same reason justify the state in fixing upon some certain quantity of property as a qualification? . . .

Depend upon it, sir, it is dangerous to open so fruitful a source of controversy and altercation as would be opened by attempting to alter the qualifications of voters; there will be no end of it. New claims will arise; women will demand a vote; lads from twelve to twenty-one will think their rights not enough attended to; and every man who has not a farthing will demand an equal voice with any other, in all acts of state. It tends to confound and destroy all distinctions and prostrate all ranks to one common level.

chosen to seven years, or three years, or for life, or make any other alterations which the society shall find productive of its ease, its safety, its freedom, or, in one word, its happiness.

A rotation of all offices, as well as of representatives and counsellors, has many advocates, and is contended for with many plausible arguments. It would be attended, no doubt, with many advantages; and if the society has a sufficient number of suitable characters to supply the great number of vacancies which would be made by such a rotation, I can see no objection to it. These persons may be allowed to serve for three years, and then be excluded three years, or for any longer or shorter term.

Any seven or nine of the legislative council may be made a quorum, for doing business as a privy council, to advise the governor in the exercise of the executive branch of power, and in all acts of state.

The governor should have the command of the militia and of all your armies. The power of pardons should be with the governor and council.

Judges, justices, and all other officers, civil and military, should be nominated and appointed by the governor, with the advice and consent of council, unless you choose to have a government more popular; if you do, all officers, civil and military, may be chosen by joint ballot of both houses; or, in order to preserve the independence and importance of each house, by ballot of one house, concurred in by the other. . . .

The Judicial Branch

The dignity and stability of government in all its branches, the morals of the people, and every blessing of society depend so much upon an upright and skilful administration of justice, that the judicial power ought to be distinct from both the legislative and executive, and independent upon both, that so it may be a check upon both, as both should be checks upon that. The judges, therefore, should be always men of learning and experience in the laws, of exemplary morals, great patience, calmness, coolness, and attention. Their minds should not be distracted with jarring interests; they should not be dependent upon any man, or body of men. To these ends, they should hold estates for life in their offices; or, in other words, their commissions should be during good behavior, and their salaries ascertained and established by law. For misbehavior, the grand inquest of the colony, the house of representatives, should impeach them before the governor and council, where they should have time and opportunity to make their defence; but, if convicted, should be removed from their offices, and subjected to such other punishment as shall be thought proper. . . .

Laws for the liberal education of youth, especially of the lower class of people, are so extremely wise and useful, that, to a humane and generous mind, no expense for this purpose would be thought extravagant. . . .

A constitution founded on these principles introduces knowledge among the people, and inspires them with a conscious dignity becoming freemen; a general emulation takes place, which causes good humor, sociability, good manners, and good morals to be general. That elevation of sentiment inspired by such a government, makes the common people brave and enterprising. That ambition which is inspired by it makes them sober, industrious, and frugal. You will find among them some elegance, perhaps, but more solidity; a little pleasure, but a great deal of business; some politeness, but more civility. If you compare such a country with the regions of domination, whether monarchical or aristocratical, you will fancy yourself in Arcadia or Elysium.

If the colonies should assume governments separately, they should be left entirely to their own choice of the forms; and if a continental constitution should be formed, it should be a congress, containing a fair and adequate representation of the colonies, and its authority should sacredly be confined to these cases, namely, war, trade, disputes between colony and colony, the post-office, and the unappropriated lands of the crown, as they used to be called.

These colonies, under such forms of government, and in such a union, would be unconquerable by all the monarchies of Europe.

You and I, my dear friend, have been sent into life at a time when the greatest lawgivers of antiquity would have wished to live. How few of the human race have ever enjoyed an opportunity of making an election of government, more than of air, soil, or climate, for themselves or their children! When, before the present epocha, had three millions of people full power and a fair opportunity to form and establish the wisest and happiest government that human wisdom can contrive? I hope you will avail yourself and your country of that extensive learning and indefatigable industry which you possess, to assist her in the formation of the happiest governments and the best character of a great people. For myself, I must beg you to keep my name out of sight; for this feeble attempt, if it should be known to be mine, would oblige me to apply to myself those lines of the immortal John Milton, in one of his sonnets:—

> I did but prompt the age to quit their clogs
> By the known rules of ancient liberty,
> When straight a barbarous noise environs me
> Of owls and cuckoos, asses, apes, and dogs.

"Rulers should be frequently chose to their office."

Popular Democracy Is the Best Form of Government

Anonymous (1776)

Most of the colonies' constitutions fashioned in 1776 and 1777 were modeled after the 1776 Virginia Constitution and reflected the ideas of John Adams and other relatively conservative colonial leaders. They featured a bicameral legislature, the separation of powers, the election of the governor and state officials by the legislature, and property qualifications for voting.

The major exception was the Pennsylvania Constitution, which was adopted in September 1776. Among its novel features was a unicameral legislature, an executive president and council elected directly by the public, and a broad franchise enabling all taxpayers and sons of taxpayers to vote.

The Pennsylvania Constitution was modeled after proposals set forth in several pamphlets and tracts published in 1776. Among these tracts was *The Interest of America*, excerpted here. It argues that America has a chance to create an entirely new form of government to best serve the interests of the people. The pamphlet's anonymous author argues against a second legislature, saying that America had no nobility equivalent to Great Britain's House of Lords. The pamphlet also calls for maintaining as much power as possible in the hands of local town and county governments.

The important day is come, or near at hand, that America is to assume a form of Government for herself. We should be very desirous to know what form is best; and that surely is best which is most natural, easy, cheap, and which best secures the rights of the people. We should always keep in mind that great truth, viz: that the good of the people is the ultimate end of civil Government. As we must (some Provinces at least) in a short time assume some new mode of Government, and the matter cannot be deferred so long as to canvass, deliberately weigh, and fully adjust everything that may hereafter appear necessary, we should leave room to alter for the better in time to come. Every Province should be viewed as having a right, either with or without an application to the Continental Congress, to alter their form of Government in some particulars; and that without being liable to raise a clamour, by some who would be glad to say that it was contrary to the Constitution that they first formed upon; that it was overturning the original plan, and leaving people at uncertainties as to the foundation they are upon, and the like. As the Government is for the people, the people, when properly represented, have a right to alter it for their advantage.

Designing a Government

The affair now in view is the most important that ever was before *America*. In my opinion, it is the most important that has been transacted in any nation for some centuries past. If our civil Government is well constructed and well managed, *America* bids fair to be the most glorious State that has ever been on earth. We should now, at the beginning, lay the foundation right. Most, if not all, other Governments have had a corrupt mixture in their very Constitution; they have generally been formed in haste, or out of necessity, or tyrannically, or in a state of ignorance; and, being badly formed, the management of them has been with difficulty. But we have opportunity to form with some deliberation, with free choice, with good advantages for knowledge; we have opportunity to observe what has been right and what wrong in other States, and to profit by them. The plan of *American* Government should, as much as possible, be formed to suit all the variety of circumstances that people may be in—virtuous or vicious, agreeing or contending, moving regularly or convulsed by the intrigues of aspiring men; for we may expect a variety of circumstances in a course of time, and we should be prepared for every condition. We should assume that mode of Government which is most equitable and adapted to the good of mankind, and trust Providence for the event; for *God*, who determines the fate of

Governments, is most like to prosper that which is most equitable; and I think there can be no doubt that a well-regulated Democracy is most equitable. An annual of frequent choice of magistrates, who, in a year, or after a few years, are again left upon a level with their neighbours, is most likely to prevent usurpation and tyranny, and most likely to secure the privileges of the people. If rulers know that they shall, in a short term of time, be again out of power, and, it may be, liable to be called to an account for misconduct, it will guard them against maladministration. A truly popular Government has, I believe, never yet been tried in the world. The most remarkable Government that has ever been, viz: the *Roman* Republick, was something near it, but not fully so; and the want of it being fully so, kept a continual contest between the Senate and Plebeians.

Popular Governments

One of the strongest proposals for a strongly democratic form of government appeared in a 1776 New Hampshire pamphlet titled "The People the Best Governors."

God gave mankind freedom by nature, made every man equal to his neighbor, and has virtually enjoined them to govern themselves by their own laws. The government which he introduced among his people the Jews abundantly proves it, and they might have continued in that state of liberty had they not desired a king. The people best know their own wants and necessities, and therefore are best able to rule themselves. Tent-makers, cobblers, and common tradesmen composed the legislature at Athens. "Is not the body (said Socrates) of the Athenian people composed of men like these?"...

It appears that the forms of government that have hitherto been proposed since the breach with Great Britain, by the friends of the American States, have been rather too arbitrary. The people are now contending for freedom; and would to God they might not only obtain, but likewise keep it in their own hands. I own myself a friend to a popular government; have freely submitted my reasons upon it.... [Popular governments] have alone secured the liberties of former ages, and a just notion of them has guarded the people against the sly insinuations and proposals of those of a more arbitrary turn, whose schemes have a tendency to deprive mankind of their natural rights.

America must consist of a number of confederate Provinces, Cantons, Districts, or whatever they may be called. These must be united in a General Congress; but each Province must have a distinct Legislature, and have as much power within itself as possible. The General Congress should not interfere or meddle with

Provincial affairs more than needs must. Every Province should be left to do as much within itself as may be; and every Province should allow each County, yea, and each Town, to do as much within themselves as possible. Small bodies manage affairs much easier and cheaper than large ones. If every County and Town manage as much business as may be within themselves, people will be better satisfied, and the Provincial Congress saved much trouble. Our Counties and Towns have heretofore been left to manage many of their own affairs; and it has been a great privilege, and their business has been managed to great advantage. Each County should now choose their own officers, which were heretofore appointed by the Crown. These matters may now be adjusted with much ease. Every Province should be allowed such full power within itself, and receive such advantages by a general union or confederation, that it would choose to continue in that union. The connection of the Provinces should be made to be for the interest of each, and be agreeable to each. This will keep them quiet and peaceable; and nothing will tend so much to this, as to let every Province have as much power and liberty within itself as will consist with the good of the whole. Neither the Continental Congress, nor any other number of men, should assume or use any power or office for their own sake, but for the good of the whole. Let *America* increase ever so much, there must never be any power like a Kingly power; no power used for its own sake, or for the advantage or dignity of any number of men, as distinct from the good of the whole; and while things are thus managed, a general union will be agreeable, and people will not complain.

Notwithstanding every Province should have all possible power within itself, yet some things must be left to the General Congress; as, 1. Making and managing war and making peace. 2. Settling differences between Provinces. 3. Making some maritime laws, or general regulations respecting trade; otherwise one Province might unjustly interfere with another. 4. Ordering a currency for the whole Continent; for it would be best that, as soon as may be, there should be one currency for the whole; the General Congress might order the quota for each Province. 5. The forming of new Provinces. 6. The sale of new lands. 7. Treaties with other nations; consequently some general directions of our *Indian* affairs.

As we are now to assume a new mode of Government, I think it ought properly to be new. Some are for keeping as near the old form of Government in each Province as can well be. But I think it is entirely wrong; it is mistaken policy. It is probable that some who propose it mean well; but I humbly conceive they have not thoroughly considered the thing. Others who propose it may have self-interest at bottom, hoping thereby to retain, or obtain, places of profit or honour. We must come as near a new form of Government as we can, without destroying private property. So far as private property will allow, we must form our Government in each Province just as if we had never any form of Government before. It is much easier to form a new Government than to patch up one partly old and partly new, because it is more simple and natural. I speak chiefly with respect to Legislature. We should by all means avoid several branches of Legislature.

One Branch of Legislature Best

One branch of Legislature is much preferable to more than one, because a plurality causes perpetual contention and waste of time. It was so in *Rome*; it has been so in *Great Britain*; and has been remarkably so in these Provinces in times past. The ever-memorable Congress now in *America* has done business infinitely better than if there had been several orders of Delegates to contest, interrupt, and be a negative one upon another.

A patched Government, consisting of several parts, has been the difficulty, I may call it the disease, of some of the best civil Governments that have been in the world—I mean the *Roman* Republick and the Government of *Great Britain*. Had the *Romans* been a true Democracy, without a Senate, or body different from the Plebeians, they might have avoided those jars and contentions which continually subsisted between those two bodies. Should we admit different branches of Legislature, it might give occasion in time to degenerate into that form of Government, or something like that, which has been so oppressive in our nation. It might open a door for ill-disposed aspiring men to destroy the State. Our having several branches of Legislature heretofore is an argument against, rather than for it, in time to come, because it is a word that not only has been abused, but in its nature tends to abuse. The simplest mode of legislation is certainly best. The *European* nations have, for some centuries past, derived most of their knowledge from the *Greeks* and *Romans*. The *Romans*, especially, have been, in a sort, an example, being excellent in many things. We have been ready to view them so in all things. We are very apt to take in, or imitate, the imperfections as well as the excellencies of those that are excellent. Hence, I suppose, it is that most, if not all, the Republicks in *Europe* have a body of Senators in their form of Government. I doubt not it will be an argument with many, that we in *America* must have something like a Senate, or Council, or Upper House, because the *Romans* and other Republicks have had. But the argument is the other way; it was their imperfection, it was a source of trouble, it was a step towards arbitrary power, and therefore to be avoided. Free Government can better, must better, subsist without it. Different branches of Legislature cause much needless expense, two ways: First, as there are more persons to maintain; and, second, as they waste time, and prolong a session by their contentions. Besides, it is a great absurdity that one branch of a Legislature, that can negative all.the rest, should be the principal Executive power in the State. There can be but little chance for proper freedom, where the making and executing the laws of a State lie in the same hand, and that not of the people in general, but of a single person. The Legislative and Executive power in every Province ought to be kept as distinct as possible. Wise, experienced, and publick-spirited persons should be in places of power, and if so, they must be sought out, chosen, and introduced. For this reason there ought not to be a number that are hereditary, for wisdom is not a birthright; nor a number put in place for life, for men's abilities and manners may change. Rulers should be frequently chose to their office. A Provincial Congress is the whole Province met by Representatives; and there is no need of a representative of a King, for we have none; nor can there be need of a Council to represent the House of Lords, for we have not, and hope never shall have, a hereditary nobility, different from the general body of the people; but if we admit different branches of the Legislature, there is danger that there may be in time.

CHAPTER 6

The Meaning of the American Revolution: Historians' Debate

Chapter Preface

Though it occurred more than two hundred years ago, the American Revolution's impact reaches to the present day. "To understand America at any time," writes historian Gordon S. Wood, "has . . . required coming to terms with the meaning of the Revolution." Historian George Athan Billias adds:

> The Revolution remains the single most important event in all of American history. Within the short span of two decades—1763-1783—Americans rejected the British monarchial system, waged a war of independence, created states out of colonies, and set up a central government based on the principles of popular rule, republicanism, and nationalism.

Billias goes on to describe one of the central questions historians face when examining the Revolution:

> These changes occurred with remarkable rapidity, but was the transformation itself sweeping enough to justify the term *revolutionary*? Did the new nation differ that much from the former colonies? Did the laws, institutions, and customs of the United States constitute a sharp break with the British heritage? Was American society radically reshaped and restructured as a result of independence? Was there a dramatic shift in the ideas, attitudes, and behavior of most Americans in the relationship between individuals and their government, the society, and with one another? Within the context of our nation's history, such issues may be reduced to a single question: How revolutionary was our Revolution?

Over the past two hundred years historians have answered that question differently. Daniel J. Boorstin, for example, argues that the American Revolution was essentially a conservative movement that sought to preserve the colonial status quo. He and other historians argue that a great deal of social change had already occurred in the century before the Revolution and that a great majority of (white, male) Americans already had political, economic, and religious freedoms and opportunities. The Revolution was fought to preserve these freedoms rather than to create new ones, Boorstin and others say. The classes of Americans that did not share in these freedoms—black slaves, women, and the very poor—were not, in this historical interpretation, much affected by the Revolution.

Other historians, however, have argued that the American insurrection was truly revolutionary. Some, such as Bernard Bailyn, have argued that the true revolution took place within the minds of Americans, affecting the way they looked at themselves and their relation to the British Empire. What had once seemed American deficiencies, such as a lack of an aristocracy, a cosmopolitan culture, and a nationally established church, were transformed into American virtues, Bailyn argues, enabling Americans to envision themselves as an independent republic.

Other historians have examined specific changes and reforms that the Revolution spurred in American society. The Revolution did create new constitutional governments. It popularized the ideals of liberty and equality. It did not abolish slavery, but it did inspire the growth of an antislavery movement (one that was partly led by free blacks demanding that America live up to its ideals as expressed in the Declaration of Independence). Many historians agree with Richard L. Bushman in arguing that the American Revolution brought more changes in American principles than in fact—but that such principles ultimately contributed to further revolutionary results. Bushman writes:

> Social and cultural change growing out of the Revolution was . . . halting and incomplete. It was for the most part a time of planting rather than harvest. Despite considerable agitation, slavery continued to the Civil War. Women, in another instance of blatant inequality, were not allowed to vote until 1920. . . . The great changes came later when the implications of revolutionary principles were more fully recognized. . . . The power of the idea of equality lay more in its enduring strength than in its immediate effect.

The following two viewpoints examine both the motives of the leaders of the American Revolution and the Revolution's ultimate impact on American life.

VIEWPOINT 1

"It seems that the rebellion against British rule allowed a certain group of the colonial elite to replace those loyal to England, give some benefits to small landholders, and leave poor white working people and tenant farmers in very much their old situation."

The War for Independence Was Not a Social Revolution

Howard Zinn (1922-)

Howard Zinn is professor emeritus of political science at Boston University. He was also a civil rights activist and opponent of the Vietnam War. Zinn's books include *Disobedience & Democracy* and *Declarations of Independence: Cross-Examining American Ideology.* His 1980 book *A People's History of the United States* was nominated for an American Book Award. The tome surveys American history from colonial times to America's bicentennial from the point of view of blacks, Native Americans, women, and other minorities and disadvantaged classes. Among the events Zinn examines from this perspective is the American Revolution.

Zinn argues that the American Revolution had little positive impact on the everyday lives of most Americans. He writes that most of the leaders of the Revolution were members of the colonial elite who wished to preserve their wealth and power. They used the war for independence from Britain as a way "to create a consensus of popular support" for their continued rule and to prevent large-scale internal changes in America's society. In this sense, Zinn concludes, the American Revolution was really a successful effort to preserve America's status quo.

Around 1776, certain important people in the English colonies made a discovery that would prove enormously useful for the next two hundred years. They found that by creating a nation, a symbol, a legal unity called the United States, they could take over land, profits, and political power from favorites of the British Empire. In the process, they could hold back a number of potential rebellions and create a consensus of popular support for the rule of a new, privileged leadership.

When we look at the American Revolution this way, it was a work of genius, and the Founding Fathers deserve the awed tribute they have received over the centuries. They created the most effective system of national control devised in modern times, and showed future generations of leaders the advantages of combining paternalism with command.

Many Rebellions

Starting with Bacon's Rebellion in Virginia, by 1760, there had been eighteen uprisings aimed at overthrowing colonial governments. There had also been six black rebellions, from South Carolina to New York, and forty riots of various origins.

By this time also, there emerged, according to Jack Greene, "stable, coherent, effective and acknowledged local political and social elites." And by the 1760s, this local leadership saw the possibility of directing much of the rebellious energy against England and her local officials. It was not a conscious conspiracy, but an accumulation of tactical responses.

After 1763, with England victorious over France in the Seven Years' War (known in America as the French and Indian War), expelling them from North America, ambitious colonial leaders were no longer threatened by the French. They now had only two rivals left: the English and the Indians. The British, wooing the Indians, had declared Indian lands beyond the Appalachians out of bounds to whites (the Proclamation of 1763). Perhaps once the British were out of the way, the Indians could be dealt with. Again, no conscious forethought strategy by the colonial elite, but a growing awareness as events developed.

With the French defeated, the British government could turn its attention to tightening control over the colonies. It needed revenues to pay for the war, and looked to the colonies for that. Also, the colonial trade had become more and more important to the British economy, and more profitable: it had amounted to about 500,000 pounds in 1700 but by 1770 was worth 2,800,000 pounds.

So, the American leadership was less in need of English rule, the English more in need of the colonists' wealth. The elements were there for conflict.

The war had brought glory for the generals, death to the privates, wealth for the merchants, unemployment for the poor. There were 25,000 people living in New York (there had been 7,000 in 1720) when the French and Indian War ended. A newspaper editor wrote about the growing "Number of Beggers and wandering Poor" in the streets of the city. Letters in the papers questioned the distribution of wealth: "How often have our Streets been covered with Thousands of Barrels of Flour for trade, while our near Neighbors can hardly procure enough to make a Dumplin to satisfy hunger?"

Gary Nash's study of city tax lists shows that by the early 1770s, the top 5 percent of Boston's taxpayers controlled 49 percent of the city's taxable assets. In Philadelphia and New York too, wealth was more and more concentrated. Court-recorded wills showed that by 1750 the wealthiest people in the cities were leaving 20,000 pounds (equivalent to about $2.5 million today).

In Boston, the lower classes began to use the town meeting to vent their grievances. The governor of Massachusetts had written that in these town meetings "the meanest Inhabitants . . . by their constant Attendance there generally are the majority and outvote the Gentlemen, Merchants, Substantial Traders and all the better part of the Inhabitants."

What seems to have happened in Boston is that certain lawyers, editors, and merchants of the upper classes, but excluded from the ruling circles close to England—men like James Otis and Samuel Adams—organized a "Boston Caucus" and through their oratory and their writing "molded laboring-class opinion, called the 'mob' into action, and shaped its behaviour." This is Gary Nash's description of Otis, who, he says, "keenly aware of the declining fortunes and the resentment of ordinary townspeople, was mirroring as well as molding popular opinion."

Using the Lower Classes

We have here a forecast of the long history of American politics, the mobilization of lower-class energy by upper-class politicians, for their own purposes. This was not purely deception; it involved, in part, a genuine recognition of lower-class grievances, which helps to account for its effectiveness as a tactic over the centuries. As Nash puts it:

James Otis, Samuel Adams, Royall Tyler, Oxenbridge Thacher,

and a host of other Bostonians, linked to the artisans and laborers through a network of neighborhood taverns, fire companies, and the Caucus, espoused a vision of politics that gave credence to laboring-class views and regarded as entirely legitimate the participation of artisans and even laborers in the political process. . . .

This accumulated sense of grievance against the rich in Boston may account for the explosiveness of mob action after the Stamp Act of 1765. Through this Act, the British were taxing the colonial population to pay for the French war, in which colonists had suffered to expand the British Empire. That summer, a shoemaker named Ebenezer MacIntosh led a mob in destroying the house of a rich Boston merchant named Andrew Oliver. Two weeks later, the crowd turned to the home of Thomas Hutchinson, symbol of the rich elite who ruled the colonies in the name of England. They smashed up his house with axes, drank the wine in his wine cellar, and looted the house of its furniture and other objects. A report by colony officials to England said that this was part of a larger scheme in which the houses of fifteen rich people were to be destroyed, as part of "a War of Plunder, of general levelling and taking away the Distinction of rich and poor."

It was one of those moments in which fury against the rich went further than leaders like Otis wanted. Could class hatred be focused against the pro-British elite, and deflected from the nationalist elite? In New York, that same year of the Boston house attacks, someone wrote to the New York *Gazette*, "Is it equitable that 99, rather 999, should suffer for the Extravagance or Grandeur of one, especially when it is considered that men frequently owe their Wealth to the impoverishment of their Neighbors?" The leaders of the Revolution would worry about keeping such sentiments within limits. . . .

In the countryside, where most people lived, there was a similar conflict of poor against rich, one which political leaders would use to mobilize the population against England, granting some benefits for the rebellious poor, and many more for themselves in the process. The tenant riots in New Jersey in the 1740s, the New York tenant uprisings of the 1750s and 1760s in the Hudson Valley, and the rebellion in northeastern New York that led to the carving of Vermont out of New York State were all more than sporadic rioting. They were long-lasting social movements, highly organized, involving the creation of countergovernments. They were aimed at a handful of rich landlords, but with the landlords far away, they often had to direct their anger against other, closer farmers who had leased the disputed land from the owners. . . .

In North Carolina, a powerful movement of white farmers was

organized against wealthy and corrupt officials in the period from 1766 to 1771, exactly those years when, in the cities of the Northeast, agitation was growing against the British, crowding out class issues. The movement in North Carolina was called the Regulator movement, and it consisted, says Marvin L. Michael Kay, a specialist in the history of that movement, of "class-conscious white farmers in the west who attempted to democratize local government in their respective counties." The Regulators referred to themselves as "poor Industrious peasants," as "labourers," "the wretched poor," "oppressed" by "rich and powerful . . . designing Monsters." . . .

A contemporary account of the Regulator movement in Orange County describes the situation:

> Thus were the people of Orange insulted by the sheriff, robbed and plundered . . . neglected and condemned by the Representatives and abused by the Magistracy; obliged to pay Fees regulated only by the Avarice of the officer; obliged to pay a Tax which they believed went to inrich and agrandise a few, who lorded it over them continually; and from all these Evils they saw no way to escape; for the Men in Power, and Legislation, were the Men whose interest it was to oppress, and make gain of the Labourer.

In that county in the 1760s, the Regulators organized to prevent the collection of taxes, or the confiscation of the property of tax delinquents. Officials said "an absolute Insurrection of a dangerous tendency has broke out in Orange County," and made military plans to suppress it. At one point seven hundred armed farmers forced the release of two arrested Regulator leaders. The Regulators petitioned the government on their grievances in 1768, citing "the unequal chances the poor and the weak have in contentions with the rich and powerful.". . .

The result of all this was that the assembly passed some mild reform legislation, but also an act "to prevent riots and tumults," and the governor prepared to crush them militarily. In May of 1771 there was a decisive battle in which several thousand Regulators were defeated by a disciplined army using cannon. Six Regulators were hanged. Kay says that in the three western counties of Orange, Anson, and Rowan, where the Regulator movement was concentrated, it had the support of six thousand to seven thousand men out of a total white taxable population of about eight thousand.

One consequence of this bitter conflict is that only a minority of the people in the Regulator counties seem to have participated as patriots in the Revolutionary War. Most of them probably remained neutral.

Fortunately for the Revolutionary movement, the key battles

were being fought in the North, and here, in the cities, the colonial leaders had a divided white population; they could win over the mechanics, who were a kind of middle class, who had a stake in the fight against England, who faced competition from English manufacturers. The biggest problem was to keep the propertyless people, who were unemployed and hungry in the crisis following the French war, under control. . . .

In Virginia, it seemed clear to the educated gentry that something needed to be done to persuade the lower orders to join the revolutionary cause, to deflect their anger against England. One Virginian wrote in his diary in the spring of 1774: "The lower Class of People here are in tumult on account of Reports from Boston, many of them expect to be press'd & compell'd to go and fight the Britains!" Around the time of the Stamp Act, a Virginia orator addressed the poor: "Are not the gentlemen made of the same materials as the lowest and poorest among you? . . . Listen to no doctrines which may tend to divide us, but let us go hand in hand, as brothers. . . ."

It was a problem for which the rhetorical talents of Patrick Henry were superbly fitted. He was, as Rhys Isaac puts it, "firmly attached to the world of the gentry," but he spoke in words that the poorer whites of Virginia could understand. Henry's fellow Virginian Edmund Randolph recalled his style as "simplicity and even carelessness. . . . His pauses, which for their length might sometimes be feared to dispell the attention, rivited it the more by raising the expectation."

Patrick Henry's oratory in Virginia pointed a way to relieve class tension between upper and lower classes and form a bond against the British. This was to find language inspiring to all classes, specific enough in its listing of grievances to charge people with anger against the British, vague enough to avoid class conflict among the rebels, and stirring enough to build patriotic feeling for the resistance movement.

Common Sense

Tom Paine's *Common Sense*, which appeared in early 1776 and became the most popular pamphlet in the American colonies, did this. It made the first bold argument for independence, in words that any fairly literate person could understand: "Society in every state is a blessing, but Government even in its best state is but a necessary evil. . . ". . . .

Common Sense went through twenty-five editions in 1776 and sold hundreds of thousands of copies. It is probable that almost every literate colonist either read it or knew about its contents. Pamphleteering had become by this time the chief theater of debate about relations with England. From 1750 to 1776 four hun-

Only Fifteen Percent of Americans Gained Freedom

Linda Grant DePauw teaches at George Washington University in Washington, D.C., and has written extensively about women's history and the colonial era. She argues in an article originally published in a 1973 issue of Maryland Historical Magazine *that the American Revolution was about freedoms for white property-owning men only—about 15 percent of the American population.*

Four groups—Negroes, servants, women, and minors—together comprised approximately 80 per cent of the two and a half million Americans in the year 1776. The legal doctrine applied to these classes excluded them from the category of persons who should enjoy the "inalienable rights" of which the Declaration speaks. But perhaps the most significant mark of their unfreedom was their usual lack of a right to vote, for the privilege of consenting to the laws was the essential right of a free man in Lockean theory. Indeed, the very word "enfranchise" was defined in the eighteenth century as the equivalent of the word "emancipate;" it meant "to make free.". . .

A fifth group of colonial Americans, adult white males with little or no property, was deprived of the vote in colonial elections and so fell short of full liberty in the Lockean sense. But they were privileged above the other unfree groups since they were legally entitled to acquire property and were protected from physical abuse except such as was administered by public authority after trial as punishment for offenses against the state. Some of these disfranchised males were idiots, invalids, or residents of workhouses. Others were simply too poor to qualify under the arbitrary property requirements of the various electoral laws. Statistically they are the least significant of the unfree, although they have had more than their share of attention from critics of consensus history. They made up between 5 and 10 per cent of the total population. If they are added to the 80 per cent of the population in the other unfree categories, which were limited not merely in their political rights but in their rights to personal liberty and property as well, then only 10 to 15 per cent of the American population remain to qualify as "freemen" in the fullest sense.

dred pamphlets had appeared arguing one or another side of the Stamp Act or the Boston Massacre or the Tea Party or the general questions of disobedience to law, loyalty to government, rights and obligations.

Paine's pamphlet appealed to a wide range of colonial opinion angered by England. But it caused some tremors in aristocrats like John Adams, who were with the patriot cause but wanted to make sure it didn't go too far in the direction of democracy. Paine had denounced the so-called balanced government of Lords and

Commons as a deception, and called for single-chamber representative bodies where the people could be represented. Adams denounced Paine's plan as "so democratical, without any restraint or even an attempt at any equilibrium or counter-poise, that it must produce confusion and every evil work." Popular assemblies needed to be checked, Adams thought, because they were "productive of hasty results and absurd judgements."

Paine himself came out of "the lower orders" of England—a staymaker, tax official, teacher, poor emigrant to America. He arrived in Philadelphia in 1774, when agitation against England was already strong in the colonies. The artisan mechanics of Philadelphia, along with journeymen, apprentices, and ordinary laborers, were forming into a politically conscious militia, "in general damn'd riff-raff—dirty, mutinous, and disaffected," as local aristocrats described them. By speaking plainly and strongly, he could represent those politically conscious lower-class people (he opposed property qualifications for voting in Pennsylvania). But his great concern seems to have been to speak for a middle group. "There is an extent of riches, as well as an extreme of poverty, which, by harrowing the circles of a man's acquaintance, lessens his opportunities of general knowledge."

Once the Revolution was under way, Paine more and more made it clear that he was not for the crowd action of lower-class people—like those militia who in 1779 attacked the house of James Wilson. Wilson was a Revolutionary leader who opposed price controls and wanted a more conservative government than was given by the Pennsylvania Constitution of 1776. Paine became an associate of one of the wealthiest men in Pennsylvania, Robert Morris, and a supporter of Morris's creation, the Bank of North America.

Later, during the controversy over adopting the Constitution, Paine would once again represent urban artisans, who favored a strong central government. He seemed to believe that such a government could represent some great common interest. In this sense, he lent himself perfectly to the myth of the Revolution—that it was on behalf of a united people.

The Declaration of Independence

The Declaration of Independence brought that myth to its peak of eloquence. Each harsher measure of British control—the Proclamation of 1763 not allowing colonists to settle beyond the Appalachians, the Stamp Tax, the Townshend taxes, including the one on tea, the stationing of troops and the Boston Massacre, the closing of the port of Boston and the dissolution of the Massachusetts legislature—escalated colonial rebellion to the point of revolution. The colonists had responded with the Stamp Act

Congress, the Sons of Liberty, the Committees of Correspondence, the Boston Tea Party, and finally, in 1774, the setting up of a Continental Congress—an illegal body, forerunner of a future independent government. It was after the military clash at Lexington and Concord in April 1775, between colonial Minutemen and British troops, that the Continental Congress decided on separation. They organized a small committee to draw up the Declaration of Independence, which Thomas Jefferson wrote. It was adopted by the Congress on July 2, and officially proclaimed July 4, 1776.

By this time there was already a powerful sentiment for independence. Resolutions adopted in North Carolina in May of 1776, and sent to the Continental Congress, declared independence of England, asserted that all British law was null and void, and urged military preparations. About the same time, the town of Malden, Massachusetts, responding to a request from the Massachusetts House of Representatives that all towns in the state declare their views on independence, had met in town meeting and unanimously called for independence: ". . . we therefore renounce with disdain our connexion with a kingdom of slaves; we bid a final adieu to Britain."

"When in the Course of human events, it becomes necessary for one people to dissolve the political bands . . . they should declare the causes. . . ." This was the opening of the Declaration of Independence. Then, in its second paragraph, came the powerful philosophical statement:

> We hold these truths to be self-evident, that all men are created equal, that they are endowed by their Creator with certain unalienable Rights, that among these are Life, Liberty and the pursuit of Happiness. That to secure these rights, Governments are instituted among Men, deriving their just powers from the consent of the governed, that whenever any Form of Government becomes destructive of these ends, it is the Right of the People to alter or to abolish it, and to institute new Government. . . .

It then went on to list grievances against the king, "a history of repeated injuries and usurpations, all having in direct object the establishment of an absolute Tyranny over these States." The list accused the king of dissolving colonial governments, controlling judges, sending "swarms of Officers to harass our people," sending in armies of occupation, cutting off colonial trade with other parts of the world, taxing the colonists without their consent, and waging war against them, "transporting large Armies of foreign Mercenaries to compleat the works of death, desolation and tyranny."

All this, the language of popular control over governments, the right of rebellion and revolution, indignation at political tyranny, economic burdens, and military attacks, was language well suited to unite large numbers of colonists, and persuade even those who had grievances against one another to turn against England.

Some Americans were clearly omitted from this circle of united interest drawn by the Declaration of Independence: Indians, black slaves, women. . . .

To say that the Declaration of Independence, even by its own language, was limited to life, liberty, and happiness for white males is not to denounce the makers and signers of the Declaration for holding the ideas expected of privileged males of the eighteenth century. Reformers and radicals, looking discontentedly at history, are often accused of expecting too much from a past political epoch—and sometimes they do. But the point of noting those outside the arc of human rights in the Declaration is not, centuries late and pointlessly, to lay impossible moral burdens on that time. It is to try to understand the way in which the Declaration functioned to mobilize certain groups of Americans, ignoring others. Surely, inspirational language to create a secure consensus is still used, in our time, to cover up serious conflicts of interest in that consensus, and to cover up, also, the omission of large parts of the human race. . . .

When the Declaration of Independence was read, with all its flaming radical language, from the town hall balcony in Boston, it was read by Thomas Crafts, a member of the Loyal Nine group, conservatives who had opposed militant action against the British. Four days after the reading, the Boston Committee of Correspondence ordered the townsmen to show up on the Common for a military draft. The rich, it turned out, could avoid the draft by paying for substitutes; the poor had to serve. This led to rioting, and shouting: "Tyranny is Tyranny let it come from whom it may." . . .

Victory over Britain

The American victory over the British army was made possible by the existence of an already-armed people. Just about every white male had a gun, and could shoot. The Revolutionary leadership distrusted the mobs of poor. But they knew the Revolution had no appeal to slaves and Indians. They would have to woo the armed white population.

This was not easy. Yes, mechanics and sailors, some others, were incensed against the British. But general enthusiasm for the war was not strong. While much of the white male population went into military service at one time or another during the war, only a small fraction stayed. John Shy, in his study of the Revolutionary army (*A People Numerous and Armed*), says they "grew weary of being bullied by local committees of safety, by corrupt deputy assistant commissaries of supply, and by bands of ragged strangers with guns in their hands calling themselves soldiers of the Revolution." Shy estimates that perhaps a fifth of the population was actively treasonous. John Adams had estimated a third opposed, a third in support, a third neutral. . . .

The Americans lost the first battles of the war: Bunker Hill, Brooklyn Heights, Harlem Heights, the Deep South; they won small battles at Trenton and Princeton, and then in a turning point, a big battle at Saratoga, New York, in 1777. Washington's frozen army hung on at Valley Forge, Pennsylvania, while Benjamin Franklin negotiated an alliance with the French monarchy, which was anxious for revenge on England. The war turned to the South, where the British won victory after victory, until the Americans, aided by a large French army, with the French navy blocking off the British from supplies and reinforcements, won the final victory of the war at Yorktown, Virginia, in 1781.

Through all this, the suppressed conflicts between rich and poor among the Americans kept reappearing. In the midst of the war, in Philadelphia, which Eric Foner describes as "a time of immense profits for some colonists and terrible hardships for others," the inflation (prices rose in one month that year by 45 percent) led to agitation and calls for action. One Philadelphia newspaper carried a reminder that in Europe "the People have always done themselves justice when the scarcity of bread has arisen from the avarice of forestallers. They have broken open magazines—appropriated stores to their own use without paying for them—and in some instances have hung up the culprits who created their distress."

In May of 1779, the First Company of Philadelphia Artillery petitioned the Assembly about the troubles of "the midling and poor" and threatened violence against "those who are avariciously intent upon amassing wealth by the destruction of the more virtuous part of the community." That same month, there was a mass meeting, an extralegal gathering, which called for price reductions and initiated an investigation of Robert Morris, a rich Philadelphian who was accused of holding food from the market. In October came the "Fort Wilson riot," in which a militia group marched into the city and to the house of James Wilson, a wealthy lawyer and Revolutionary official who had opposed price controls and the democratic constitution adopted in Pennsylvania in 1776. The militia were driven away by a "silk stocking brigade" of well-off Philadelphia citizens.

It seemed that the majority of white colonists, who had a bit of land, or no property at all, were still better off than slaves or indentured servants or Indians, and could be wooed into the coalition of the Revolution. But when the sacrifices of war became more bitter, the privileges and safety of the rich became harder to accept. About 10 percent of the white population (an estimate of Jackson Main in *The Social Structure of Revolutionary America*), large landholders and merchants, held 1,000 pounds or more in personal property and 1,000 pounds in land, at the least, and these men owned nearly half the wealth of the country and held as slaves one-seventh of the country's people.

The Continental Congress, which governed the colonies through the war, was dominated by rich men, linked together in factions and compacts by business and family connections. . . .

Ronald Hoffman says: "The Revolution plunged the states of Delaware, Maryland, North Carolina, South Carolina, Georgia, and, to a much lesser degree, Virginia into divisive civil conflicts that persisted during the entire period of struggle." The southern lower classes resisted being mobilized for the Revolution. They saw themselves under the rule of a political elite, win or lose against the British.

Social Control

In Maryland, for instance, by the new constitution of 1776, to run for governor one had to own 5,000 pounds of property; to run for state senator, 1,000 pounds. Thus, 90 percent of the population were excluded from holding office. And so, as Hoffman says, "small slave holders, non-slaveholding planters, tenants, renters and casual day laborers posed a serious problem of social control for the Whig elite."

With black slaves 25 percent of the population (and in some counties 50 percent), fear of slave revolts grew. George Washington had turned down the requests of blacks, seeking freedom, to fight in the Revolutionary army. So when the British military commander in Virginia, Lord Dunmore, promised freedom to Virginia slaves who joined his forces, this created consternation. A report from one Maryland county worried about poor whites encouraging slave runaways:

> The insolence of the Negroes in this county is come to such a height, that we are under a necessity of disarming them which we affected on Saturday last. We took about eighty guns, some bayonets, swords, etc. The malicious and imprudent speeches of some among the lower classes of whites have induced them to believe that their freedom depended on the success of the King's troops. We cannot therefore be too vigilant nor too rigourous with those who promote and encourage this disposition in our slaves.

Even more unsettling was white rioting in Maryland against leading families, supporting the Revolution, who were suspected of hoarding needed commodities. The class hatred of some of

253

these disloyal people was expressed by one man who said "it was better for the people to lay down their arms and pay the duties and taxes laid upon them by King and Parliament than to be brought into slavery and to be commanded and ordered about as they were." A wealthy Maryland landowner, Charles Carroll, took note of the surly mood all around him:

> There is a mean low dirty envy which creeps thro all ranks and cannot suffer a man a superiority of fortune, of merit, or of understanding in fellow citizens—either of these are sure to entail a general ill will and dislike upon the owners.

Despite this, Maryland authorities retained control. They made concessions, taxing land and slaves more heavily, letting debtors pay in paper money. It was a sacrifice by the upper class to maintain power, and it worked. . . .

In general, throughout the states, concessions were kept to a minimum. The new constitutions that were drawn up in all states from 1776 to 1780 were not much different from the old ones. Although property qualifications for voting and holding office were lowered in some instances, in Massachusetts they were increased. Only Pennsylvania abolished them totally. The new bills of rights had modifying provisions. North Carolina, providing for religious freedom, added "that nothing herein contained shall be construed to exempt preachers of treasonable or seditious discourses, from legal trial and punishment." Maryland, New York, Georgia, and Massachusetts took similar cautions.

The American Revolution is sometimes said to have brought about the separation of church and state. The northern states made such declarations, but after 1776 they adopted taxes that forced everyone to support Christian teachings. William G. McLoughlin, quoting Supreme Court Justice David Brewer in 1892 that "this is a Christian nation," says of the separation of church and state in the Revolution that it "was neither conceived of nor carried out. . . . Far from being left to itself, religion was imbedded into every aspect and institution of American life."

One would look, in examining the Revolution's effect on class relations, at what happened to land confiscated from fleeing Loyalists. It was distributed in such a way as to give a double opportunity to the Revolutionary leaders: to enrich themselves and their friends, and to parcel out some land to small farmers to create a broad base of support for the new government. Indeed, this became characteristic of the new nation: finding itself possessed of enormous wealth, it could create the richest ruling class in history, and still have enough for the middle classes to act as a buffer between the rich and the dispossessed. . . .

Edmund Morgan sums up the class nature of the Revolution this way: "The fact that the lower ranks were involved in the contest should not obscure the fact that the contest itself was generally a struggle for office and power between members of an upper class: the new against the established." Looking at the situation after the Revolution, Richard Morris comments: "Everywhere one finds inequality." He finds "the people" of "We the people of the United States" (a phrase coined by the very rich Gouverneur Morris) did not mean Indians or blacks or women or white servants. In fact, there were more indentured servants than ever, and the Revolution "did nothing to end and little to ameliorate white bondage."

Carl Degler says (*Out of Our Past*): "No new social class came to power through the door of the American revolution. The men who engineered the revolt were largely members of the colonial ruling class." George Washington was the richest man in America. John Hancock was a prosperous Boston merchant. Benjamin Franklin was a wealthy printer. And so on.

On the other hand, town mechanics, laborers, and seamen, as well as small farmers, were swept into "the people" by the rhetoric of the Revolution, by the camaraderie of military service, by the distribution of some land. Thus was created a substantial body of support, a national consensus, something that, even with the exclusion of ignored and oppressed people, could be called "America.". . .

It seems that the rebellion against British rule allowed a certain group of the colonial elite to replace those loyal to England, give some benefits to small landholders, and leave poor white working people and tenant farmers in very much their old situation.

VIEWPOINT 2

"It was the Revolution, more than any other single event, that made America into the most liberal, democratic, and modern nation in the world."

The War for Independence Was a Social Revolution

Gordon S. Wood (1933-)

One of the questions facing students of American history is whether the American Revolution can be considered a true revolution—a fundamental change or overthrow of the rulers of America. Some historians have answered no, stating that the war for independence from Great Britain had little effect in changing the internal leadership and social structure of the colonies. In comparing the American Revolution to other revolutions, such as the French Revolution of 1789 and the Russian Revolution of 1917, they argue that the American Revolution had comparatively little impact on the ruling political and social structures.

Gordon S. Wood is one of the most prominent historians who has taken an opposing view—that the American Revolution was a transforming event that greatly altered the lives of all Americans. A professor of history at Brown University in Providence, Rhode Island, Wood is the author of many articles and two noteworthy books. In 1969 he published *The Creation of the American Republic*, a massive study of political ideology in America as it developed from the time of the Declaration of Independence to the making of the U.S. Constitution. He argued in that book that the republicanism of America's founders was radical for its time. His 1992 *The Radicalism of the American Revolution*, from which this viewpoint is excerpted, examines how the American Revolution changed American society. Wood argues that the changes the American Revolution brought on were profound. One of the most significant changes, he asserts, was the creating of a sense of equality for all Americans.

We Americans like to think of our revolution as not being radical; indeed, most of the time we consider it downright conservative. It certainly does not appear to resemble the revolutions of other nations in which people were killed, property was destroyed, and everything was turned upside down. The American revolutionary leaders do not fit our conventional image of revolutionaries—angry, passionate, reckless, maybe even bloodthirsty for the sake of a cause. We can think of Robespierre, Lenin, and Mao Zedong as revolutionaries, but not George Washington, Thomas Jefferson, and John Adams. They seem too stuffy, too solemn, too cautious, too much the gentlemen. We cannot quite conceive of revolutionaries in powdered hair and knee breeches. The American revolutionaries seem to belong in drawing rooms or legislative halls, not in cellars or in the streets. They made speeches, not bombs; they wrote learned pamphlets, not manifestos. They were not abstract theorists and they were not social levelers. They did not kill one another; they did not devour themselves. There was no reign of terror in the American Revolution and no resultant dictator—no Cromwell, no Bonaparte. The American Revolution does not seem to have the same kinds of causes—the social wrongs, the class conflict, the impoverishment, the grossly inequitable distributions of wealth—that presumably lie behind other revolutions. There were no peasant uprisings, no jacqueries, no burning of châteaux, no storming of prisons.

Of course, there have been many historians—Progressive or neo-Progressive historians, as they have been called—who have sought, as Hannah Arendt put it, "to interpret the American Revolution in the light of the French Revolution," and to look for the same kinds of internal violence, class conflict, and social deprivation that presumably lay behind the French Revolution and other modern revolutions. Since the beginning of the twentieth century these Progressive historians have formulated various social interpretations of the American Revolution essentially designed to show that the Revolution, in Carl Becker's famous words, was not only about "home rule" but also about "who was to rule at home." They have tried to describe the Revolution essentially as a social struggle by deprived and underprivileged groups against entrenched elites. But, it has been correctly pointed out [by Bernard Bailyn], despite an extraordinary amount of research and writing during a good part of this century, the purposes of these Progressive and neo-Progressive historians—"to portray the origins and goals of the Revolution as in some significant measure expressions of a peculiar economic malaise or of the social protests and aspirations of an impoverished or threatened mass population—have not been fulfilled." They have not been fulfilled because the social conditions that generically are supposed to lie behind all revolutions—poverty and economic deprivation—were not present in colonial America. There should no longer be any doubt about it: the white American colonists were not an oppressed people; they had no crushing imperial chains to throw off. In fact, the colonists knew they were freer, more equal, more prosperous, and less burdened with cumbersome feudal and monarchical restraints than any other part of mankind in the eighteenth century. Such a situation, however, does not mean that colonial society was not susceptible to revolution.

Precisely because the impulses to revolution in eighteenth-century America bear little or no resemblance to the impulses that presumably account for modern social protests and revolutions, we have tended to think of the American Revolution as having no social character, as having virtually nothing to do with the society, as having no social causes and no social consequences. It has therefore often been considered to be essentially an intellectual event, a constitutional defense of American rights against British encroachments ("no taxation without representation"), undertaken not to change the existing structure of society but to preserve it. For some historians the Revolution seems to be little more than a colonial rebellion or a war for independence. Even when we have recognized the radicalism of the Revolution, we admit only a political, not a social radicalism. The revolutionary leaders, it is said [by Bailyn], were peculiar "eighteenth-century radicals concerned, like the eighteenth-century British radicals, not with the need to recast the social order nor with the problems of the economic inequality and the injustices of stratified societies but with the need to purify a corrupt constitution and fight off the apparent growth of prerogative power." Consequently, we have generally described the Revolution as an unusually conservative affair, concerned almost exclusively with politics and constitutional rights, and, in comparison with the social radicalism of the other great revolutions of history, hardly a revolution at all.

A Radical Revolution

If we measure the radicalism of revolutions by the degree of social misery or economic deprivation suffered, or by the number of people killed or manor houses burned, then this conventional emphasis on the conservatism of the American Revolution becomes true enough. But if we measure the radicalism by the amount of social change that actually took place—by transformations in the relationships that bound people to each other—then the American Revolution was not conservative at all; on the contrary: it was as radical and as revolutionary as any in history. Of course, the American Revolution was very different from other revolutions. But it was no less radical and no less social for being different. In fact, it was one of the greatest revolutions the world has known, a momentous upheaval that not only fundamentally altered the character of American society but decisively affected the course of subsequent history.

It was as radical and social as any revolution in history, but it was radical and social in a very special eighteenth-century sense. No doubt many of the concerns and much of the language of that premodern, pre-Marxian eighteenth century were almost entirely political. That was because most people in that very different distant world could not as yet conceive of society apart from government. The social distinctions and economic deprivations that we today think of as the consequence of class divisions, business exploitation, or various isms—capitalism, racism, etc.—were in the eighteenth century usually thought to be caused by the abuses of government. Social honors, social distinctions, perquisites of office, business contracts, privileges and monopolies, even excessive property and wealth of various sorts—all social evils and social deprivations—in fact seemed to flow from connections to government, in the end from connections to monarchical authority. So that when Anglo-American radicals talked in what seems to be only political terms—purifying a corrupt constitution, eliminating courtiers, fighting off crown power, and, most important, becoming republicans—they nevertheless had a decidedly social message. In our eyes the American revolutionaries appear to be absorbed in changing only their governments, not their society. But in destroying monarchy and establishing republics they were changing their society as well as their governments, and they knew it. Only they did not know—they could scarcely have imagined—how much of their society they would change. J. Franklin Jameson, who more than two generations ago described the Revolution as a social movement only to be roundly criticized by a succeeding generation of historians, was at least right about one thing: "the stream of revolution, once started, could not be confined within narrow banks, but spread abroad upon the land."

By the time the Revolution had run its course in the early nineteenth century, American society had been radically and thoroughly transformed. One class did not overthrow another; the poor did not supplant the rich. But social relationships—the way people were connected one to another—were changed, and decisively so. By the early years of the nineteenth century the Revolution had created a society fundamentally different from the colonial society of the eighteenth century. It was in fact a new society unlike any that had ever existed anywhere in the world. . . .

That revolution did more than legally create the United States; it transformed American society. Because the story of America has turned out the way it has, because the United States in the twentieth century has become the great power that it is, it is difficult, if not impossible, to appreciate and recover fully the insignificant and puny origins of the country. In 1760 America was only a collection of disparate colonies huddled along a narrow strip of the Atlantic coast—economically underdeveloped outposts existing on the very edges of the civilized world. The less than two million monarchical subjects who lived in these colonies still took for granted that society was and ought to be a hierarchy of ranks and degrees of dependency and that most people were bound together by personal ties of one sort or another. Yet scarcely fifty years later these insignificant borderland provinces had become a giant, almost continent-wide republic of nearly ten million egalitarian-minded bustling citizens who not only had thrust themselves into the vanguard of history but had fundamentally altered their society and their social relationships. Far from remaining monarchical, hierarchy-ridden subjects on the margin of civilization, Americans had become, almost overnight, the most liberal, the most democratic, the most commercially minded, and the most modern people in the world.

And this astonishing transformation took place without industrialization, without urbanization, without railroads, without the aid of any of the great forces we usually invoke to explain "modernization." It was the Revolution that was crucial to this transformation. It was the Revolution, more than any other single event, that made America into the most liberal, democratic, and modern nation in the world. . . .

These changes were radical, and they were extensive. To focus, as we are today apt to do, on what the Revolution did not accomplish—highlighting and lamenting its failure to abolish slavery and change fundamentally the lot of women—is to miss the great significance of what it did accomplish; indeed, the Revolution made possible the anti-slavery and women's rights movements of the nineteenth century and in fact all our current egalitarian thinking. The Revolution not only radically changed the personal and social relationships of people, including the position of women, but also destroyed aristocracy as it had been understood in the Western world for at least two millennia. The Revolution brought respectability and even dominance to ordinary people long held in contempt and gave dignity to their menial labor in a manner unprecedented in history and to a degree not equaled elsewhere in the world. The Revolution did not just eliminate monarchy and create republics; it actually reconstituted what Americans meant by public or state power and brought about an entirely new kind of popular politics and a new kind of democratic officeholder. The Revolution not only changed the culture of Americans—making over their art, architecture, and iconography—but even altered their understanding of history, knowledge, and truth. Most important, it made the interests and prosperity of ordinary people—their pursuits of happiness—the goal of society and government. The Revolution did not merely create a political and legal environment conducive to economic expansion; it also released powerful popular entrepreneurial and commercial energies that few realized existed and transformed the economic landscape of the country. In short, the Revolution was the most radical and most far-reaching event in American history. . . .

Conditions for Revolution

By the late 1760s and early 1770s a potentially revolutionary situation existed in many of the colonies. There was little evidence of those social conditions we often associate with revolution (and some historians have desperately sought to find): no mass poverty, no seething social discontent, no grinding oppression. For most white Americans there was greater prosperity than anywhere else in the world; in fact, the experience of that growing prosperity contributed to the unprecedented eighteenth-century sense that people here and now were capable of ordering their own reality. Consequently, there was a great deal of jealousy and touchiness everywhere, for what could be made could be unmade; the people were acutely nervous about their prosperity and the liberty that seemed to make it possible. With the erosion of much of what remained of traditional social relationships, more and more individuals had broken away from their families, communities, and patrons and were experiencing the anxiety of freedom and independence. Social changes, particularly since the 1740s, multiplied rapidly, and many Americans struggled to make sense of what was happening. These social changes were complicated, and they are easily misinterpreted. Luxury and conspicuous consumption by very ordinary people were increasing. So, too, was religious dissent of all sorts. The rich became richer, and aristocratic gentry everywhere became more conspicuous and self-conscious; and the numbers of poor in some cities and the numbers of landless in some areas increased. But social classes based on occupation or wealth did not set themselves against one another, for no classes in this modern sense yet existed. The society was becoming more unequal, but its inequalities were not the source of the instability and anxiety. Indeed, it was the pervasive equality of American society that was causing the problems. . . .

A True Revolution

Edmund S. Morgan is Sterling Professor of History Emeritus at Yale University in New Haven, Connecticut. His books include Inventing the People: The Rise of Popular Sovereignty in England and America *and* American Slavery, American Freedom. *In the following excerpt from his* New York Review of Books *article on Gordon S. Wood's book* The Radicalism of the American Revolution, *Morgan supports Wood's contention that the American Revolution was a true social revolution.*

The Revolution did revolutionize social relations. It did displace the deference, the patronage, and social divisions that had determined the way people viewed one another for centuries and still view one another in much of the world. It did give to ordinary people a pride and power, not to say an arrogance, that have continued to shock visitors from less favored lands. It may have left standing a host of inequalities that have troubled us ever since. But it generated the egalitarian view of human society that makes them troubling and makes our world so different from the one in which the Revolutionists had grown up. It was not a Marxist revolution, not the overthrow of a ruling class, not the rising of an oppressed class. But if we can escape from the stereotypes that have governed our thinking about it, we will recognize that it is time to stop apologizing for its conservatism (or praising it) and see it as indeed "the most radical and most far-reaching event in American history."

This extraordinary touchiness, this tendency of the colonists in their political disputes to argue "with such vehemence as if all had been at Stake," flowed from the precariousness of American society, from its incomplete and relatively flattened character, and from the often "rapid ascendency" of its aristocracy, particularly in the Deep South, where families "in less than ten years have risen from the lowest rank, have acquired upward of £100,000 and have, moreover, gained this wealth in a simple and easy manner." Men who had quickly risen to the top were confident and aggressive but also vulnerable to challenge, especially sensitive over their liberty and independence, and unwilling to brook any interference with their status or their prospects.

For other, more ordinary colonists the promises and uncertainties of American life were equally strong. Take, for example, the lifelong struggle of farmer and sawmill owner Moses Cooper of Glocester, Rhode Island, to rise from virtual insignificance to become the richest man in the town. In 1767-68, at the age of sixty, Cooper was finally able to hire sufficient slaves and workers to do all his manual labor; he became a gentleman and justice of the peace and appended "Esq." to his name. Certainly by this date he could respond to the rhetoric of his fellow Rhode Islanders talking about their colony as "the promised land . . . a land of milk and honey and wherein we eat bread to the full . . . a land whose stones are iron . . . and . . . other choice mines and minerals; and a land whose rivers and adjacent seas are stored with the best of fish." And Cooper might well have added, "whose forests were rich with timber," for he had made his money from lumber. Yet at the same time Cooper knew only too well the precariousness of his wealth and position and naturally feared what Britain's mercantile restrictions might mean for his lumber sales to the West Indies. What had risen so high could as readily fall: not surprisingly, he became an enthusiastic patriot leader of his tiny town of Glocester. Multiply Cooper's experience of uneasy prosperity many thousandfold and we have the stuff of a popular revolutionary movement. . . .

Patriots vs. Courtiers

The great social antagonists of the American Revolution were not poor vs. rich, workers vs. employers, or even democrats vs. aristocrats. They were patriots vs. courtiers—categories appropriate to the monarchical world in which the colonists had been reared. Courtiers were persons whose position or rank came artificially from above—from hereditary or personal connections that ultimately flowed from the crown or court. Courtiers, said John Adams, were those who applied themselves "to the Passions and Prejudices, the Follies and Vices of Great Men in order to obtain their Smiles, Esteem, and Patronage and consequently their favors and Preferments." Patriots, on the other hand, were those who not only loved their country but were free of dependent connections and influence; their position or rank came naturally from their talent and from below, from recognition by the people. "A real patriot," declared one American in 1776, was "the most illustrious character in human life. Is not the interest and happiness of his fellow creatures his care?". . .

It is in this context that we can best understand the revolutionaries' appeal to independence, not just the independence of the country from Great Britain, but, more important, the independence of individuals from personal influence and "warm and private friendship." The purpose of the Virginia constitution of 1776, one Virginian recalled, was "to prevent the undue and over-whelming influence of great landholders in elections." This was to be done by disfranchising the landless "tenants and retainers" who depended "on the breath and varying will" of these great men and by ensuring that only men who owned their own land could vote.

A republic presumed, as the Virginia declaration of rights put it, that men in the new republic would be "equally free and inde-pendent," and property would make them so. Property in a re-public was still conceived of traditionally—in proprietary terms—not as a means of personal profit or aggrandizement but rather as a source of personal authority or independence. It was regarded not merely as a material possession but also as an at-tribute of a man's personality that defined him and protected him from outside pressure. A carpenter's skill, for example, was his property. Jefferson feared the rabble of the cities precisely because they were without property and were thus dependent. . . .

In a monarchical world of numerous patron-client relations and multiple degrees of dependency, nothing could be more radical than this attempt to make every man independent. What was an ideal in the English-speaking world now became for Americans an ideological imperative. Suddenly, in the eyes of the revolution-aries, all the fine calibrations of rank and degrees of unfreedom of the traditional monarchical society became absurd and degrad-ing. The Revolution became a full-scale assault on dependency.

Dependency and Slavery

At the beginning of the eighteenth century the English radical whig and deist John Toland had divided all society into those who were free and those who were dependent. "By *Freeman*," wrote Toland, "I understand men of property, or persons that are able to live of themselves; and those who cannot subsist in this independence, I call *Servants*." In such a simple division everyone who was not free was presumed to be a servant. Anyone tied to someone else, who was someone's client or dependent, was servile. The American revolutionary movement now brought to the surface this latent logic in eighteenth-century radical whig thinking.

Dependency was now equated with slavery, and slavery in the American world had a conspicuous significance. "What is a slave," asked a New Jersey writer in 1765, "but one who depends upon the will of another for the enjoyment of his life and prop-erty?" "Liberty," said Stephen Hopkins of Rhode Island, quoting Algernon Sidney, "solely consists in an independency upon the will of another; and by the name of slave we understand a man who can neither dispose of his person or goods, but enjoys all at the will of his master." It was left to John Adams in 1775 to draw the ultimate conclusion and to destroy in a single sentence the entire conception of society as a hierarchy of graded ranks and degrees. "There are," said Adams simply, "but two *sorts* of men in the world, freemen and slaves." Such a stark dichotomy collapsed all the delicate distinctions and dependencies of a monarchical society and created radical and momentous implications for Americans.

Independence, declared David Ramsay in a memorable Fourth of July oration in 1778, would free Americans from that monarchical world where "favor is the source of preferment," and where "he that can best please his superiors, by the low arts of fawning and adulation, is most likely to obtain favor." The revolutionaries wanted to create a new republican world in which "all offices lie open to men of merit, of whatever rank or condition." They believed that "even the reins of state may be held by the son of the poorest men, if possessed of abilities equal to the important station." They were "no more to look up for the blessings of government to hungry courtiers, or the needy dependents of British nobility"; but they had now to educate their "own children for these exalted purposes." Like Stephen Burroughs, the author of an extraordinary memoir of these years, the revolutionaries believed they were "so far . . . republican" that they considered "a man's merit to rest entirely with himself, without any regard to family, blood, or connection." We can never fully appreciate the emotional meaning these commonplace statements had for the revolutionaries until we take seriously their passionate antagonism to the prevalence of patronage and family influence in the *ancien régime.*

Of course, the revolutionary leaders did not expect poor, humble men—farmers, artisans, or tradesmen—themselves to gain high political office. Rather, they expected that the sons of such humble or ungenteel men, if they had abilities, would, as they had, acquire liberal and genteel republican attributes, perhaps by attending Harvard or the College of New Jersey at Princeton, and would thereby rise into the ranks of gentlemen and become eligible for high political office. The sparks of genius that they hoped republicanism would fan and kindle into flame belonged to men like themselves—men "drawn from obscurity" by the new opportunities of republican competition and emulation into becoming "illustrious characters, which will dazzle the world with the splendor of their names." Honor, interest, and patriotism together called them to qualify themselves and posterity "for the bench, the army, the navy, the learned professions, and all the departments of civil government." They would become what Jefferson called the "natural aristocracy"— liberally educated, enlightened gentlemen of character. For many of the revolutionary leaders this was the emotional significance of republicanism—a vindication of frustrated talent at the expense of birth and blood. For too long, they felt, merit had been denied. In a monarchical world only the arts and sciences had recognized talent as the sole criterion of leadership. Which is why even the eighteenth-century *ancien régime* called the world of the arts and sciences "the republic of letters." Who, it was asked, remembered the fathers or sons of Homer and Euclid? Such a question was a republican dagger driven into the heart of the old hereditary order. "Virtue," said Thomas Paine simply, "is not hereditary.". . .

Laws of Inheritance

In their revolutionary state constitutions and laws the revolutionaries struck out at the power of family and hereditary privilege. In the decades following the Revolution all the new states abolished the legal devices of primogeniture and entail where they existed, either by statute or by writing the abolition into their constitutions. These legal devices, as the North Carolina statute of 1784 stated, had tended "only to raise the wealth and importance of particular families and individuals, giving them an unequal and undue influence in a republic, and prove in manifold instances the source of great contention and injustice." Their abolition would therefore "tend to promote that equality of property which is of the spirit and principle of a genuine republic.". . .

Women and children no doubt remained largely dependent on their husbands and fathers, but the revolutionary attack on patriarchal monarchy made all other dependencies in the society suspect. Indeed, once the revolutionaries collapsed all the different distinctions and dependencies of a monarchical society into either freemen or slaves, white males found it increasingly impossible to accept any dependent status whatsoever. Servitude of any sort suddenly became anomalous and anachronistic. In 1784 in New York, a group believing that indentured servitude was "contrary to . . . the idea of liberty this country has so happily established" released a shipload of immigrant servants and arranged for public subscriptions to pay for their passage. As early as 1775 in Philadelphia the proportion of the work force that was unfree—composed of servants and slaves—had already declined to 13 percent from the 40 to 50 percent that it had been at mid-century. By 1800 less than 2 percent of the city's labor force remained unfree. Before long indentured servitude virtually disappeared. . . .

One obvious dependency the revolutionaries did not completely abolish was that of nearly a half million Afro-American slaves, and their failure to do so, amidst all their high-blown talk of liberty, makes them seem inconsistent and hypocritical in our eyes. Yet it is important to realize that the Revolution suddenly and effectively ended the cultural climate that had allowed black slavery, as well as other forms of bondage and unfreedom, to exist throughout the colonial period without serious challenge. With the revolutionary movement, black slavery became excruciatingly conspicuous in a way that it had not been in the older monarchical society with its many calibrations and degrees of unfreedom; and Americans in 1775-76 began attacking it with a vehemence that was inconceivable earlier.

Slavery

For a century or more the colonists had taken slavery more or less for granted as the most base and dependent status in a hierarchy of dependencies and a world of laborers. Rarely had they felt the need either to criticize black slavery or to defend it. Now, however, the republican attack on dependency compelled Americans to see the deviant character of slavery and to confront the institution as they never had to before. It was no accident that Americans in Philadelphia in 1775 formed the first anti-slavery society in the world. As long as most people had to work merely out of poverty and the need to provide for a living, slavery and other forms of enforced labor did not seem all that different from free labor. But the growing recognition that labor was not simply a common necessity of the poor but was in fact a source of increased wealth and prosperity for ordinary workers made slavery seem more and more anomalous. Americans now recognized that slavery in a republic of workers was an aberration, "a peculiar institution," and that if any Americans were to retain it, as southern Americans eventually did, they would have to explain and justify it in new racial and anthropological ways that their former monarchical society had never needed. The Revolution in effect set in motion ideological and social forces that doomed the institution of slavery in the North and led inexorably to the Civil War.

With all men now considered to be equally free citizens, the way was prepared as well for a radical change in the conception of state power. Almost at a stroke the Revolution destroyed all the earlier talk of paternal or maternal government, filial allegiance, and mutual contractual obligations between rulers and ruled. The familial image of government now lost all its previous relevance, and the state in America emerged as something very different from what it had been.

Chronology

1763   *February 10* The Seven Years War between England and France ends with the Treaty of Paris. England is victorious over France in the battle for the colonial possession of North America but is exhausted, faces huge debts, and begins to look to her North American colonies as a potential source of new revenue.

      October 7 England establishes the Proclamation Line along the Appalachian Mountains, temporarily blocking westward expansion by the colonists and separating white Americans from Native Americans.

1764   *April 5* Parliament, under the leadership of George Grenville, enacts the Sugar Act, to raise money and tighten the mercantile system by more vigorously blocking smuggling activities and trying suspected smugglers in vice-admiralty courts rather than by jury trials. The law prompts a May town meeting in Boston, at which time James Otis first raises the issue of taxation without representation.

      August Boston merchants pledge to stop buying British luxury goods. The nonimportation protest movement gradually spreads to other colonies.

1765   *March 22* Parliament, at the urging of the Grenville ministry, passes the Stamp Act designed to tax documents circulating within the colonies. The tax is scheduled to take effect on November 1, 1765. Parliament also passes a Quartering Act to force civil authorities in the colonies to provide housing and provisions for British troops.

      May 29 The Virginia legislature, at the urging of Patrick Henry, passes resolutions condemning the Stamp Act. The resolutions are but part of the storm of colonial protest over the measures. Secret organizations known as the Sons of Liberty are formed and use violence and intimidation to prevent the Stamp Act's enactment.

      October The Stamp Act Congress, a forerunner of the future Continental Congress, is held in New York City. Delegates from nine colonies petition Parliament for repeal and reiterate the colonies' right to be taxed only by their own representatives.

1766   The Regulator Movement begins in North Carolina. Western farmers organize their opposition to the planter aristocracy.

March 18 Parliament repeals the Stamp Act but passes the Declaratory Act, which holds that Parliament reserves the right to pass any law affecting the colonies.

1767   *June 29* The Townshend Duties are enacted. A series of external taxes on goods entering the colonies are now in place. The colonies again respond by organizing an economic boycott of British goods.

October The New York assembly is suspended by Parliament because of its refusal to financially support British troops stationed there.

November John Dickinson begins to publish his "letters from a farmer in Pennsylvania" objecting to the Townshend Duties and the Parliament's interference with representative government in the colonies.

1768   *October 1* British troops are deployed in and around Boston in response to requests by customs officials.

1770   *March 5* The Boston Massacre occurs. Five colonists are killed by British gunfire.

April 12 Parliament rescinds the Townshend Duties, save for a tax on tea. The colonial nonimportation movement ceases despite Boston's efforts to maintain it until the tax on tea is removed.

1772   *June 13* Governor Thomas Hutchinson of Massachusetts announces that he will receive his salary from the crown. Massachusetts judges make a similar announcement in August. The development of the executive and judiciary branches being taken out of the colonists' control prompts the formation of Committees of Correspondence in Massachusetts and other colonies.

1773   *May 10* Parliament passes a Tea Act, which grants duty relief to the East India Tea Company, enabling it to undersell smugglers and other merchants and potentially monopolize the tea trade. Ships carrying the East India tea are denied permission to dock in Philadelphia, New York, and Charleston. In Boston the ships are able to dock but are prevented from unloading their shipment.

December 16 The Boston Tea Party occurs. Angry colonists disguised as Indians board the three tea ships and dump all the tea into the harbor.

1774   *March 31* Parliament passes the first of the Coercive Acts (also known as the Intolerable Acts) in response to the Boston Tea Party, closing the port of Boston. The Massachusetts assembly is later dissolved.

May 30 Parliament adds insult to injury by passing the Quebec Act guaranteeing the French in Quebec their Catholic religion and extending the boundaries of the province to the Ohio River.

July Thomas Jefferson publishes his pamphlet *A Summary View of the Rights of British America,* which asserts that the colonists' natural rights are preeminent to their duties to England and the empire.

September The First Continental Congress meets in Philadelphia to plan a response to the Coercive Acts. A plan by delegate Joseph Galloway to create an American parliament in conjunction with the British Parliament is proposed and defeated. Congress passes declarations decrying the Coercive Acts and the Quebec Act as unjust and organizes a Continental Association to create and enforce efforts to stop all trade with Great Britain. The congress adjourns October 22 with plans to meet the following year if grievances are not met.

1775   *April 19* The "shot heard 'round the world" is fired at Lexington and Concord.

May American forces under Ethan Allen and Benedict Arnold capture British garrisons at Ticonderoga and Crown Point.

May 10 The Second Continental Congress begins its deliberations in Philadelphia.

June Bunker Hill (actually Breed's Hill) outside Boston is seized by the Americans. The British retake it but suffer heavy casualties.

October The British burn Falmouth (Portland), Maine.

December Colonial invasion of Canada under Benedict Arnold fails.

1776   *January* Thomas Paine publishes his pamphlet *Common Sense,* which challenges the legitimacy of the king.

June Richard Henry Lee of Virginia offers a resolution that the United Colonies "ought to be free and independent states." Thomas Jefferson is assigned the task of drafting a declaration of independence.

July The British fleet appears off New York.

Streams of loyalists leave the country, and the persecution of the remaining loyalists intensifies.

July 2 The Continental Congress votes in favor of Lee's resolution of independence.

July 4 American independence is declared.

December Gen. George Washington surprises and captures thousands of Hessian troops at Trenton.

1776-1780 Fourteen states draft new, more democratic state constitutions.

1777 The Articles of Confederation are drafted.

September British general Howe moves on Philadelphia.

October The British are humiliated in the Battle of Saratoga.

1777-1778 Washington's army freezes at Valley Forge.

1778 *February 6* An alliance with France is agreed to, thereby committing the French to the success of the American Revolution.

1778-1780 Georgia is overrun by British troops.

Gen. George Rogers Clark wages his campaign against the British and their Indian allies in the Ohio valley.

1779 French treaty with Spain indirectly brings another European nation to the support of the revolution.

The Continental Congress moves to requisition money and supplies from the states.

Proposals are advanced in South Carolina and Georgia to enlist slaves in the war effort.

1780 Benedict Arnold turns traitor.

May 12 Charleston, South Carolina, falls to the British.

1781 British defeat at Yorktown signals the end of the British commitment to defeating the Americans.

1783 The Treaty of Paris is signed, recognizing the independence of the United States.

Annotated Bibliography

Willi Paul Adams, *The First American Constitutions*. Chapel Hill: University of North Carolina Press, 1980. A history of the state constitutions that were drafted during the Revolution.

American Enterprise Institute for Public Policy Research, *America's Continuing Revolution*. Washington, DC: American Enterprise Institute for Public Policy Research, 1975. A collection of lectures on the American Revolution sponsored by the conservative public policy research institution. The contributors include Irving Kristol, Daniel J. Boorstin, Caroline Robbins, and Gordon S. Wood.

David Ammerman, *In the Common Cause: American Response to the Coercive Acts of 1774*. Charlottesville: The University Press of Virginia, 1974. For many colonists the Coercive Acts served as the straw that broke the camel's back. This history chronicles the individual and collective colonial response to this exercise of British legislative power.

Charles M. Andrews, *Colonial Background of the American Revolution*. New Haven, CT: Yale University Press, 1924. A series of essays arguing that the British Empire at the time of the American Revolution was run by men who were fair-minded administrators rather than stubborn tyrants.

Bernard Bailyn, *The Ideological Origins of the American Revolution*. Cambridge, MA: Harvard University Press, 1967. An intellectual history of the American Revolution, based on a close reading of the pamphlets of the revolutionary era.

Bernard Bailyn, *The Ordeal of Thomas Hutchinson*. Cambridge, MA: Harvard University Press, 1974. A superb biography of one of the targets of the Stamp Act mobs and one of the leading loyalists of the American Revolution.

Bernard Bailyn, *The Origins of American Politics*. New York: Knopf, 1968. A slender but crucial volume which supplements the arguments advanced in *The Ideological Origins of the American Revolution*.

Charles A. Beard, *An Economic Interpretation of the Constitution of the United States*. New York: Macmillan, 1913. An argument by the dean of American progressive era historians that contends that the Constitution was written by and for men of wealth.

Carl Becker, *The Declaration of Independence*. New York: Knopf, 1922. The classic history of the ideas embodied in America's founding document.

George Athan Billias, ed., *The American Revolution: How Revolutionary Was It?* 4th ed. Fort Worth, TX: Holt, Rinehart and Winston, Inc., 1990. This anthology charts the changing historical interpretations of the American Revolution over the past two hundred years.

George Athan Billias, ed., *George Washington's Opponents*. New York: D. Appleton-Century, 1969. A series of essays dealing with British military policies and strategies.

Richard Bissell, *New Light on 1776 and All That*. Boston: Little, Brown, 1975. An irreverent account of the American Revolution by a novelist and Broadway playwright.

Colin Bonwick, *English Radicals and the American Revolution*. Chapel Hill: University of North Carolina Press, 1977. A study of British opponents of British imperial policy at the time of the Revolution.

Carl Bridenbaugh, *The Spirit of '76: The Growth of American Patriotism Before Independence*. New York: Oxford University Press, 1975. An intellectual and political history of the building of American patriotism, as opposed to American nationalism.

John Brooke, *King George III*. New York: McGraw-Hill, 1972. An even-handed biography of this controversial figure.

Robert E. Brown, *Middle Class Democracy and the Revolution in Massachusetts*. Ithaca, NY: Cornell University Press, 1955. A microcosmic examination of a single colony, this volume attempts to refute the notion that the Constitution was drafted solely for economic reasons.

John L. Bullion, *A Great and Necessary Measure: George Grenville and the Genesis of the Stamp Act, 1763-1765*. Columbia: University of Missouri Press, 1983. A history of the background to the crucial British decision to impose this controversial tax.

Robert M. Calhoon, *The Loyalists in Revolutionary America, 1760-1781*. New York: Harcourt Brace Jovanovich, 1973. The best single-volume synthesis of the history of colonial loyalists.

Christopher Collier, *Roger Sherman's Connecticut: Yankee Politics and the American Revolution*. Middletown, CT: Wesleyan University Press, 1971. Simultaneously a biography of a colony-turned-state and a leading figure of the Revolution and after.

Edward Countryman, *The American Revolution*. New York: Hill and Wang, 1985. This is the best brief single-volume general history of the American Revolution. The author is especially effective in treating the intellectual history of the Revolution.

Jeffrey Crow and Larry Tise, eds., *The Southern Experience in the American Revolution*. Chapel Hill: University of North Carolina Press, 1978. A series of essays on the American South during and after the Revolution.

John D. Dann, *The Revolution Remembered: Eyewitness Accounts of the War for Independence*. Chicago: University of Chicago Press, 1980. This is a collection of firsthand accounts of those who served as ordinary soldiers in the Revolution.

Thomas Flemming, *1776: Year of Illusion*. New York: Norton, 1975. A social and political history of the decision for independence.

Thomas Flexner, *George Washington*. Boston: Little, Brown, 1968. The best single-volume biography of Washington.

Jay Fliegelman, *Prodigals and Pilgrims*. New York: Cambridge University Press, 1982. A history of the Revolution that attempts to link the movement for independence with a decline in patriarchal authority.

Eric Foner, *Tom Paine and Revolutionary America*. New York: Oxford University Press, 1976. The best recent single-volume biography of Paine, this book combines biography with excellent social history.

Philip S. Foner, *Labor and the American Revolution*. Westport, CT: Greenwood Press, 1977. This volume attempts to trace the history of working people during the course of the Revolution.

William M. Fowler Jr. and Wallace Coyle, eds., *The American Revolution: Changing Perspectives*. Boston: Northeastern University Press, 1979. A collection of essays by British and American historians examining the social causes and consequences of the American Revolution.

Douglas Southall Freeman, *George Washington*. 7 vols. New York: Charles Scribner, 1948-57. This is the definitive multi-volume biography of Washington.

Felix Gilbert, *To the Farewell Address: Ideas of Early American Foreign Policy*. Princeton, NJ: Princeton University Press, 1961. A superb intellectual history of American foreign policy, foreign policymakers, and the American commitment to neutrality.

Lawrence Henry Gipson, *The Coming of the Revolution, 1763-1775*. New York: Harper and Row, 1962. A distillation of his life's work, Gipson's volume echoes Andrews's defense of British imperial rule.

Barbara Graymont, *The Iroquois in the American Revolution*. Syracuse, NY: Syracuse University Press, 1972. A history of the impact of the Revolution on the Iroquois.

Jack Green, *The Quest for Power: The Lower Houses of Assembly in the Southern Royal Colonies, 1689-1776*. Chapel Hill: University of North Carolina Press, 1963. An excellent study of an institution crucial in the history of republican government and a breeding ground for potential revolutionaries.

Philip Greven, *Four Generations: Population, Land and Family in Colonial Andover, Massachusetts*. Ithaca, NY: Cornell University Press, 1970. A demographic study of declining expectations and prospects in a small New England town over the course of the century preceding the Revolution.

Philip Greven, *The Protestant Temperament*. Ithaca, New York: Cornell University Press, 1977. While not directly concerned with the American Revolution, this volume provides excellent background for understanding the religious underpinnings of the Revolution.

Robert Gross, *The Minutemen and Their World*. New York: Hill and Wang, 1976. A social and political history of Concord, Massachusetts, preceding, during, and following the Revolution.

Alan Heimert, *Religion and the American Mind*. Cambridge, MA: Harvard University Press, 1966. A history of the Revolution that emphasizes the significance of the Great Awakening in the making and energizing of the American Revolution.

H. James Henderson, *Political Parties in the Continental Congress*. New York: McGraw-Hill, 1974. This history traces the development of political partisanship after independence had been declared.

Don Higginbotham, *The War of American Independence*. New York: Macmillan, 1971. An excellent general military history of the Revolution.

Dirk Hoerder, *Crowd Action in Revolutionary Massachusetts, 1765-1780*. New York: Academic Press, 1977. A history of the American Revolution from the bottom up, this history is an important corrective to the focus on the leaders of the Revolution.

Peter Charles Hoffer, *Revolution and Regeneration*. Athens: University of Georgia Press, 1982. A generational and demographic study of the revolutionary era.

J. Franklin Jameson, *The American Revolution Considered as a Social Movement*. Princeton, NJ: Princeton University Press, 1926. An early statement of the idea that "who should rule at home" was just as important to some members of the revolutionary generation as home rule.

Merrill Jensen, *The Articles of Confederation*. Madison: University of Wisconsin Press, 1940. A history of the first national constitution and a statement in support of this document, this volume is also a denial that the "critical period" following the Revolution was really that critical.

Merrill Jensen, *The Founding of a Nation: A History of the American Revolution, 1763-1776*. New York: Oxford University Press, 1968. A general history of the American Revolution written by a historian sympathetic to the American cause, but not necessarily in sympathy with those Americans who neglected to remember the words and commitments of the Declaration of Independence.

Alice Hanson Jones, *Wealth of a Nation to Be*. New York: Columbia University Press, 1980. A monumental economic history of the American colonies at the onset of the Revolution.

Michael Kammen, *A Rope of Sand: The Colonial Agents, British Politics, and the American Revolution*. Ithaca, NY: Cornell University Press, 1968. An important study of colonial American lobbyists operating in London prior to 1776.

Michael Kammen, *A Season of Youth: The American Revolution and the Historical Imagination*. New York: Knopf, 1976. A cultural and political history of the Revolution and revolutionary generation.

Linda Kerber, *Women of the Republic: Intellect and Ideology in Revolutionary America*. Chapel Hill: University of North Carolina Press, 1980. A history of female and male attitudes and female activities, political and military, in the midst of war and its aftermath.

Benjamin Labaree, *The Boston Tea Party*. New York: Oxford University Press, 1964. An examination of one of the most famous events in the history of the Revolution.

Jan Lewis, *The Pursuit of Happiness: Family and Values in Jefferson's Virginia*. Cambridge, MA: Cambridge University Press, 1983. An intellectual and social history of the locale that produced the author of the famous phrase, the "pursuit of happiness."

Forrest McDonald, *We the People: The Economic Origins of the Constitution.* Chicago: University of Chicago Press, 1958. An economic and political history of the postwar 1780s that culminated in the ratification of a new constitution.

Pauline Maier, *From Resistance to Revolution.* New York: Knopf, 1972. A history of the decade prior to 1776 when the colonies moved from hesitant resistance to open rebellion.

Pauline Maier, *The Old Revolutionaries: Political Lives in the Age of Samuel Adams.* New York: Knopf, 1980. A series of essays on important, if lesser known, revolutionary figures who opted for a break with England well before it was popular to do so.

Jackson Turner Main, *The Antifederalists: Critics of the Constitution, 1781-1788.* Chapel Hill: University of North Carolina Press, 1961. A history of those who supported the Revolution only to question the necessity for a centralizing constitution.

Jackson Turner Main, *The Social Structure of Revolutionary America.* Princeton, NJ: Princeton University Press, 1965. A social and political history of the Revolution.

Dumas Malone, *Thomas Jefferson.* Berkeley: University of California Press, 1963. This is the definitive multi-volume biography of Jefferson.

Robert Middlekauf, *The Glorious Revolution.* New York: Oxford University Press, 1982. A volume in the Oxford history of the United States, this is a comprehensive history of the American Revolution.

Edmund S. Morgan, *American Slavery, American Freedom: The Ordeal of Colonial Virginia.* New York: Norton, 1975. A valuable history of the growth of slavery in Virginia and of its impact on the thinking of the revolutionary generation, many of whom were slaveholders themselves and anxious to be free of British slavery.

Edmund S. Morgan and Helen M. Morgan, *The Stamp Act Crisis: Prologue to Revolution.* Chapel Hill: University of North Carolina Press, 1953. A detailed history of the colonial response to the tax that galvanized the colonies a decade prior to the Revolution.

Richard B. Morris, *The Peacemakers: The Great Powers and American Independence.* New York: Harper and Row, 1965. A complex but rewarding history of international diplomacy during the American Revolution.

Gary B. Nash, *The Urban Crucible.* Cambridge, MA: Harvard University Press, 1979. A study of growing political awareness in the cities of colonial America prior to the Revolution.

Mary Beth Norton, *The British-Americans: The Loyalists in Exile in England, 1774-1789.* Boston: Little, Brown, 1972. A study of those who were first scorned as loyalists in the colonies and then scorned as Americans in England.

Mary Beth Norton, *Liberty's Daughters: The Revolutionary Experience of American Women, 1750-1800.* Boston: Little, Brown, 1980. A pioneering study of a neglected field, namely the role of women in the American Revolution.

Howard Peckham, *The Toll of Independence*. Chicago: University of Chicago Press, 1974. A history of battles and battle casualties of the Revolution.

Merrill Peterson, *Thomas Jefferson and a New Nation*. New York: Oxford University Press, 1970. The best single-volume biography of Jefferson.

Benjamin Quarles, *The Negro in the American Revolution*. Chapel Hill: University of North Carolina Press, 1961. A history which emphasizes the military contributions of black Americans, slave and free alike.

Jack N. Rakove, *The Beginnings of National Politics: An Interpretive History of the Continental Congress*. New York: Knopf, 1979. A highly detailed but important political history of the nation during the revolutionary war.

Caroline Robbins, *The Eighteenth Century Commonwealthman*. Cambridge, MA: Harvard University Press, 1959. A study of the English background to the American Revolution with special emphasis on liberal thinkers in the eighteenth century.

Donald Robinson, *Slavery in the Structure of American Politics*. New York: Harcourt Brace Jovanovich, 1970. A history of the looming issue of slavery in the midst of war. It details the impact of slavery on military policy, political thinking, and constitution making.

Clinton Rossiter, *Seedtime of the Republic*. New York: Harcourt Brace, 1953. A study of the rhetoric of the American Revolution.

Charles Royster, *A Revolutionary People at War*. Chapel Hill: University of North Carolina Press, 1979. A careful study of both officers and men who served in the American Revolution and a study of the impact of the war on the forming of the American character.

Richard Alan Ryerson, *The Revolution Is Now Begun: The Radical Committees of Philadelphia, 1765-1776*. Philadelphia: University of Pennsylvania Press, 1978. A study of popular committees, rather than Pennsylvania elite, in the years leading up to the Revolution.

John Shy, *A People Numerous and Armed*. New York: Oxford University Press, 1976. A series of essays on the social and military history of the Revolution.

Kenneth Silverman, *A Cultural History of the American Revolution*. New York: Thomas Crowell, 1976. An attempt to examine the phenomenon of republicanism in the context of painting, music, and literature.

Jack M. Sosin, *The Revolutionary Frontier, 1765-1783*. New York: Holt, Rinehart and Winston, 1967. A history of the colonial west, which produced many egalitarian movements during the era of the Revolution.

W.A. Speck, *Stability and Strife: England, 1714-1760*. Cambridge, MA: Harvard University Press, 1977. An excellent starting point for students interested in the English background to the American Revolution.

David Szatmary, *Shays' Rebellion: The Making of an Agrarian Insurrection.* Amherst: University headed by Massachusetts Press, 1980. A history of the post-revolutionary revolt headed by an army veteran, which failed, and which helped to trigger the Constitutional Convention of 1787.

Robert W. Tucker and David C. Hendrickson, *The Fall of the First British Empire.* Baltimore: Johns Hopkins University Press, 1982. An excellent general history of the origins of the Revolution.

John C. Wahlke, ed., *The Causes of the American Revolution.* 3rd ed. Lexington, MA: D. C. Heath, 1973. A collection of essays by historians examining the social conditions and ideological beliefs that led to the American Revolution.

James Walker, *The Black Loyalists.* New York: Holmes and Meier, 1976. A study of a neglected group, black Americans who preferred to align themselves with the British or with black nationalism rather than an independent United States.

Anthony Wallace, *The Death and Rebirth of the Seneca.* New York: Knopf, 1970. The best single-volume history of the Seneca.

Garry Wills, *Explaining America: The Federalist.* New York: Doubleday, 1981. An intellectual history of the Federalist Papers and their authors.

Garry Wills, *Inventing America: Jefferson's Declaration of Independence.* New York: Doubleday, 1978. An intellectual biography of Thomas Jefferson that places him closer to the communitarian thinking of the Scottish Enlightenment than to the individualistic thinking of John Locke.

Gordon S. Wood, *The Creation of the American Republic, 1776-1787.* Chapel Hill: University of North Carolina Press, 1969. A political and intellectual history of the shift from the decentralizing Articles of Confederation to the centralizing Constitution.

Gordon S. Wood, *The Radicalism of the American Revolution.* New York: Knopf, 1992. An analysis of the American Revolution that claims it was a radical movement that transformed American society and culture.

Alfred Young, ed., *The American Revolution: Explorations in the History of American Radicalism.* De Kalb: Northern Illinois University Press, 1976. A series of essays by primarily New Left historians seeking to take the American Revolution beyond a simple struggle over questions of imperial rule.

Anne Y. Zimmer, *Jonathan Boucher: Loyalist in Exile.* Detroit: Wayne State University Press, 1978. A biography of an Anglican clergyman and outspoken loyalist.

Primary Source Collections

Mortimer J. Adler and Wayne Moquin, eds., *The Revolutionary Years.* Chicago: Encyclopedia, Inc., 1976. A collection of articles, speeches, letters, and other accounts by people of varied perspectives describing the events before, during, and after the American Revolution.

Bernard Bailyn, ed., *Pamphlets of the American Revolution.* Cambridge, MA: Harvard University Press, 1965. Bailyn reprints important American political pamphlets covering the years 1750 to 1765 and adds extensive commentary and background information.

Morton Borden and Penn Borden, eds., *The American Tory*. Englewood Cliffs, NJ: Prentice-Hall, 1972. Collection of writings by and about American loyalists.

Henry Steele Commager and Richard B. Morris, eds., *The Spirit of 'Seventy-Six*. New York: Harper and Row, 1967. A massive collection of primary source documents describing the American Revolution. Includes Parliamentary debates, American and British eyewitness accounts, letters, diaries, and even songs and ballads of the period.

William P. Cumming and Hugh Rankin, *The Fate of a Nation*. London: Phaidon Press, 1975. A narrative of the American Revolution interspersed with contemporary descriptions, accounts, and illustrations.

Elizabeth Evans, *Weathering the Storm*. New York: Charles Scribner's Sons, 1975. An anthology of writings by women of the American Revolution, taken mostly from diaries and journals.

Jack P. Greene, ed., *Colonies to Nation, 1763-1789*. New York: Norton, 1975. An anthology of public and private documents covering the period from the 1763 customs service disputes to the making of the U.S. Constitution.

Thomas Jefferson, *Writings*. Edited by Merrill D. Peterson. New York: The Library of America, 1984. A comprehensive collection of the writings of the author of the Declaration of Independence, including many letters and articles pertaining to the American Revolution.

Merrill Jensen, ed., *Tracts of the American Revolution*. New York: The Bobbs-Merrill Company, Inc., 1967. Collection of political pamphlets written between 1763 and 1776 attacking and defending British policy toward the colonies and the colonies' proper response.

Jackson T. Main, ed., *Rebel Versus Tory: The Crises of the Revolution, 1773-1776*. Chicago: Rand McNally, 1963. A selection of debates from the Continental Congress and elsewhere on the three pivotal years leading up to the Declaration of Independence.

Richard B. Morris, ed., *The American Revolution, 1763-1783*. Columbia: University of South Carolina Press, 1970. Morris documents the rising tensions between the Americans and British, the debates over independence, and the effects of the war.

Thomas Paine, *The Complete Writings of Thomas Paine*. Edited by Philip S. Foner. New York: Citadel Press, 1969. Collection of writings by the author of *Common Sense* and *The Crisis*.

J. R. Pole, ed., *The Revolution in America, 1754-1788*. Stanford, CA: Stanford University Press, 1970. A large selection of public documents covering both the debates over independence from Great Britain and the internal reforms of the colonial governments.

Leslie F. S. Upton, ed., *Revolutionary Versus Loyalist*. Waltham, MA: Blaisdell Publishing Company, 1968. A collection of pamphlets and writings covering 1774-1784, collected by a Canadian historian who argues that loyalist writings have been unfairly neglected.

For Discussion

Chapter One

1. In this excerpt from John Locke's writings, what ideas do you see echoed in the Declaration of Independence and other writings of the leaders of the American Revolution? Cite specific examples.

2. How would you define Charles-Louis de Montesquieu's concept of political virtue? Does it reflect something that Great Britain lacked in 1776? Why or why not? Does the United States have such virtue today? Explain.

Chapter Two

1. What sort of attitude does Soame Jenyns have toward the colonies? Daniel Dulany toward the British? Do their writing styles strengthen or weaken their arguments? Explain.

2. What arguments do Soame Jenyns and Martin Howard make to refute the colonists' assertion that the colonies are being unfairly taxed without representation? Do Jenyns's and Howard's arguments offer any room for compromise on the issue?

3. On what matters do the accounts of the Boston Massacre agree? On what points do they disagree? What underlying agendas of the authors might explain their differences?

Chapter Three

1. Do you believe that the Joseph Galloway plan of union between the colonies and Britain could have worked? Why or why not?

2. On what points are the Continental Congress's declarations on taxes consistent with the viewpoints protesting taxes in the previous chapter? On what points have the colonists' views on taxes changed?

3. On what issues do John Dickinson, Charles Inglis, and Samuel Seabury agree? What consequences of independence do they fear the most?

4. How are the language and approach used by Thomas Paine different from those of other anti-British viewpoints in this and the previous chapter? Why do you think Paine's *Common Sense* was a bestseller?

Chapter Four

1. How does John Carmichael justify violence and war against the British? Do you believe his arguments are an adequate answer to the pacifism expressed by the Quakers in the first viewpoint?

2. What reasons does Jacob Duché use in trying to convince George Washington to surrender? What reasons does William Livingston provide in his exhortations to Americans to continue the Revolution? Are Duché and Livingston directly opposed or just focusing on different things?

3. Does the anonymous author of the fifth viewpoint, calling for harsh measures against loyalists, rely primarily on reason or emotion as a basis for his arguments? Are his arguments more or less convincing than those of Aedanus Burke, author of the sixth viewpoint?

Chapter Five

1. Why does Jonathan Boucher find the idea of natural rights as expressed by Samuel Adams and others so threatening? Do you agree with any of his objections? Why or why not?

2 What objections does Thomas Paine have to the English constitution? What do you think are the reasons many revolutionary leaders, including John Adams, opposed many of Paine's ideas concerning democracy?

3. Which of the viewpoints in this chapter do you believe most clearly reflects the influence of John Locke? Which most reflects the influence of Charles-Louis de Montesquieu?

Chapter Six

1. What does Howard Zinn call the central myth of the Revolution? Why does he call it a myth? Do you agree or disagree?

2. In what respects was the American Revolution radical, according to Gordon S. Wood? In what ways was it conservative? How does Wood's analysis differ from Zinn's?

General

1. Do you believe that the colonists' decision to declare independence was inevitable? What alternatives or compromises do you believe could have been worked out? List the viewpoints that support your conclusions.

2. Describe the main ways the debate over the colonies' connection to Britain evolved from 1763 to 1776.

3. Was the American Revolution truly revolutionary? Why or why not?

Index

285